Preventive Justice and the Power of Policy Transfer

Preventive Justice and the Power of Policy Transfer

James Thomas Ogg

First published 2015 by
PALGRAVE MACMILLAN

Palgrave Macmillan in the UK is an imprint of Macmillan Publishers Limited,
registered in England, company number 785998, of Houndmills,
Basingstoke, Hampshire RG21 6XS.

Palgrave Macmillan in the US is a division of St Martin's Press LLC,
175 Fifth Avenue, New York, NY 10010.

Palgrave Macmillan is the global academic imprint of the above companies
and has companies and representatives throughout the world.

Palgrave® and Macmillan® are registered trademarks in the United States,
the United Kingdom, Europe and other countries.

ISBN: 978-1-137-49501-3

This book is printed on paper suitable for recycling and made from fully
managed and sustained forest sources. Logging, pulping and manufacturing
processes are expected to conform to the environmental regulations of the
country of origin.

A catalogue record for this book is available from the British Library.

A catalog record for this book is available from the Library of Congress.

For my parents, Sue and Alan

Contents

List of Figures

List of Statutes

Anti-Social Behaviour Act 2003
Anti-Terrorism, Crime and Security Act 2001
Company Directors Disqualification Act 1986
Computer Misuse Act 1990
Convention for the Protection of Human Rights and Fundamental
  Freedoms
Crime and Courts Act 2013
Crime and Disorder Act 1998
Criminal Justice Act 2003
Criminal Justice and Court Services Act 2000
Criminal Justice and Immigration Act 2008
Criminal Justice and Police Act 2001
Criminal Justice and Public Order Act 1994
Domestic Violence, Crime and Victims Act 2004
Drug Trafficking Offences Act 1986
Family Law Act 1996
Football Spectators Act 1989
Football (Disorder) Act 2000
Football (Offences and Disorder) Act 1999
Gaming Act 1968
Housing Act 1996
Licensed Premises (Exclusion of Certain Persons) Act 1980
Magistrates' Court Act 1980
Misuse of Drugs Act 1971
Police Reform Act 2002
Policing and Crime Act 2009
Powers of Criminal Courts (Sentencing) Act 2000
Prevention of Terrorism Act 2005
Proceeds of Crime Act 2002
Protection from Harassment Act 1997
Public Order Act 1986
Road Traffic Act 1988
Road Traffic Offenders Act 1988
Serious Crime Act 2007
Serious Organised Crime and Police Act 2005
Sexual Offences Act 2003

Terrorism Prevention and Investigation Measures Act 2011
Theft Act 1968
Violent Crime Reduction Act 2006

Foreign Legislation

Racketeer Influence Corrupt Organization Act 1970
The Italian Code of Criminal Procedure *[Article 416 bis]*

List of Cases

A and others *v.* Secretary of State for the Home Department [2004]
UKHL 56

AS (Pakistan) *v.* Secretary of State for the Home Department [2008]
EWCA Civ 1118

Clingham (formerly C) (a minor) *v.* Royal Borough of Kensington and
Chelsea; R (McCann) *v.* Crown Court at Manchester [2002] UKHL 39

Engel *v.* Netherlands [1976] 1 EHRR 647

R (McCann) *v.* Crown Court at Manchester [2001] 1 WLR 358

R (McCann) *v.* Crown Court at Manchester [2003] 1 AC 787

R *v.* Cuthbertson [1981] AC 470

Secretary of State for the Home Department *v.* AF and another [2009]
UKHL 28

Secretary of State for the Home Department *v.* E and another [2007]
UKHL 47

Secretary of State for the Home Department *v.* JJ and others [2007]
UKHL 45

Secretary of State for the Home Department *v.* MB and others [2007]
UKHL 46

Welch *v.* UK [1995] 20 EHRR 247

Acknowledgements

I would like to first sincerely thank Professor Lucia Zedner for her guidance and support. I am privileged and feel fortunate to have been able to work with such an astute academic in my field. She was able at all times to provide me with expert critique as my work developed, and this was always balanced with warmth, kindness, and a demonstrated understanding of the pressures of (academic) life.

There are numerous other people that supported my academic journey to whom I would like to show my appreciation. I would like to thank the Centre for Criminology and the Faculty of Law at the University of Oxford for providing me with studentship funding and resources. The need for anonymity means that I cannot properly acknowledge many people who made my research possible. Suffice to say I am indebted and hugely thankful to those ministers and civil servants in the Home Office and Serious Organised Crime Agency who assisted me and agreed to be interviewed.

To me this book represents some of the best and worst times of my life, and I acknowledge the personal support of those who have got me through at different stages. I am grateful to my friends and colleagues from LMH (Marinella, Helen, Paulina, Bhaveet, Gordon, and Stephen) and the Centre for Criminology (Maria-Cristina, Jess, Marie, Alex, Stephen, Gavin, Paolo, Julian, Chris, and Harry) who brightened up the many dark and cold English winters.

To my now life partner Eliza, you met me at my lowest point – as a friend at my last push to finish writing. I am enormously grateful for your tolerance and understanding, and your sharp proofreading. *You* are the greatest and most original finding of my studies – and I would do it all over again just to meet you: *Con Cuore e Cortesia, AML.*

Most importantly I would like to thank my parents, Sue and Alan. You have given me your time, and unfailing academic guidance and love throughout my life. I am certain that without your limitless and selfless support I would not have succeeded to bridge my way back into university – let alone reach this moment in which I find myself publishing a book. I therefore dedicate this book to you both.

List of Abbreviations

ACPO	Association of Chief Police Officers
ASBO	Anti-Social Behaviour Order
CPS	Crown Prosecution Service
CT	Counter Terrorism
CUREC	University of Oxford Central University Researcher Ethics Committee
ECHR	European Convention on Human Rights
HMCE	Her Majesty's Customs and Excise
IPP	Imprisonment for Public Protection
LP	Cabinet Legislative Programme Committee
NCA	National Crime Agency
NCIS	National Criminal Intelligence Service
NCS	National Crime Squad
NOMS	National Offender Management Service
PC	Parliamentary Counsel
RCPO	Revenue and Customs Prosecutions Office
RICO	Racketeer-Influenced Corrupt Organizations Act 1970
RSHO	Risk of Sexual Harm Order
SCA	Serious Crime Act 2007
SCPO	Serious Crime Prevention Order
SFO	Serious Fraud Office
SOCA	Serious Organised Crime Agency
SOCPA	Serious Organised Crime and Police Act 2005
SOPO	Sexual Offences Prevention Order
TPIM	Terrorism Prevention and Investigation Measure

1
Introduction

At the heart of this book lies an urge to understand better the nature of criminal justice policy and decision-making in the United Kingdom, during a time of complex reform. Over the decade of the former New Labour government, there were marked shifts in criminal law and criminal justice policy. In particular, during the period 1997–2007, the UK saw a rapid expansion of crime control policies and an increased number of new (many wide-reaching) criminal laws passed by parliament (Morris 2006; Lacey 2007: 174–175). The Act at the core of this book, the Serious Crime Act 2007, marked the 60th piece of Home Office legislation during this 10-year period, whereas by contrast there 'were only 48 pieces of Home Office legislation in the previous 100 years' (Brimelow 2007: 1).[1] This increase in legislative activity has provided academics interested in criminal justice with numerous new fields of analysis. These analyses have typically concerned the consequences of such expansion (such as problems of overcriminalisation and a growing prison population) and criticism of excessively wide-reaching powers, and the creation of new measures, particularly in the state's response to anti-social behaviour and terrorism (Garland 2001: 75–76; Matthews and Young 2003: 7; Crawford 2009). However, researchers have tended to concentrate on one substantive policy arena (for example, anti-social behaviour or terrorism) rather than on the apparent pattern of new measures, which together mount a strong attack on the rights of those accused or suspected of involvement in criminal activity (and on the criminal trial; see Ashworth and Zedner 2008). That is, there is a general trend among these new developments to introduce legislation that makes prosecution easier or even non-essential.[2]

An important sub-group of these new measures, and the focus of this book, is a family of preventive orders, many of which involve a civil and criminal proceedings. Hybrid orders diminish the accused or suspected individuals by avoiding the criminal trial altogether (Simester and von Hirsch 2006: 175). As these orders are described as 'civil' and 'preventive' (and not criminal and punitive), they have the benefit of being applied in proceedings with a lowered civil standard of proof, and less stringent controls over the admission of evidence (for example, the admission of hearsay evidence). Moreover, they have the additional benefit (though not for the accused person) of creating criminal offences for breach of the terms of an order, which can carry heavier punishments than conventional High Court powers of contempt (and are arguably often disproportionate to the original behaviour that triggered the order to be imposed) (Ashworth 2004: 279).

While the literature concerning the rights of accused individuals has discussed the principles and underlying efficacy of these orders, there has been limited engagement in understanding *why* these developments have occurred in the first place (Lacey 2009: 946). Criminology as a discipline has ingenuously accepted the explanation of a politicisation of crime control without adequate consideration of (or search for) alternative explanations for these developments. The widely accepted explanation is based on a perception by the state that a trade-off exists between the competing demands of the rights of the accused and those of the public,[3] and that there has been a political aspiration to 'rebalance the Criminal Justice System in favour of the law-abiding majority' (Home Office 2006b).[4] Crime control undeniably became a more pronounced instrument of political exertion in the 20th century – the beginnings often attributed to the election manifestos of the Conservative Party in 1979, but then later escalated under New Labour.[5] Other global phenomena such as *Governing Through Crime* (Jonathan Simon 2007) and a *Culture of Control* (David Garland 2001) suggest governments have (for good or ill) exploited perceptions of crimes to introduce programmes, measures, and practices that powerfully affect the lives of many. However, politicisation has become an overused, catch-all explanation, which has led to a simplified presumption that politicians and political agendas are wholly responsible for the new direction in criminal justice (that is, a 'top-down' view of policy-making). This book shows that a more nuanced examination of the dynamics of policy-making can augment the simplistic political explanations for these new developments, by recognising the structural forces that are also at play in the policy-making process.

The aim of this book is to explain the proliferation of preventive orders across a wide and diverse range of areas of crime policy in the

UK (including anti-social behaviour, domestic violence, football-related violence, sexual offences, terrorism, and organised crime). This is achieved through a detailed case study analysis of the process involved in developing one of the more controversial (yet less scrutinised) civil preventive orders, the Serious Crime Prevention Order (hereafter SCPO).[6] Analysis of the genesis of this single measure is also used as a springboard to explore three under-researched themes in criminal justice scholarship: new developments in serious and organised crime control in the UK; a prevailing preventive ideology in criminal justice, or 'preventive justice'; and 'policy transfer' as a common part of the domestic policy-making process. These three contemporaneous topics can be connected through an analysis of the SCPO. Three broad research questions shape this book's enquiry:

1. How can we best explain the spread of the preventive order model as a key response in crime control?
2. What can a detailed study of the policy process tell us about the increased prevalence of new preventive practices in crime control?
3. To what extent, if any, does policy transfer play a role in the domestic process of policy-making and innovation?

Accordingly, two specific empirical research questions guide the analysis of the origins of the SCPO (in Part II of this book):

1. What was the nature and extent of the role played by the preceding preventive orders in the formulation of the SCPO?
2. Did decision-makers knowingly formulate the SCPO and other preventive orders as part of a broader goal to foster an alternative system of preventive justice?

It is argued that domestic policy transfer is a driving force in everyday policy-making, and, as a result, enhanced systems could be developed to accommodate and facilitate the process of transfer. The SCPO, a novel measure in organised crime control, is argued to be the consequence of incremental processes of policy transfer that have evolved the preventive order model across distinct areas of crime control (encompassing Anti-Social Behaviour Orders, Football Banning Orders, Sexual Offender Orders, and terrorism Control Orders[7] among others). This incremental process may also be indicative of the broader shift towards a system of (criminal) preventive justice. The dynamics of this mechanism of policy transfer are developed into an exploratory framework. At a broader level, it is also argued that those who study criminal justice (referred to throughout this book as criminologists) should engage in the empirical analysis of legislative and policy practices that lie behind the development of new instruments (laws and measures) or any new policy direction, so often criticised by them as a form of deliberate and malevolent government action. The examination of policy transfer in this book shows how even large-scale policy changes can occur through pathways which are paved by unconscious and/or incremental developments by policy-makers, where the intentions cannot, in any way, be characterised as malevolent.

I proceed in two parts. Part I explores the three distinct areas of research that intersect when conducting a detailed examination of the SCPO. Chapter 2 looks at the SCPO in the context of the broader organised crime control agenda in the UK. Prior strategies and responses to organised crime control are reviewed, and the new legislative trend towards a definition of 'serious crime' is appraised. It is argued that the SCPO is a novel and innovative response to organised crime that was not derived from past responses in this policy arena. Chapter 3 explores the role of preventive ideology in criminal justice policy. It provides a brief overview of the family of preventive orders, of which the SCPO is a member. The chapter argues that there has been a rise in the role of a preventive ideology in contemporary criminal justice, which can be seen to underpin some of the presiding discourses in contemporary criminology such as security, risk, and dangerousness. Chapter 4 examines policy transfer as a mechanism to explain the rise of this new family of preventive orders that led to the SCPO. A policy transfer framework is developed to explore how specific ideas 'catch on', take hold, and come to dominate the work of policy-makers and decision-makers.

Part II constitutes the empirical component of this book. Chapter 5 sets out the methodology used to explore the spread of the preventive order, and specifically the genesis of the SCPO. It outlines the method of 'process-tracing', based on a research design incorporating documentary analyses (of both policy documents and statute law) and 'elite interviews' with key decision-makers. This chapter also outlines the procedures taken in the analysis of these sources, including case selection, content analysis, coding, sampling, and the design of the interview schedule. Chapter 6 provides an analysis of the legislative proliferation of the preventive order model. This analysis shows that not only has proliferation occurred in numbers of preventive orders, but there has also been an expansion of the provisions of these orders (for example, permitting a longer period during which an order can be applied, longer custodial sentences for breaching an order, and wider forms of application such as through civil procedure). Consequently, the SCPO, a more recent addition to this family, embodies some of the widest provisions that are open to judicial discretion. Chapter 7 focuses directly on the policy process involved in developing the SCPO. It combines results of the analyses of public and departmental policy documents and interviews completed with key decision-makers involved at the early stage of policy gestation. It tests the responses of interviewees for evidence of policy transfer and explores whether there was a preventive ideology during formulation. Lastly, Chapter 8 provides a final discussion, where conclusions are drawn and key implications are discussed.

This book intends to make an important contribution to the field of academic research by providing a method for examining the detail of the processes by which criminal justice policy is made. It also has some important implications for practitioners (particularly in the Home Office) in relation to the structure and operation of policy-making, whereby a greater recognition of the role of policy transfer could appreciably facilitate the process of policy development and make the procedures undertaken more efficient.

Part I

2
'Serious' Shifts in Organised Crime Control

The state's prescribed responses to 'serious crime' present novel changes in criminal justice policy and criminal law that have received very little scrutiny, particularly in academic discourses and analyses. This chapter addresses the concept of serious crime and its relationship with past policies dealing with organised crime. It provides a background to 'serious and organised crime', a concept reinforced by substantive legislative and executive activity in the UK, namely, through the establishment of a Serious Organised Crime Agency (hereafter SOCA)[1] (pursuant to the Serious Organised Crime and Police Act 2005 [hereafter SOCPA 2005]) and the SCPO (under the Serious Crime Act 2007 [hereafter SCA 2007][2]). The chapter has two key objectives: the first is to place the SCPO against a background of past policies in this policy arena; and the second is to provide a more detailed statutory description of this new order within the broader context of the 2007 Act in which it is situated.

Prior to the 2005 and 2007 Acts, the concept of 'serious crime' was primarily either one of general parlance relating to an informally conceived category of crimes (murder, rape, terrorism, and/or any other subjectively selected offences), a concept in international law (related to war crimes and genocide) or one of common law discourses relating to degrees of 'seriousness', seriousness thresholds, and/or standards (to distinguish, for example, indictable and summary offences). The specific offences that could be categorised as 'serious' and those which could not were generally not formally stipulated or legally defined as such. The SCA 2007 changed this tradition by providing a schedule of 'serious crimes' and legislative guidance as to its definition, supplying this category of crimes with a statutory base. Under the SCA 2007, Schedule 1, this category of crimes broadly includes trafficking in drugs, people, and arms; prostitution and child sex; armed robbery; financial offences (money laundering, fraud, tax/revenue evasion, and counterfeiting); corruption and bribery; blackmail; intellectual property offences; and environmental offences.

Two elements of this defined list of serious offences are immediately curious. First, many offences which are most commonly perceived as 'serious' (for example, murder, terrorism, genocide, and other indictable offences) are omitted, while blackmail, copyright infringement, and environmental offences such as salmon fishing are included under the legislative definition of serious crime. Second, all the offences listed in Schedule 1 of the SCA 2007 are already statutorily recognised in other established acts and legislation. For example, drug trafficking is an offence under the Misuse of Drugs Act 1971 and the Drug Trafficking Offences Act 1986 (numerous distinct sections relating to the importation, production, and supply of illicit drugs) and blackmail is an offence under s.21 of the Theft Act 1968. Therefore there remains the question as to why these offences were deemed serious over a list of other arguably more serious offences, and why it was necessary to identify them as serious at all if there was legislation already in place to deal with each of these offences?

The answers to these questions are explicable only by reference to the concept of 'organised crime'. Organised crime is the central motivation behind the legislature's enactment of the SCA 2007. However, interestingly, the concept of 'organised crime' (and its definition) is intentionally absent from the acts which address it, such as the SCA 2007 and the SOCPA 2005 (Owen et al. 2005: 22; Fortson 2008: 18). This chapter examines and explains this relationship, and indeed the distinction, between 'serious' and 'organised' crime.

Organised crime is an intricate and complex area of study that elicits contention within public and academic debate (in relation to its conceptual definition), within the current knowledge about its nature and extent across the globe, and within the government policies that seek to respond to this type of criminal activity (Varese 2010: 35–36). This category of crimes has risen dramatically in importance on the UK political agenda over the last few decades, from initially being only loosely conceived and largely unrecognised by the legislature to its current status as a 'national security threat' (Harfield 2008: 71). This dramatic shift has culminated in the enactment of the SCA 2007, which embodies a number of responses to 'organised/serious crime' including the ability to use the SCPO to prevent individuals from engaging in organised/serious criminal activity. The chapter proceeds to analyse these newer responses in the context of the measures and responses that preceded them.

It is shown that the SCPO is anomalous and a novel departure from orthodox counter-organised crime policy in the UK.

However, it is also shown how the SCPO is evidence of a wider, more gradual shift away from *post hoc* responses and procedure (investigation, arrest, prosecution, criminal trial, and sentence) to *pre hoc*[3] remedies that aim to disrupt and regulate organised criminal activity.

2.1 History of responses to organised crime in the UK

In the UK, 'organised crime' control policy held a low profile until the beginning of the 1990s. As in most other jurisdictions, early responses that were designed to inhibit the development and growth of organised criminal groups were offence-focused. For example, the Gaming Act 1968 established a Gaming Board in an attempt to regulate the occurrence of illicit gambling rackets; Her Majesty's Customs and Excise (HMCE) investigated occurrences of fraud; and 'specialised detective squads', such as vice squads and drug squads, focused on breaking up trafficking networks (Levi 2006: 825–826). The Drug Trafficking Offences Act 1986, while still focusing on one distinct offence category of narcotics trading, introduced two important policy measures for broader organised crime control: mandatory reporting by banks and other financial institutions of 'suspicious activity' (potential fraud or money-laundering activity) and a provision that enabled the state to confiscate the proceeds of crime if the defendants could not prove that their assets were legitimate. The 1986 Act was implemented principally in response to the outcome of 'Operation Julie', the largest LSD trafficking 'bust' in Britain where, after initial investigatory confiscations, the convicted drug traffickers were returned millions of pounds, which were allegedly associated with their crimes (*R v Cuthbertson* [1981]; Nicol 1988: 75–76). The provision to confiscate the proceeds of the crime was particularly innovative as it placed the burden of proof on the defendant and was also retrospective, meaning that convicted traffickers could be made to defend the legitimacy of their assets post-conviction (*Welch v UK* [1995]).[4]

In the 1990s there was a marked shift in organised crime control, particularly in the executive branch, towards multi-offence categories through the formulation of departments, agencies, and policies targeting 'organised', 'major', and 'serious' crime. With the establishment of the Organised and International Crime Division of the Home Office, the National Crime Squad (NCS), and the National Criminal Intelligence Service (NCIS), there was a shift in organised crime control towards more national and collaborative law enforcement. For example, the

NCIS replaced the former National Drugs Intelligence Unit; the formation of the NCS was an amalgamation of formerly separate UK Regional
Crime Squads; and Serious and Major Crime Units were an amalgamation of former drug squads, fraud squads, and vice squads (Levi 2006:
831–832; Harfield 2008: 66–67). Levi (1998: 366) maintains that the
threat of organised crime and the 'Russian Mafia' 'were used to persuade
British politicians and others to set up the National Criminal Intelligence
Service and the National Crime Squad'. This is despite the fact that these
more centralised policing models were developed against a great British
tradition of local policing, historically deeply rooted in British suspicion
of the French and Napoleon's national centralised police model (Levi
1998: 342).

A raft of changes since 2005 saw responses to organised crime control
continue this apparent movement towards non-specific redefinition and
centralisation of law enforcement institutions and policy measures. The
SOCPA 2005 established the SOCA, which further unified the various
institutional initiatives discussed above. In effect, SOCA was an amalgamation of the NCIS and the NCS, as well as other areas of law enforcement such as the (non-taxation related) intelligence and investigative
arms of HMCE (Owen et al. 2005: 1; Levi 2006: 839). The investigation
of tax-related fraud and crime became the responsibility of Her Majesty's
Revenue and Customs (HMRC), a merger of HMCE and Inland Revenue.
The National Crime Agency (NCA), which replaced SOCA under the
Crime and Courts Act 2013, again merged functions of SOCA and the
Child Exploitation and Online Protection Centre, and absorbed some
responsibilities from the UK Borders Agency and the (now abolished)
National Police Improvement Agency. Similarly, the SCA 2007 represents, in large part, a culmination of policy measures that have been
used in past UK counter-organised crime policy – with one important
exception. The 2007 Act contains provisions in relation to three familiar
areas: encouraging or assisting crime, prevention of fraud, and recovery
of the proceeds of crime. These three provisions are summarised below,
prior to the more detailed description of the fourth provision of the
2007 Act – and the novel exception – the SCPO.

First, the 'encouraging or assisting crime' provision of the SCA 2007
abolished the existing (allegedly ineffective) common law offence of
incitement (s.59) and created three new offences: intentionally encouraging or assisting an offence (s.44), encouraging or assisting an offence
believing it will be committed (s.45), and encouraging or assisting
offences believing one or more will be committed (s.46). This is a large
and complex area of law reform that was recommended by the Law

Commission,[5] which aimed to refashion the law in relation to secondary liability and involvement in crime such as attempts, incitement, and conspiracy to commit crime (Fortson 2008: 63). Second, the provision relating to the 'prevention of fraud' in the SCA 2007 formally permits data sharing (s.68) and data matching (s.73) between government bodies. Data matching, as specified in Schedule 7 of the SCA 2007, was already operating under the National Fraud Initiative, and the 2007 Act merely provides this provision with a statutory basis (Peck et al. 2007: 58). Third, the provision relating to 'recovering the proceeds of crime' is principally bureaucratic, transferring the powers and functions of the Assets Recovery Agency to SOCA and the National Policing Improvement Agency (s.74). It also extends powers under the Proceeds of Crime Act 2002 to other law enforcement officials and financial investigators (ss.75–86). Clearly these three measures essentially extend, redefine, or enhance powers and policy measures that were already in operation under pre-existing legislation. The expansive nature of these existing provisions is an important theme re-examined later in this chapter. However, the more uncharacteristic fourth provision of the SCA 2007 (and the nucleus of this book), the SCPO, requires a detailed description.

2.2   The Serious Crime Prevention Order

The SCPO is a civil order that can impose prohibitions and restrictions on individuals or companies which, if breached, result in criminal sanctions. The court[6] may impose an SCPO if there are reasonable grounds to believe on the civil standard of proof, the balance of probabilities (with a heightened standard within that standard[7]), that an individual has either 'committed a serious offence', 'facilitated the commission by another person of a serious offence', or 'conducted himself [sic] in a way that was likely to facilitate the commission by himself or another person of a serious offence' (s.2). This expansive definition of 'involvement' – from actual commission to conduct that might indirectly facilitate a serious offence – is also examined in Section 2.3 of this chapter as it is potentially problematic, particularly in the light of the fact that the SCA 2007 does not provide a statutory definition of the term 'facilitate' (Fortson 2008: 35).

An SCPO has two possible applications. First, Section 5(3) of the SCA 2007 states that an SCPO may prohibit, restrict, or make requirements in relation to an individual's travel, financial arrangements, property, business, employment, as well as the people with whom they might associate, the premises that they are permitted to access, or the items they are permitted to use. Second, Section 5(4) of the 2007 Act states that these 'prohibitions, restrictions or requirements' can be placed on organisations or groups of individuals such as 'bodies corporate, partnerships and unincorporated associations'. These provisions can apply to the financial or business operations of an organisation, including arrangements regarding employment of staff or goods and services. Non-compliance with the conditions of an SCPO (a civil order) results in an individual being liable to criminal sanctions, including (for an indictable offence) imprisonment for up to five years, a fine, or both (s.25); the forfeiture of criminal possessions (s.26); and with specific regard to organisations or other bodies, the 'winding up of a company' (s.27(2)). This two-step approach provides the state with powers to place heavy restrictions on individuals and companies, backed up by substantial punishments – powers that law enforcement agencies have not had throughout the history of organised crime control. It is therefore important to examine the policy-making environment that nurtured this novel measure (this is the primary focus of Part II of this book).

A 'serious offence' is defined in Schedule 1 of the SCA 2007 to include the following comprehensive list of offences: drug trafficking (s.1); people trafficking (s.2); arms trafficking (s.3); prostitution and child sex (s.4); armed robbery (s.5); money laundering (s.6); fraud (s.7); offences in relation to public revenue (for example, tax evasion or fraud) (s.8); corruption and bribery (s.9); counterfeiting (s.10); blackmail (s.11); intellectual property (for example, copyright infringement) (s.12); environment (for example, illicit salmon fishing, waste disposal, or the purchase or sale of endangered species) (s.13); and inchoate offences (for example, conspiracy, attempt, aiding, abetting, counselling, or procuring) (s.14).[8] As suggested previously, this list of 'serious crimes' is strikingly peculiar as it does *not* include murder or other indictable offences, which would undoubtedly be more commonly regarded as more 'serious' than, for example, salmon fishing or copyright infringement. These omissions are the result of the Legislature's primary intention to address 'organised crime', that is, criminal activity that is organisational or business-like. While an illicit business operating in contract killing (murder) is possible, it is clear that the crimes listed in Schedule 1 of the SCA 2007 are related to obtaining monetary gains or profits from the illicit activities. This leads to an examination of the complexities and rhetorical significance of the terms 'serious' and 'organised' crime. Fortson (2008: 18) observes:

[T]he legislature has wisely resisted the temptation to use the expression 'organised crime', or 'serious organised crime'. It is a temptation that was not resisted when Parliament enacted the Serious Organised Crime and Police Act 2005. The expression 'organised crime' is misleading because a significant amount of serious crime is committed in an elementary fashion, or even haplessly, and it can be perpetrated by a person acting alone but who succeeds in inflicting considerable damage nonetheless.

However, in defining the crimes targeted in the SCA 2007 as 'serious', it has arguably lost some of the meaning carried by the term 'organised', relating to a business or organisational operation. This significant distinction between the terms 'serious' and 'organised' is worthy of closer examination.

2.3   Organised crime, serious crime, serious organised crime, or *any* crime?

[W]e could think of comparing organized crime to the British Common Cold: we all know something about it but we do not completely understand how it acts and above all, there is always a more dangerous illness we should be protecting ourselves against. (Allum 2008: 2–3)

Nomenclature and taxonomical discourse in the 'organised crime' literature has become commonplace in academic research and writing, so much so that almost every publication on this topic contains a paragraph or section on the associated definitional issues (Varese 2010). In the UK, in both policy-making and academic circles, this debate is less impassioned, though it is clear that this term and its meaning present a key area of struggle. Through the enactment of the SCA 2007, policy- and law-makers attempted to elude the conceptual problem that 'organised crime' presents by using 'serious crime' instead. The serious crimes listed in Schedule 1 of the SCA 2007 encapsulate the activities most commonly associated with the rhetoric of organised crime – and beyond. It is important to briefly consider these definitional debates in order to understand that which the legislature in the UK has sought to overcome. Two essential distinctions must be made when discussing organised crime in policy terms: its rhetorical use and its operational definition.

The early lack of recognition of the term 'organised crime' can be ascribed to the perceived absence of mafia-type organised crime groups in the UK (Anderson 1993: 294). In the late 20th century, the main experience and acknowledgement of organised crime groups in the UK related to those from the Irish Republican Army (IRA) in Northern Ireland, as well as some notable cases of serious fraud[9] (Anderson 1993: 298–300). Anderson (1993: 294) argues that prior to 1994, law enforcement agencies in the UK believed that criminal syndicates which monopolised illicit markets did not exist in the UK. That is, any threats of this kind were not 'homegrown', but rather came from abroad through immigration or cross-border trade (Anderson 1993: 295). Over the last decade, there has been a gradual recognition of homegrown organised criminal activity, particularly in the domains of drug and people trafficking. However, the precise categorisation of these criminal groups is blurred and confounded by false impressions. For example, Peter Stelfox, Detective Superintendent of Greater Manchester Police (1998: 399), proposed that the operational definition could be extended to include gangs, so-called 'lower-level' organised crime. In addition, Gilmour (2008: 20) maintains that these early conceptions remain in the current dominant discourse (public, media, and even academic commentary), depicting a false picture of organised crime as 'mafia' activity rather than the closer reality of loose networks of criminal activity (see also Hobbs 1988; Woodiwiss 1999. Moreover, the enduring ideas of organised crime as a foreign problem have also arguably compounded problems in other policy domains, for example, asylum and immigration policy, where 'highly restrictive' policies have been the result (Anderson 1993: 307).

In the UK, there is no statutory definition of 'organised crime' (Harfield 2008: 63). In fact, there has never been such a definition and there has been strong resistance to it by the legislature and parliament. This does not mean, however, that there are no laws, specialised law enforcement agencies, or policing operations aimed at detecting, preventing, and prosecuting organised criminal activity. As mentioned above, the UK has various laws targeting organised criminal activity (including the SCA 2007). Since 2006, SOCA and subsequently the NCA were charged with the duty of specifically reducing the harm caused by organised crime. Prior to 2006, separate law enforcement agencies such as the NCIS, HMCE, and the NCS were charged with this responsibility of investigating organised criminal activity (Harfield 2008: 64). In the UK police service's three-tiered policing model, two of the three levels (Levels 2 and 3) are aimed at organised criminal activity (John and Maguire 2004: 3; Gilmour 2008: 19).[10] In addition, a specialised division of the Crown Prosecution Service (CPS) is dedicated to prosecuting organised crime (Organised Crime Division), as well as the Revenue and Customs Prosecutions Office (RCPO) and the Serious Fraud Office (SFO), which also deal with cases of organised crime. Operational responses to organised crime are therefore well established and long-standing. Harfield (2006: 743; 2008: 64) maintains that organised crime in the UK is identified by these law enforcement agencies through applying the 'duck recognition conceptual model': 'something that looks, walks, quacks, and generally behaves like a duck is recognisable as such'. Levi (2006: 831) suggests that parliament, and the legislature in particular, has struggled with the conceptual and operational ambiguities of the term 'organised', which has resulted in a stronger policy focus on the concept of 'serious' crime. However, arguably these operational ambiguities have been exacerbated by the introduction of the term 'serious'. Detective Chief Inspector Stan Gilmour, Thames Valley Police, satirically captured the pragmatic difficulties of these definitions, stating: '[M]y policing role is therefore clear – I will tackle organised crime or even organised serious crime but not serious organised crime' (Gilmour 2008: 3). In addition, Levi and Maguire (2004: 458) warn of a potential loss of recognition of the 'organic nature' of these networks given that the offences they commit are 'greater than the sum of their individual crime elements', that is, the offence might be prosecuted but the organisation behind the offence can endure through transubstantiation (for example, by replacing any key individuals who might be prosecuted).

The avoidance of the term 'organised' is not only based on the grounds of the potential conceptual ambiguities. Crime control policies endeavouring to deal with 'organised crime' would also elicit responses aimed at criminalising group membership or crimes of association. Examples of such legislation are observable around the world, most notably the US Racketeer Influenced and Corrupt Organizations (RICO) Act 1970. This 1970 Act criminalises any 'enterprise'[11] involved in a pattern (two or more specified offences) of racketeering (s.1962). Section 1962(c) also makes provision for the criminalisation of membership of such groups or enterprises (for individuals either 'employed by or associated with'). In addition, the *Associazione di un tipo Mafiosi* (Mafia Association) legislation in Italy criminalises membership of mafia-type associations of groups consisting of three or more persons (*Article 416 bis* of the Italian Penal Code). This type of activity challenges fundamental premises of the British common law, wherein justice and punishment are individualised.

British law has been concerned with *individual responsibility* [emphasis added] for criminal acts. People can be prosecuted as accomplices or accessories or as participants in a conspiracy or under Scots law for 'art and part guilt' (group criminality) but they cannot be prosecuted, except in exceptional circumstances, for being members of an organisation. (Anderson 1993: 293)

Consequently, this type of US legislative model has been resisted in the UK (Levi and Smith 2002). Rather the concept of 'serious crime' and the use of measures in the SCA 2007, such as the SCPO and provisions pertaining to encouraging and assisting crime, are favoured as they uphold the British legal tradition of focusing on 'individual responsibility' for complicity.

Given that the UK Parliament has resisted calling the 'organised crime duck' a 'duck', it is questionable as to why this terminology has continued to 'hatch' in recent parliamentary 'bills'. This inclusion of the 'organised duck' is clearly apparent in policy-making activities under examination (for example, the Serious 'Organised Crime' and Police Act 2005 and the Serious 'Organised Crime' Agency). While the operational definition of organised crime for the purposes of policy-making is often vague or unknown, it remains an important and recognised issue to focus on:

> [O]rganised crime [was] at the top of the 1998 UN criminological agenda. . . . This great political confluence has led to international pressure to harmonize the fight against organised crime, even if people do not always have a clear understanding of what 'it' is. (Levi 1998: 337)

There are two principal explanations for the persistent use of this terminology. First, it is clear that there is an extant, evocative, and rhetorical meaning of organised crime (which might be different to the reality of the organised criminal activity).

> If a series of very real criminal problems can be grouped under a term which makes an impact on both professional and popular audiences, the pressure to use it becomes overwhelming. (Anderson 1993: 308)

That is to say, there is a strong political incentive to use the language of organised crime in the drafting of bills or in public debate, as it conjures up images (whether entirely accurate or not) of some of the most serious criminal activities in society. Second, as referred to above, the influence of international harmonisation in the response to this type of serious criminal activity has undoubtedly compelled the use of this term in policy circles. The influence of US policy has added to the confusion in the UK in relation to the organised crime/serious crime distinction. The UK cooperates with the US and other countries in areas of 'mutual legal assistance' (for example, extraditions or legal cooperation), 'policy coordination' (for example, treaties and shared information), and 'operational activities' (for example, intelligence and data/information sharing).[12] Similarly, joint task forces, committees, and law enforcement initiatives within Europe have clearly played an analogous role.

> All these types of cooperation are officially concerned with serious crime rather than organised crime, although the term organised crime is often mentioned in their deliberations and documents. Participation in these overlapping circles provides part of the explanation for the introduction of the term organised crime on to the UK political agenda. (Anderson 1993: 305)

This environment of international cooperation has arguably made it difficult for the UK to avoid using the popular expression of organised crime (Anderson 1993: 305). Contemporary legislative and policy responses, particularly the SCA 2007, mark a significant shift away from the confusion created by the organised crime (operational) definition; however, they are not without their own set of ambiguities.

2.3.1   Any crime?

In the white paper (Home Office 2004: 4) *One Step Ahead: A 21st-Century Strategy to Defeat Organised Crime*, the government stated its intention to be 'lawfully audacious' by using anything in its reach to deal with the harms of organised crime. The white paper outlined the new agency that would acquire responsibility for this so-called audacious direction and operation. Soon after, the SOCPA 2005 established this agency, SOCA. The white paper also stressed that SOCA would need new superior 'technologies and methods' in order to achieve its position of being one step ahead (Home Office 2004: 4). Accordingly, a consultation (green) paper was published in 2006, entitled *New Powers Against Organised and Financial Crime*, which essentially put forward those measures listed in the SCA 2007, discussed above – principally creating, but also extending data-sharing initiatives, amending participatory offences such as encouraging and assisting crime, creating 'Organised Crime Prevention Orders',[13] and amending proceeds of crime legislation (Home Office 2006a). Both the white and green papers sought to deal with various perceived 'gaps' in criminal law and policy, which have allegedly rendered law enforcement and the criminal justice system vulnerable to those at the 'edges', or on the 'fringes', of serious and organised crime (Home Office 2004: 15, 30, 41; Home Office 2006b: 10, 26, 29). The government's reference in these papers to the fringes (or edges) of this criminal activity refers to both those who manage to avoid prosecution and those who encourage and assist criminal acts (Fortson 2008: 13). The SOCPA 2005 principally provided an enhanced law enforcement agency to deal with those on the fringes of serious/organised crime,[14] while the SCA 2007 provided the means to reach those on the fringes.

Despite the declared intention to respond to serious and organised crime, the two resultant pieces of legislation (SOCPA 2005; SCA 2007) reach far beyond this category of offences. First, while it was the intention that SOCA deal with Level 3 crime, it was *not* bound by the SOCPA 2005 in relation to its investigative ambit: '[D]espite its name, SOCA's work is not in fact restricted to crime which is either serious or organised' (Owen et al. 2005: 10). For example, Part 3 of SOCPA 2005 in relation to police powers including powers of arrest without a warrant (s.110), power to direct a person to leave a place (s.112), and power to take fingerprints (s.117) or impressions of footwear (s.118) applied to criminal investigations for *all* offences regardless of seriousness (Owen et al. 2005: 72). Similarly, SOCA's powers relating to intelligence extended to all types of crime, including 'non-serious crime' (SOCPA 2005: s.5(30);[15] Fitzpatrick 2006: 130). The Joint Committee on Human Rights (2005: 2.11) expressed apprehension about this issue during the drafting of the Serious Organised Crime and Police Bill:

> We are concerned that the Government appears to be invoking a particularly serious threat (from serious organised crime) to justify taking exceptional powers to interfere with the individual's private life, which it then uses in relation to the lesser threat posed by ordinary crime. This is how civil liberties are gradually eroded over time.

The government argued, however, that this open authority was justified owing to the non-specific and nebulous nature of serious and organised criminal activity.

> [E]ven lone operators, who are not motivated by profit, could inflict considerable damage to persons and institutions and it was therefore left to the SOCA to decide for itself which areas of criminal activity warrant its attention, whether or not the conduct in question would ordinarily be regarded as organised. (Owen et al. 2005: 2)

The discussion of the SCA 2007 above showed that there are a number of expansive provisions which merit more detailed examination. These liberal provisions in the SCA 2007 can be extended to *any* crimes, not just serious crime. There are few restrictions proscribed in numerous parts of the SCA 2007: 'Despite the reference in the short title of the 2007 Act, to "Serious Crime", a significant number of provisions of that Act apply to *all* crimes of varying gravity' (Fortson 2008: 3). First and foremost, Part 2 of the SCA 2007, *Encouraging or Assisting Crime*, is certainly not limited to the serious offences outlined above in Schedule 1 of the Act. That is, throughout all the sections of Part 2 (ss.44–67), there is no limiting language – there are merely references made to 'an offence' – thus the Act can be interpreted to apply to the encouraging or assisting of all offences.[16] Equally, Part 3 (Chapter I) of the SCA 2007, *Prevention of Fraud*, contains no definition of fraud for the purposes of the Act. This suggests that the data-sharing provisions in the SCA 2007 can be invoked for all cases of fraud, with no measure of 'serious fraud' and 'no monetary thresholds' (Fortson 2008: 3).

Finally, Part 1 of the SCA 2007, *Serious Crime Prevention Orders*, which sets out provisions for the use of SCPO, also has the potential to be exceptionally wide-reaching. An SCPO can be issued if either the High Court on application or the Crown Court on conviction

> is satisfied that a person has been involved with serious crime . . . [and the Court] has reasonable grounds to believe that the order would protect the public by preventing, restricting or disrupting involvement by the person in serious crime. (SCA 2007: s.1(1))

There are two apparent conditions in this section that demonstrate the 2007 Act's broad applicability. First, while a 'serious offence' in the SCA 2007 (s.2(2)(a)) principally refers to those offences listed in Schedule 1 of the Act (delineated above), there is a second provision (s.2(2)(b)) which states that a serious offence

> is one which, in the particular circumstances of the case, the court considers to be sufficiently serious to be treated for the purposes of the application or matter as if it were so specified.

There are grounds to question the intention of the legislature and the meaning of the notion of 'sufficiently serious'. In particular, it is unclear whether judges should interpret s.2(2)(b) based on whether the particulars of the case are serious enough when weighed against the relative seriousness of the offences listed in Schedule 1, or rather in relation to the judicial requirement to be satisfied that an order is necessary to protect the public (Fortson 2008: 33). If it is left to judicial discretion to decide what is sufficiently serious with respect to *public protection*, conceivably any offence or ('serious') social threat could constitute reasonable grounds for an order.

The second expansive aspect relates to the definition of 'involvement' in the Act. As outlined above, the Act provides that a person has been involved in serious crime if they have either 'committed a serious offence' (s.2(1)(a)), 'facilitated the commission by another person of a serious offence' (s.2(1)(b)), or 'conducted himself [sic] in a way that was likely to facilitate the commission by himself or another person of a serious offence' (s.2(1)(c)). The first element of *committing* an offence (s.2(1)(a)) is arguably less problematic given that the court must determine that a person has actually been engaged in a criminal act. However, even this seemingly straightforward condition raises doubts as to whether an SCPO should be used at all in these circumstances. That is, if there is ample evidence to persuade the court that a person has committed an offence, why should that person *not* be subject to criminal prosecution, with all of its safeguards? This is particularly pertinent given that it is expected that, after the House of Lords decision in *McCann* (*R v Manchester Crown Court* [2003]), the civil standard of proof to issue an SCPO will be heightened to the level of the criminal standard, that is, beyond all reasonable doubt (Explanatory Note 2007; SCA 2007).

The second two classifications of involvement in serious crime present further complications, as each requires the *facilitation* of a serious offence. Facilitation is not defined in the SCA 2007 itself, although the Explanatory Notes (2007: 4) specify that it should take 'its natural meaning of "to make easier"'. Fortson (2008: 35) exemplifies the complexity of determining whether an accused person has made it easier for another person (P) in the commission of a serious offence:

> [B]y selling a car to P, believing that P would use it to commit a robbery (which he did) . . . [t]he subject's purpose was to make a profit from the sale of a car, but he was indifferent about whether P would commit the offence or not. But would it be permissible for the court to construe the word 'facilitating' as amounting to no more than indifference on the part of the subject (or a lack of awareness) that his/her acts had facilitated the commission of an offence?

This question essentially goes to the accused's *intention in facilitating* the serious offence, which is somewhat nebulous and difficult to substantiate. Furthermore, s.2(1)(c) provides grounds for application if an accused has 'conducted himself in a way that was likely to facilitate the commission by himself or another person of a serious offence'. This goes one step further by providing that for an SCPO to be applied, intention to facilitate a serious crime is not a necessary requirement (indirect facilitation satisfies the lowest threshold of inchoate activity).

The legislature's solution to the conceptual complexities posed by the term organised crime has been to avoid its definition altogether and replace it with much broader concepts relating to serious crime. The open statutory scope of 'serious crime' (potentially classifying any crime as serious), and the inclusion of indirect facilitation as a basis for inchoate liability make the 2007 Act an exceptionally broad-reaching instrument of state control. The SCPO is no exception to the expansive powers in the 2007 Act, reaching beyond the confines of criminal law as a civil–criminal hybrid order. In subsequent chapters, the SCPO is analysed in the context of other hybrid orders.[17] However, in the last section of this chapter, the SCPO is examined within a framework of regulatory approaches to organised crime control.

2.4   Reactionary and regulatory responses to organised crime

Levi and Maguire (2004: 398) argue that responses to organised crime should focus on both harmful *acts* (targeting serious offences) and harmful *actors* (suppressing growth and disrupting the structures of organised crime groups and associations). At the broadest level there are two categories of responses which target harmful acts and actors: conventional, post hoc, reactionary responses through law enforcement and prosecution of criminal offences, and newer, pre hoc, regulatory and disruptive responses that sit outside the criminal law. Pre hoc responses that prioritise the disruption of criminal activity are less concerned with prosecuting those engaging in such activity. Levi and Maguire's (2004) analyses of these two models suggest that the central paradigm for global organised crime control policy remains one of a post hoc law enforcement approach, although pre hoc methods are becoming deeply entrenched. These two categories of approach are briefly canvassed in this last section of the chapter to demonstrate how contemporary efforts, namely those examined above (SOCPA 2005; SCA 2007), appear to be tilting towards regulatory, pre hoc methods. Such methods, developed outside the mainstream criminal justice system, are a potential problematic as they risk escaping judicial scrutiny and oversight that would afford the usual safeguards against governmental excess.

Under past agencies such as NCIS, NCS, and HMCE organised crime had conventionally been managed through post hoc law enforcement procedures, namely through stages of suspicion, detection, arrest, charge, prosecution, trial, conviction, and sentence (Harfield 2008). This type of reactionary response tends to focus on harmful *acts* (waiting for a criminal offence to occur) rather than the *actors* involved. While some actors are clearly affected by post hoc responses (that is, the perpetrators of a serious offence who are successfully convicted), in many cases, organised criminal groups have the capacity simply to replace convicted individuals and continue their involvement in illicit activities. The effectiveness of state intervention to redress the problems of organised crime through these methods, for example, the prosecution of individuals for specific offences, is questionable if ultimately the patterns of harmful action endure (Levi and Maguire 2004: 401). The shortcomings of post hoc procedures are also recognised in government and law enforcement circles that believe the criminal justice system has 'tilted the balance excessively towards the defence', and that criminal law protections and safeguards can easily be exploited by professional criminals (Home Office 2004: 44).

Harfield (2008: 67, 72) suggests that organised crime is beyond the reach of the traditional criminal justice system of trial and prosecution, though not necessarily owing to exploitable procedural rules. Rather, there are deficient resources and agency coordination, which are necessary to prosecute this type of criminal behaviour: first, there are often no witnesses, for example, for conspiracy charges; second, prosecutions of this scale require sophisticated intelligence; and finally, there is a lack of communication and cooperation between law enforcement agencies (Harfield 2008). This lack of agency communication was vividly depicted in an account given by a prosecutor who was interviewed by Harfield (2008: 65), of a case in which nine investigative teams within three distinct agencies were investigating the same criminal group. The lack of cooperation was attributed to agency demands to reach performance targets and make key arrests and seizures (Harfield 2008: 65). It is clear that some of the measures contained in SOCPA 2005 and SCA 2007 (examined above) are expanding criminalisation, and therefore enhance post hoc law enforcement and prosecutorial approaches. For example, the provision in relation to encouraging and assisting crime creates new inchoate offences that criminalise the involvement in or facilitation of serious criminal acts. This generates new offences on the fringe of

organised criminal activity. However, it is apparent that these two statutory acts also indicate the state's proclivity for pre hoc approaches in
organised crime control.

2.5   Pre hoc approaches

There are a number of pre hoc methods used to respond to serious/
organised crime, which can be broken down into three categories: *community approaches*, principally local crime prevention strategies such as
interest groups, public education and dedicated 'tip-off hotlines'; *regulatory approaches*, including data sharing between government agencies,
international agency cooperation, and financial regulation of illicit
business activity through corporate governance and surveillance such as
reporting of suspicious transactions; and *private sector approaches*, including private sector statutory requirements and public–private sector collaboration (Levi and Maguire 2004: 411–423). The SOCPA 2005 and SCA
2007 contain numerous instances of a pre hoc approach. For example,
the provisions relating to data matching and asset recovery advance
the cooperation within and between the public and private sectors, and
regulate the financial activities of criminal groups. However, the central
provisions of each act (the development of both SOCA and the SCPO,
respectively) provide the most compelling illustrations of the pre hoc
approach which chiefly aspires to regulate and disrupt the activities of
individuals involved in organised crime before its commission.[18]

   The law enforcement model for SOCA represented a paradigmatic
shift to 'intelligence and disruption rather than detection and prosecution' (Harfield 2008: 68). Arguably, post hoc responses can also operate
through policing practices that *disrupt*, and intervene in, the workings
of organised crime groups. For example, Gilmour (2008: 18) argues that
organised crime groups are often undermined through prosecuting the
individuals involved with 'minor offences, such as benefit fraud and
anti-social behaviour'.[19] Nonetheless, SOCA's concentration on disruption rather than prosecution marked a significant shift away from traditional post hoc law enforcement procedures. According to SOCA's annual
report (2006–2007: 7), the agency's priorities were to be intelligence-led,
to reduce the 'underlying harms' associated with organised crime, to disrupt and dislocate (to outside the UK) criminal markets, and to recover
assets and proceeds of crime. Unlike conventional policing agencies that
operate within the purview of traditional law enforcement, SOCA's priority was not necessarily to prosecute. Moreover, Fitzpatrick (2006: 135)
argues that SOCA played a large role in disallowing 'phone-tap' evidence

to be admitted in serious criminal hearings because it believed that the use of its surveillance as court evidence would compromise the secrecy of its surveillance techniques. Again this indicates SOCA's preference for intelligence and regulation rather than (or at least as a priority to) enhancing traditional forms of prosecution.

The white paper (Home Office 2004: 12) that preceded both the 2005 and 2007 Acts proposed the following three objectives for responding to organised crime: (1) reduce the profit opportunities for organised crime, (2) disrupt organised crime businesses and markets, and (3) increase direct state intervention targeting members of organised crime groups. For the first two objectives, it is apparent that the desired responses are based on non-prosecutorial disruption and regulation of the *product or output* of illicit activity, particularly by

> using all the regulatory and other powers at our disposal, including our tax powers, our financial recovery powers and our powers to bear down on money laundering. (Home Office 2004: 12)

The third objective, direct state intervention, would traditionally be achieved through criminalisation to increase the risk of prosecution for the *producers* of organised crime (individual actors). However, contemporary responses have opted for an earlier form of intervention that restricts and prohibits an individual's behaviour by issuing an SCPO (though this may also eventually result in prosecution if an order is breached). The SCPO with its powers to make requirements, restrictions, and prohibitions on an individual can surely be classified as regulatory, if not punitive.[20] However, the SCPO can be distinguished from other regulatory measures in this field since it operates through direct intervention targeting individuals (rather than output), and can achieve its purpose by stepping outside the criminal law (placing tailored prohibitions on individuals without first proving their guilt). This ambitious and overextended form of regulation risks obscuring its basic claims and intention:

> Arguably, therefore, regulation has proved to be less about withdrawal of the state than the ushering in of a period of hyper-activity marked by legislative frenzy; an expanding apparatus of control; and a colonizing impulse quite at odds with the minimalism to which the regulatory state pretended. (Ashworth and Zedner 2008: 40)

The SCPO can be applied either pre hoc (through civil application in the High Court) or post hoc (as part of sentencing). In post hoc (criminal) circumstances, the application of an SCPO is less objectionable because the criminal trial privileges and safeguards have been afforded to the individual who has already been convicted. For example, Harfield (2008: 64) maintains that two criminal trial privileges are paramount: that oral evidence is provided by witnesses in court, and that defendants are given the opportunity to cross-examine witnesses. Such privileges are not afforded in the circumstances of pre hoc application, as the orders are imposed in civil court procedure where hearsay evidence (such as that which may be included in written witness statements) is admissible, and cross-examination is generally not possible.

Therefore, the SCPO is clearly traversing new territory. While it falls within the theoretical scope of pre hoc regulatory and disruptive measures employed in an attempt to be 'one step ahead' of serious offenders and their illicit activities, the SCPO also moves multiple steps in numerous other innovative directions. The SCPO marks a step away from past policies in this arena, and a step around the terminology of 'organised' crime. It moves a step beyond (blanket) regulatory measures by focusing on the regulation of specific individual action. And it takes a step sideways, outside the long-honoured tradition of common law criminal trial procedures and protections.

> Organized crime is today a great, unmanageable threatening fact in the lives of our communities. It is not enough to ask whether the machinery of law enforcement is good, we must go further, call in question the wisdom of the laws themselves and discover whether or not some of our experiments are not as menacing in their effect as criminal activities. (Chamberlin 1932: 668–669)

These remarks by Chamberlin in 1932 resonate with the current analysis of the SCPO, which is clearly a measure that is part of some interesting experiments in 21st-century crime control. Yet remarkably little is known (or written) about the nature and origins of the SCPO and how it came to occupy such a prominent place on the organised crime control agenda.

This chapter has assessed the SCPO in the broader context of the developments in serious and organised crime control in the UK, including shifts to a 'serious' crime definition, and an apparent preference for pre hoc regulatory responses. In the next chapter, the SCPO and pre hoc regulatory responses will be shown to be part of a much larger theoretical transformation in criminal justice, driven by a pervading preventive ideology.

3
A State of Prevention

While the SCPO is a new and innovative response to organised crime, it has strong foundations in other areas of crime control. The nature, form, and function of the SCPO, outlined in Chapter 2, mirror a broader set of 'preventive orders' in the UK, including the Anti-Social Behaviour Order (hereafter ASBO), terrorism Control Order, and Football Banning Order, to name the most notorious examples.[1] The essential components of the preventive order model are threefold: first, it can place prohibitions and/or restrictions on an individual or other entity,[2] second, it is intended to prevent harms (or risks of harm) associated with a *specific offence category*, and third, the breach of an order constitutes a strict liability criminal offence.[3] These three criteria are explored further in Chapter 6, which provides a legislative analysis of the development of the preventive order model over time.

This chapter develops a conceptual framework to assist in understanding the expanded (and extensive) use of preventive orders in the UK. The framework that is developed throughout the chapter examines the role of prevention and preventive discourses in shaping and changing the approach to criminal justice and its crime control policies. It examines the historical role of prevention in shaping criminal justice practices and institutions, and assesses the more recent observations by criminal justice professionals and criminologists that indicate a new proclivity towards a greater role for a preventive jurisprudence. Historically, the criminal justice system has worked largely retrospectively, encompassing reactive policing, investigation, a criminal trial, and (if guilty) post hoc punishment. However, the movements discussed in this chapter highlight an apparent proactive state ideology, and a range of future-orientated measures to prevent various degrees of harm. This expands the discussion in Chapter 2 about the legislative trend in the field of

d organised crime towards regulatory, pre hoc measures. It is
.at a preventive ideology lies behind many of the key con-
emporary themes in criminological discourse (including regulation, risk, and security). These themes are driving the creation of new crime control responses, which together embody a questionable system of 'preventive justice'.

The first section of this chapter contains a brief overview of the existing literature that has noted a pre-emptive turn in criminal justice. The second section (3.2) conceptualises the broader spectrum of preventive state action in the UK, particularly the relationship between preventive orders and preventive detention (or indeterminate sentences of imprisonment for public protection [hereafter IPP], introduced by the Criminal Justice Act 2003). The next two sections (3.3 and 3.4) examine the historical role of prevention and emphasise the abiding challenge that this concept presents to some of the central pillars of criminal justice (namely, the distinction between civil and criminal procedure, and justifications for punishment). In the fifth and final section (3.5), it is shown that prevention is the imperative driving the new penology and state developments based on regulation, risk, and security.

3.1 The preventive state, pre-emptive turn, and preventive justice

The preventive or pre-emptive turn in criminal justice has been identified to acknowledge new policy approaches that aim to anticipate future harm, based on uncertain information and risk (Zedner 2009). This has been argued to mark a shift from a reactive to a proactive state in seeking out new risk-based techniques (Janus 2004: 33). As a consequence, several commentators have called for greater recognition and analysis of the function of the 'preventive state', and the constitutional limits and constraining legal principles that should apply to the use of coercive state action in the name of prevention (Steiker 1998; Janus 2004; Ashworth and Zedner 2014). One early commentator, Steiker (1998), observed that there are existing rules or limits for the state in relation to how and when it can investigate, and how and when it can punish. These rules are established within criminal law and procedure to guarantee fundamental fairness and justice, such as established due process protections and constraint on police powers and practices.[4] For example, fair trial and high standards of proof and rules of evidence are required before the state can punish; likewise stop, search, and seizure powers are curbed by the requirement that there must be reasonable grounds for suspicion so as to maximise the protection of the right to liberty and freedom from arbitrary investigation. However, Steiker (1998: 774) stressed that these rules are less clear when the state wishes to prevent:

> [C]ourts and commentators have had much less to say about the related topic of the limits of the state not as punisher (and thus, necessarily as investigator and adjudicator of criminal acts) but rather as preventer of crime and disorder generally. Indeed, courts and commentators have not yet even recognized this topic *as* a distinct phenomenon either doctrinally or conceptually. . . . The state can also attempt to identify and neutralise dangerous individuals before they commit crimes by restricting their liberty in a variety of ways.

Steiker's (1998: 776–777) focus was on doctrinal issues such as the question of what constitutes punishment and is thus subject to constitutional protections, and what limits remain for measures that are not punitive but rather preventive: 'What constitutional and/or policy limits are there on the non-punitive "preventive" state?' In particular, there has been a growth in developments 'giving the police more authority to intervene earlier to prevent' through, for example, police powers related to loitering, 'move-on', and stop and search, as well as legislative 'restraints' or 'prophylactic measures' that aim to deal with dangerous individuals, including sex offender registrations and sexual predator laws (Steiker 1998: 774–776). In fact, various criminal justice institutions (and related institutions) employ preventive measures and powers as part of the crime control function. These preventive functions operate within various institutions of criminal justice, such as policing (stop and search, detention for questioning), criminal courts (pre-trial detention, preventive orders), mental health (commitment of individuals who are found to be mentally ill), civil courts (injunctions, civil preventive orders), and juvenile detention and prisons (civil commitment). Steiker (1998: 778) argues that these measures have all been assessed separately as discrete measures and that the inherent similarities between these measures should be acknowledged and scrutinised further under a broader framework of prevention. These specific manifestations of the preventive state are examined in Section 3.2.

A further distinction is made by Janus (2004: 2), who distinguishes between 'radical' and 'routine' prevention:

> First, radical prevention seeks to intervene where there is some sort of 'propensity' or risk of *future* harm, whereas routine prevention

responds to actual or attempted harm. Second, radical prevention operates by substantially curtailing people's liberty *before* harm results, whereas in routine prevention individuals suffer deprivations of liberty only after actual harm is done or attempted.[5]

Janus (2004: 2) asserts that radical prevention policies target outsider groups in exceptional cases, such as sex offenders, terrorists, and the mentally ill. Varied examples of defunct radical preventive laws of the past are provided as illustrations, including legislation targeting: sexual predators, sterilisation, race-based discrimination, Japanese prisoners of war, homosexuality, vagrancy, anti-loitering, 'political speech' during war time, and bio-terrorism in emergency times (Janus 2004: 17). It is argued that this creates a jurisprudence of 'the other', which allows coercive action to be taken against individuals deemed dangerous, without 'triggering' public concern and outcry about the rights-derogating and punitive aspects of these policies (Janus 2004: 24). Accordingly, Janus (2004: 31) warns that there is a danger that we will

> awaken our old addiction, supporting an expansive use of outsider logic, just at a time when we thought we had gotten some control over that destructive and immoral practice.

Furthermore, in recognising this orientation of the preventive state, it is also important to realise that the formation of this new body of measures constructs an additional arm of state control:

> The most significant development in the crime control field is not the transformation of criminal justice institutions but rather the development, alongside these institutions, of a quite different way of regulating crime and criminals. Alongside policing and penalty there has grown up a third 'governmental' sector – the new apparatus of prevention and security. (Garland 2001: 170)

This third sector can be seen as divorced from customary proceedings (arrest, trial, prosecution, and sentence). This is an important distinction when conceptualising the role of prevention, as new measures arguably add to (rather than replace) existing coercive measures established within the criminal justice system. Conversely, as this third sector is separated from the criminal law, it has also been conceptualised as a form of '*counter-law* with the primary aim of getting around the legal barriers to the use of coercive institutions or confinement as a preventive strategy' (emphasis added, Hebenton and Seddon 2009:

347; see generally, Ericson 2007[6]). Robinson (2001: 1455–1456) argues that preventive measures[7] have become 'cloaked' by the criminal justice system, but they should be recognised in a separate preventive system. The benefit is that they would be rendered more transparent and accountable, as well as being subject to debate, rather than being hidden behind the structures of criminal justice (Robinson 2001). This has led to questions about the potential of and for a system of 'preventive justice'.[8] Zedner (2003: 174–175) suggests that a preventive justice framework could adopt some principles from the criminal law, but new preventive standards might also need to be devised.[9] One issue with the term 'preventive justice' is that it inherently suggests that such practices are, or can be, *just*. While outside the necessary scope of this book, this assumption that adequate standards or principles underpin the practices and policies associated with prevention is open to debate.

Finally, the reasons for the recent ascendancy of prevention are also contested and unresolved. O'Malley and Hutchinson (2009: 206) contend that while the 'preventive government' is not new, there has been a re-emergence of this concept as part of the 'rise of liberalism'. However, there is some general agreement in the literature that these developments should be perceived in part as an 'aggressive preventive agenda' in response to terrorism (Janus 2004: 1). Many scholars, including Tadros (2007: 664), contend that notions of prevention and pre-emption in government and policy circles have heightened after the events in the US on 11 September 2001 involving terrorist attacks in New York and Washington (hereinafter referred to as 9/11). Similarly, Zedner (2007a: 174) asserts that 'the growth of terrorist activity has generated an emerging genre of preventive justice'. Despite these contentions, Crawford (2006: 455 and 2009: 18) suggests that in the UK the anti-social behaviour agenda is largely responsible for having paved the way towards such preventive thinking. It is a central premise of this book that the combination of these two policy agendas (terrorism and anti-social behaviour), which are broadly at opposite ends of the spectrum of seriousness of offences, left a sizeable gap in crime control. More importantly, this gap has inevitably been filled with legislative and policy responses emanating from these two extremes. This suggests that policy precedents can be created (either intentionally or unintentionally) which might facilitate the spread of ideas, in this case resulting in an increased preventive ideology. Later chapters develop more detailed theoretical explanations for the rise of the preventive state, particularly through the lens of the policy-making process. However, the focus of this chapter is on the *evidence* and *implications* of the preventive state, in order to establish whether or not it can be said with certainty that the UK is in a state of prevention.

3.2 Conceptualising the interventions of a preventive state

An increasing amount of law and policy is being implemented by successive governments in the US and UK that allows intrusive state intervention, which is defended in the name of prevention. Many of these new measures use coercive *means*, which resemble coercive techniques historically associated with punishment and sentence. These can be conceptually divided into two types of coercive measures: those which result in more serious *deprivations* of liberty and those resulting in *restrictions* of liberty. This has also become legally significant because deprivation (as opposed to restriction) of liberty is only warranted under certain specific conditions. The jurisprudence of the Strasbourg Court (see, for example, in *Engel and others v Netherlands* [1976: paras. 60–66]) delimits the point at which restrictions become deprivations, in relation to military sanctions (including 'light arrest', 'aggravated arrest', 'strict arrest', and 'committal to a disciplinary unit'). In UK cases relating to the detention of terrorists this has resulted in 18-hour home detention being determined a deprivation of liberty, whereas 12 or 14 hours were both accepted by the House of Lords as mere restrictions on liberty.[10] This 'murky distinction between restrictions and deprivation of liberty' makes a clear division difficult to delimit (Zedner 2007a: 183). However, the conceptual utility of creating a distinction is of particular value in understanding the degree of restriction imposed by various preventive measures. A depiction of a number of preventive measures and their level of limitation on liberty is presented in Figure 3.1.

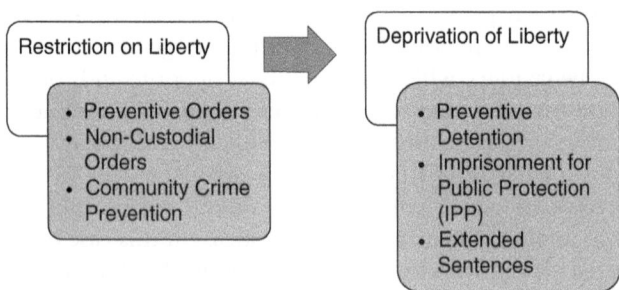

Figure 3.1 Degree of limitation on liberty

Figure 3.1 shows how policy measures containing restrictions (partial deprivations) of liberty lie at one end of the spectrum of limitations (for example, preventive orders), while more complete deprivations of liberty lie at the other end (for example, preventive detention). This spectrum can be further appropriated to acknowledge the various intermediary levels of limitation on liberty. For example, Zedner's (2007a: 188) analysis indicates that community crime-prevention initiatives would be at the far lower and 'anodyne' end of the spectrum. In addition, further distinctions could be made *between* different preventive orders. For example, the severe restrictions and conditions imposed by a terrorism Control Order (including periodic home detention) could be conceptualised as lying closer to deprivations of liberty when compared to other orders such as the ASBO or Football Banning Order. Indeed some of the terms of Control Orders were deemed by the courts to constitute a deprivation of liberty and therefore unlawful and in contravention of Article 6 of the ECHR (namely, 18-hour home curfew), whereas fewer hours of home detention are deemed to constitute mere restriction (see *Secretary of State for the Home Department v JJ and others* [2007: para. 105]; *v E and another* [2007: para. 11]; *v MB and others* [2007: para. 10]).

Interestingly, directly following the 9/11 attacks, the Control Order regime under the Prevention of Terrorism Act 2005 essentially replaced preventive detention measures which were enacted under the Anti-Terrorism, Crime and Security Act 2001 (see the 'Belmarsh Case', *A and others v Secretary of State for the Home Department* [2004]). Therefore, the preventive order model could be seen as an alternative to the more severe deprivations imposed by imprisonment. Ashworth and Zedner (2010: 79) argue that 'deprivation of liberty for purely preventive purposes may be justifiable *in extremis* and *as a last resort*, when nothing less will provide adequate public protection' (emphasis added). It is the second component of this assertion, 'as a last resort', which suggests preventive orders are being imposed as an alternative to detention. This rule of last resort emphasises the potential utility of restrictions on liberty being utilised before the more hastened use of deprivations. The regime of preventive orders could be seen as an alternative to preventive detention, but also as an alternative to mainstream imprisonment resulting from conviction:

I suspect that some kinds of deprivation of liberty or property will provide the most adequate and humane forms of punishment, even if the deprivation of liberty should not take the form of imprisonment as commonly as it presently does. (Tadros 2007: 661)

This approach also links to broader principles of minimal state intervention in punishment that have corollary advantages in diluting the punitive state and reducing imprisonment. Indeed Slobogin (2005: 123) maintains that 'individual prevention should become the predominant goal of the criminal justice system'. If we embrace the preventive model, there may be significant benefits:

> Imprisonment, which is the most common type of punishment, is in a deep sense not commensurate with blame; depriving someone virtually all of his freedom because he raped, robbed or assaulted someone is a gigantic moral non-sequitur. (Slobogin 2005: 146)

Furthermore, Slobogin (2005: 147) asserts that complete deprivation of liberty, as in the common practice of imprisonment, is not always fair because 'as a constitutional matter, the degree of liberty deprivation should be limited to that necessary to achieve the government's prevention aims'. It is argued that more accurate responses would either be the 'eye-for-an-eye shibboleth' (a more accurate retributivist punishment, but widely morally unacceptable) or reparation and restorative justice (which is more accurate as it pays back victims and society, but is not acceptable to retributivists) (Slobogin 2005: 146). These *prima facie* potential benefits of the preventive order model at sentencing should not be overlooked (the role of preventive measures and retributive punishment is analysed further in Section 3.4.2).

Some categories of conduct can potentially attract both preventive restrictions and preventive deprivations of liberty (particularly violent and sexual offending), while others can only be addressed by restrictions. There have been no specific provisions in respect of serious and organised crimes in the UK (drug and people trafficking, major fraud, etc.) which permit preventive detention (neither post-conviction nor pre-trial). Therefore, if the state wishes to intervene to limit the liberty of individuals who are believed to be engaged in serious criminal activity, the state can attempt either to deprive their liberty through imprisonment (after trial and prosecution) or to make preventive restrictions on liberty pre-trial (using an SCPO).

Steiker (1998: 778) has criticised the lack of acknowledgement of the relationship between preventive measures: '[E]ach individual preventive practice has been treated as *sui generis* rather than as a facet of a larger question in need of a more general conceptual framework.' However, there is an equal danger of treating these measures as all the same, where, for example, preventive orders or even preventive detention might be justified in relation to terrorism (perhaps on a temporary basis during times of emergency), but this use might not be generalisable to other categories of serious crime. Nonetheless, it is important to recognise these measures as being part of the same spectrum of state intervention on liberty, as 'together this growing raft of preventive measures suggest a larger change that might appear all the more palpable if the parallels between these various measures were recognized' (Zedner 2007a: 189). In this task of drawing such parallels, and unifying theories of the state of prevention, it is stressed that it is equally important to assess the discrete utility and justification for each new measure. Given that restrictions (preventive orders) and deprivations (preventive detention) can be conceived as being on the same scale of state coercive intervention, those measures which deprive the liberty of an individual (the ultimate end of the scale) are examined briefly in the next section.

3.2.1   Preventive detention and the imprisonment
for public protection order

The practice of preventive detention reflects the state's tendency to intervene earlier to prevent crime and deal with risks of harm. The logic behind and rationale for preventive detention is straightforward: 'identifying "dangerous" people and depriving them of their liberty *before* they can do harm' (Janus 2004: 1). However, any deprivation of liberty must also be considered lawful under Article 5 of the ECHR. Prevention provides an avenue for forging exceptions to Article 5, where detention is made lawful in subsections (1)(c) 'when it is reasonably considered necessary to *prevent* his [sic] committing an offence' and (1)(e) 'for the *prevention* of the spreading of infectious diseases, [and] of persons of unsound mind, alcoholics or drug addicts or vagrants' (emphasis added). In the UK, under the Criminal Justice Act 2003 new preventive powers were given to the courts, namely, extended sentences (s.225) and indeterminate sentences (s.227), whereby a prisoner's 'release [is] made by the Parole Board on the basis of assessments of risk to the public' (Hebenton and Seddon 2009: 348). These so-called 'dangerous offender' provisions – and the provision for IPP in particular – enable the judiciary to make decisions based on a precautionary logic (Hebenton and Seddon 2009: 348). Since their inception, these provisions have resulted in a large number of prisoners on indeterminate sentences (approximately 1,000 after the first year of implementation), which have incarcerated prisoners beyond the term allocated for punishment or 'tariff' (Jacobson and Hough 2010: 9). Owing to wide criticism of the results of this policy leading to an unsustainable prison population and also the unjust nature of extended prison terms, the IPP provision was amended by the Criminal Justice and Immigration Act 2008 to remove the mandatory requirement on judges to sentence using an IPP if certain minimum conditions were met.[11] However, the IPP provision is still widely used by courts at sentencing and the population of IPP prisoners continues to rise, from 1,079 in June 2006 to 5,828 in January 2010 (Jacobson and Hough 2010: 12; see also Hebenton and Seddon 2009, and Ramsay 2012).[12]

In the US, the literature on preventive detention suggests that this policy is more entrenched. Historically, the quarantine (for example, of 'disease-carrying ships') might be one of the earliest known uses of preventive detention (Richards 1989: 332–333). However, Floud and Young (1981: 41) make an important distinction between this previous policy and the current developments, arguing that '[q]uarantine as a precaution against unintentional harm is one thing; preventive detention as a precaution against wrong-doing is another matter altogether'. The key circumstances under which preventive detention is deployed are in the detention of 'material witnesses', juveniles, mentally ill, sexual predators, and accused persons pre-trial (Dershowitz 1973: 1282–1287; Corrado 1996). Dershowitz (1973: 1283–1293) proposes three points on a 'preventive continuum' where these measures typically fall: pure prevention; actual suspicion; and indefinite confinement. For example, the detention of material witnesses can be determined as 'pure prevention' as individuals are detained either for their own safety or to prevent them from fleeing, their testimony being assessed as crucial to the criminal prosecution in which they have become involved. The detention of individuals pre-trial, however, is based on 'actual suspicion' where there is a criminal charge and the accused person presents a risk of absconding. Finally, those convicted of crimes but, at the end of the service of their sentence, found to be mentally ill or possessing some other perceived qualities of dangerousness (such as 'sexual psychopaths') fall within the category of requiring continued or 'indefinite confinement' (similar to the IPP in the UK).

While the former two categories of preventive detention ('pure prevention' and 'actual suspicion') are arguably more defensible as they are a *temporary* part of criminal procedure,[13] indefinite confinement is more problematic. Indefinite confinement, such as in cases of the IPP, runs the risk of undermining basic principles that underpin sentencing, including the need for certainty of punishment and proportionality of sentence. This can result in the pattern of punishment across more serious and less serious criminal offences becoming indistinguishable or 'flattened'

(Keyzer, Pereira and Southwood 2004: 249). This use of indefinite confinement has proved to be particularly problematic in the US, as it has been increasingly employed in relation to even relatively minor offences (Dershowitz 1973: 1294; Auerhahn 2003).[14] These preventive sentencing practices are grounded on the fact that wrongdoing has already been proved beyond reasonable doubt at trial, and a judge is satisfied that an individual has the potential for future harm (Dershowitz 1973: 1282). However, Robinson (2001: 1452) strongly asserts that at sentencing

> it is difficult enough to determine a person's present dangerousness. . . . [but it is] much more difficult . . . [to determine] whether he would commit an offence if released at the end of the deserved punishment term in the future.

Despite this, Duff (2001: 174) contends that indefinite confinement of 'a very small class of "dangerous" offenders' might be morally defensible, but *only* based on past criminal conduct. That is, some persistent violent offenders might reach a point where determinations can be made about their inherent quality of dangerousness; however, this is argued to be based on an exceptional form of retribution (for the past actions of the offender) and not on preventive predictions about their potential for future harm (Duff 2001: 168–174).

These more extreme measures that deprive the liberty based on preventive rationales clearly contribute to the broader picture of a preventive justice system that is being created. The notion that preventive orders might be justified based on retribution for past criminal harm (for example, at sentencing) is discussed in Section 3.4.2. However, the next section shows how the notion of prevention has a long-held position in criminal justice.

3.3   Historical role of prevention

Prevention and 'preventive justice' are certainly not new concepts of criminal justice and the operation of crime control. Several early criminal law theorists, including Blackstone (cited in Lewis 1922: 1649), discussed the notion of prevention as a central concept guiding the operation of criminal justice practices, institutions, and modes of punishment:

> The policy of preventive justice is the old one of 'an ounce of prevention'. If crime can be prevented at the outset, how much simpler and easier our way of life – this, indeed, is a worthy objective. (Del 1940: 346)

A number of historical examples can be given to demonstrate the role of prevention. First, practices such as the binding-over powers of magistrates to keep the peace were justified on preventive grounds, owing to a perception during the period of King Edward III that 'the machinery of the criminal law . . . [was] unable to preserve the peace of the realm' (Del 1940: 332; see also Ashworth and Zedner 2014: 75). In addition, within the civil law the concept of 'foresight' has long existed in contracts and torts (O'Malley 2004: 4). During the 19th century, there was also a growth of preventive drug, public health and health-and-safety legislation, and new regulatory and urban planning laws aimed at preventing potential harm (O'Malley 2004). Early theorists also held that prevention was the 'only universal purpose of punishment' (Justice Oliver Wendell Holmes; cited in Williams 2009: 68), and indeed 'preferable' to punitive models of justice: '[P]reventive justice is upon every principle, of reason, of humanity, and of sound policy, preferable in all respects to *punishing* justice' (emphasis in original; Blackstone, cited in Lewis 1922: 1649). Finally, the founding principles of the institution of British policing exhibited a central adherence to preventive philosophy as espoused by Robert Peel (Reiner 1992: 768). Community policing was the fundamental pillar of Peel's model, which encompassed preventive patrols and proactive police action.[15]

It is arguable that the debate about the role of prevention in guiding these criminal justice practices, institutions, and theories of punishment has not progressed very far since the days of these early theorists. The inherent ambiguities surrounding the appropriate role of prevention remain unresolved. For example, many of the issues raised early in the debate by Del (1940: 333–334) in relation to binding-over powers, such as their classification as civil or criminal, or the appropriate evidence and standard of proof, are reflected in current debates about the use of new preventive orders.[16] Moreover, debates about the role of prevention in punishment have been subsumed by retributive demands (see Section 3.4.2). That is, there appears to have been little development in delineating a comprehensive framework (conceptual, normative, or otherwise) for preventive justice. However, as stated above, there is recent renewed interest in exploring such frameworks as the various new legislative developments indicate a more proactive state approach to crime control.

The ideology of prevention has also permeated crime control policy through more indirect state means (that is, through its non-legislative arms). Local authorities and non-state actors have engaged in localised, preventive practices based on theories of social and situational crime prevention, which have gained significant public and political support in the last two decades of the 20th century (O'Malley 1996: 189; Ashworth 2005: 68). The situational preventive measures focus on reducing the opportunity to commit crime through target-hardening strategies (such as utilising locks and CCTV) and other opportunity reduction programmes (O'Malley 1996: 189–191). Social crime-prevention initiatives focus on changing the attitudes of potential offenders through local community programmes, such as the Home Office 'Prevent' strategy which attempts to identify, challenge, and change radical Islamic views of individuals and extremist organisations across Britain (Home Office 2011b). These indirect state practices, conducted at the individual or community level, have the benefit of reducing the burden on state law enforcement institutions (Ashworth 2005: 69). However, such crime-prevention strategies can be distinguished from the enquiry into the preventive state. These are *indirect* preventive approaches that aim to change environmental factors to 'design-out' crime or change the conditions conducive to crime, rather than to create preventive measures (such as the SCPO) or laws allowing the imposition of *direct* state coercive action over individuals, in attempts to amend and control their behaviour.[17] A distinction might therefore be drawn between 'situational (general) crime prevention' (focusing on unidentified potential offenders) and, to coin a phrase, 'individual (specific) crime prevention'[18] (focusing on an identified potential offender). These types of individual-targeted sanctions which potentially lead to imprisonment present a challenging new structure, one that has been historically associated with the system of criminal law and criminal prosecution (a system that provides an accompanying set of requisite fundamental protections for accused individuals).

Finally, it is worth noting that preventive measures have also historically been employed as exceptional powers during times of emergency and war. Cole and Lobel (2007: 28) maintain that the US preventive state has manifested itself most obviously in the Bush administration's anti-terrorism policies, using preventive detention, 'coercive interrogation', 'rendition',[19] torture, and other tactics that have stepped outside the rule of law. These exceptional powers are part of a paradigm shift that occurs when the state declares a situation of emergency and derogates from the norm (Cole and Lobel 2007: 29). Gross (2003: 1024) explains how such derogations are based on a political realist claim that during (violent) crises, democracies should actually follow constitutional principles *less strictly* in order to preserve the Constitution. That is, we should not sacrifice a Constitution by making amendments for exceptional individual cases requiring emergency powers; rather we must temporarily derogate from the constitutional principles, thereby upholding the Constitution. In addition, Lowe (2005: 185) argues that during times of emergency it is not uncommon to have 'temporary derogations from the normal rules' if there is discernible 'clear and present danger'.[20] For example, a distinction might be made here between 'preventive detention' and 'punitive restraint' (Corrado 1996). According to Corrado (1996: 790), the use of preventive detention is unlikely to be defensible where there is no immediate 'intended harm', even if an individual is dangerous and 'highly likely to intend harm in the future'. Conversely, it is seemingly defensible to use 'punitive restraint' so long as it is short-term and where there is immediate (clear and present) intention to harm a particular individual or the public generally. That is, for 'punitive restraint' (but not for all forms of preventive detention) some element of *blame* can be attributed for an individual's fledging involvement. This corresponds with other measures in the criminal law, for example, liability for attempts (and other inchoate offences) and stalking legislation, as well as preventive police powers, such as apprehending an individual suspected of planning a criminal or terrorist act (Corrado 1996: 790). Therefore, the goal might be to develop a system which

> allows short-term emergency measures but draws the line against permanent restrictions. Above all else, we must prevent politicians from exploiting momentary panic to impose long-lasting limitations on liberty. (Ackerman 2004: 1030)

While few would argue with this statement as a goal or a statement of clear principle, in practice it is sometimes difficult to resist the attempts to capitalise on critical incidents that impose otherwise unpalatable solutions. Cole (2004: 1799) postulates that, in practice, the goal of 'short-term' temporary solutions is often unrealistic given that, for example, acts of 'terrorism are not susceptible to strict time limitations'. In addition, Ackerman (2004: 1060) emphasises the difficulty in actually identifying and measuring malleable terms such as 'clear and present danger', which opens the door for 'political manipulation'.[21] Above all, Gross (2003: 1027) argues that this derogation creates a more fundamental strain on democratic values: 'Times of crisis pose the greatest and most serious danger to constitutional freedoms and principles.' That is, even if the arguments defending temporary derogations were accepted, there is a corollary danger of apathy and complacency: 'Our acceptance of the growing role of the executive branch as natural may be attributed, in part, to our conditioning during times of emergency' (Gross 2003: 1030). Similarly, Ramraj (2008: 5) also emphasises other broader or less conspicuous flow-on effects of emergency situations suggesting, for example, that terrorism might have arguably normalised the secrecy of intelligence information,[22] where governments are now able to use such enormous threats to public safety and security as a justification for the use of extreme measures in the control of other areas of serious crime. Another more nebulous side effect of preventive detention in emergency situations is that it might create an acceptable norm for restricting liberty without trial (since restrictions and deprivations are on the same spectrum, as demonstrated above). That is, restrictions on liberty achieved through the Control Order may have been, in part, attributed to the conditioning and normalisation of more austere, liberty-depriving emergency powers (namely, preventive detention). The restrictions on liberty accepted in respect of the Control Order may have in turn continued to influence and perhaps promote the acceptance of new forms of preventive orders such as the SCPO. This normalisation process can be thought of as occurring through a succession of policy precedents.[23] The danger of making policy without proper recognition of policy precedents is that any subsequent measures that are developed can become quite different from the original emergency powers, which might include the loss of specifically designed safeguards such as the use of sunset clauses to ensure a date of expiry (and possible renewal), and thus an opportunity for reflection and review of the utility of the measures.

In addition, Cole and Lobel (2007: 29) note that the creation of a 'preventive paradigm' can be facilitated by the use of the language of wartime, such as the portrayal of 'enemy combatants' attempting to commit 'acts of war'. This paradigm shift changes the landscape of state coercive intervention:

[T]he preventive paradigm turns to detention as a preventive matter and employs it against individuals deemed suspect by virtue of their group identity or political affiliations. (Cole and Lobel 2007: 33)

Therefore, it is argued that, under a 'preventive paradigm', a distinction must be made between state coercive action in wartime and peacetime: emergency powers are distinguishable as 'wartime exceptions' whereas the criminal law relates to peacetime norms (Cole and Lobel 2007: 66–69). Such preventive powers should be viewed as both *exceptional* and *temporary*, and it is implied that when 'wartime' ends, so should any preventive measures and techniques.

Preventive ideology therefore has long played a strong role in crime control policy and has influenced the powers held by various criminal justice institutions, such as the magistracy (binding-over), police (street patrols), the courts at sentencing (deterrence and incapacitation), and local government strategies (situational crime prevention). In times of emergency, the adoption of a 'preventive paradigm' appears to be a facile channel to rapidly develop exceptionally coercive state powers. While Zedner (2006: 5) rightly asserts that we should not 'overlook [these] continuities' of the role of prevention in customary forms of criminal justice, the recent heightened preference for prevention is clear. This has some important implications for the administration of criminal justice.

3.4   Preventive ideology and blurred notions of criminal justice

The proliferation of a preventive ideology is impinging on a number of established boundaries in criminal justice. The discussions hitherto have touched on several key complexities, including the blurring boundaries of civil and criminal procedure, the distinction between prevention and punishment, and the role of prevention in retributive theories of punishment. These equivocal concerns require further brief consideration.

3.4.1   Prevention and civil law: A marriage of convenience

It is clear from the analysis thus far that 'the power of the state to intervene to prevent crime is more easily justified than the power to punish' (Corrado 1996: 790). This is intrinsically associated with the convenient marriage of prevention to civil law, as punishment is to the criminal law. The marriage of criminal law and punishment is part of a long common law tradition, and ensures that before the state can employ severely coercive measures to punish citizens, it must do so following a criminal procedure that upholds established principles of justice and fairness. It is entrenched in constitutional norms (both domestic and those of the ECHR) that the state's purpose of *punishment* should not be achieved through civil procedure, where there are fewer basic protections for individuals and lower thresholds of proof and evidence. That is, Article 6 guarantees in the ECHR apply only to criminal proceedings. However, the purpose of prevention does not have the same jurisprudential or doctrinal foundation as punishment. This means that if a *severely coercive measure* can be deemed preventive, it is therefore (1) not punitive and (2) procedurally polygamous, that is, able to engage with either civil or criminal law. This is demonstrated in the Civil Court of Appeal decision in *McCann v Crown Court at Manchester* [2001: para. 39], where Lord Phillips stated that:

> Many injunctions in civil proceedings operate severely upon those against whom they are ordered. In matrimonial proceedings a husband may be ordered to leave his home and not to have contact with his children. . . . But such an order is imposed not for the purpose of punishment but for protection of the family. This demonstrates that, when considering whether an order imposes a penalty or punishment, it is necessary to look beyond its consequence and to consider its purpose.

Therefore, on the surface it would seem that the most powerful forms of constitutional guardianship can be avoided by a simple claim to a preventive purpose.[24] Zedner (2007a: 185) argues that this can create a simplified (and flawed) dichotomy, which is only concerned with 'whether these procedures are ECHR-compliant or not . . . [that is] technically ECHR-compliant'. The raft of 'civil' preventive orders epitomises the resultant blurring of civil and criminal procedure, and preventive and punitive purpose.

Dershowitz (1973: 1296) claims that the civil/criminal classification of statutory sanctions is often a game played between accused individuals and the state: the individual strives to make the charge criminal (offering heightened protections), while the state strives for civil proceedings (where lower standards of evidence are required). As Coffee (1992: 1887) asserts, 'procedural informality benefits the prosecution'. The consequence of this 'game' has been a merging of civil and criminal procedure. Accordingly the new preventive order model in the UK, including the SCPO and ASBO, has struggled to identify a clear basis for its statutory classification. For example, one elementary way to determine the classification of new provisions might be to look to its statutory location as either within criminal or civil codes: '[W]e must class [the law] where we find it placed by its authors' (Dershowitz 1973: 1299). However, while these preventive measures are statutorily defined as civil orders – that is, civil standards of proof and evidence nominally apply – they are imbedded in criminal statutes, for example, the SCPO in the SCA 2007, and the ASBO in the Crime and Disorder Act 1998.

In the past, some conceptual distinctions have been made between the character of criminal and civil law. For example, the distinction in *purpose* between the criminal law and civil law has been argued to be one of *prohibitions* and *pricing* respectively, while the distinction in *method* is that the criminal law deals in *sanctions* and the civil law deals in *penalties* (Coffee 1992: 1876). Both of these distinctions can be understood in economic terms as being relative to the 'social costs' in response to a given transgression. The criminal law aims to *exceed* the social cost of offending in order to punish and prohibit the actions of individuals; whereas the civil law aims to meet the social cost (but does not go beyond it), issuing a penalty which is priced to balance the demands of compensation (restoration to victims) and deterrence (a disincentive to future transgression) (Coffee 1992: 1882–1883). This suggests that measures in the civil law should have no purpose of prohibiting an individual's behaviour:

> Clearly, their purpose is not prohibitory in the sense of forbidding entirely the activity in question by imposing penalties greater than the social costs created by the activity. Indeed, if the defendant's benefit from the conduct exceeds the victim's loss (adjusted to reflect the limited likelihood of apprehension), the defendant is free under optimal deterrence theory to engage in conduct that harms others at will, so long as the defendant pays all compensation. (Coffee 1992: 1883)

This distinction is also clearly not upheld by the SCPO and other 'civil' preventive orders. They do not fit this characterisation of the civil law, where their focus is foremost on creating prohibitions, restrictions, and requirements on individuals, and contain no compensatory component.

Finally, Ashworth (2000: 5) contends that the character of criminal proceedings can be distinguished by two structural ingredients:

> The key procedural elements that distinguish criminal from civil proceedings are that criminal proceedings are generally brought by a public official as prosecutor, and that they can result in the conviction of the defendant and in the passing of a sentence.

The Strasbourg Court, in *Engel and others v Netherlands* [1976: para. 82], sustains the latter element of risk of conviction, stating that we must 'take into consideration the degree of severity of the penalty that the person concerned risks incurring'. If any of the conditions of a civil preventive order are breached, punishment and conviction ensue. Therefore, Ashworth (2000: 6) argues that if the two procedural stages associated with civil preventive orders (application and breach) were recognised as one hybrid process, then such orders would be categorised as criminal, as they contain both elements of being brought by a public authority and the risk of conviction (which are not part of the civil process). Several legal academics have since argued that these 'two-step' prohibitions should be viewed together (Simester and von Hirsch 2006; Ashworth and Zedner 2008: 46). However, Lord Steyn opposed this view in the appeal by *Clingham and McCann* (2002: para. 23):

> I do not agree. These are separate and independent procedures. The making of the order will presumably sometimes serve its purpose and there will be no proceedings for breach. It is in principle necessary to consider the two stages separately.

Despite this claim that these stages are independent and separate, the House of Lords arguably affirms a link through acknowledging the severity of a potential criminal outcome in the first stage of civil application by requiring a criminal standard of proof:

> [T]he heightened civil standard and the criminal standard are virtually indistinguishable. . . . But in my view pragmatism dictates that the task of magistrates should be made more straightforward by ruling that they must in all cases under s 1 apply the criminal standard. (Lord Steyn, *Clingham and McCann*, 2002: para. 37)

Clearly, the notion of prevention can obscure both the civil/criminal divide and the boundaries of punishment – and this is plainly represented by new civil preventive orders, such as the SCPO. These are civil orders contained in criminal statutes. They allow civil standards to be applied during a hearing, such as in relation to the admission of evidence (for example, hearsay), but must be proved at the criminal standard (or heightened civil standard). Moreover, a public authority taking civil action seeking the imposition of prohibitions makes the state a 'party' in the civil hearing presenting evidence (akin to prosecution in criminal trials), whereas historically disputes in the civil courts were brought between two private citizens or as a result of commercial arrangements between a government or government entity and another such entity or citizen. It is arguable that too much of an advantage may be given to the state in civil cases, as it gathers evidence (intelligence) taken from state police agencies, and then is a party in the civil hearing where less stringent rules of evidence are applied. That is, the application of coercive state action through the civil courts where criminal punishment might follow on breach could be seen to 'un-level' the playing field that is more rigorously balanced in the criminal courts.

3.4.2 Retribution in a state of prevention

Theories of retributive punishment are also being challenged by the emerging preventive state. To understand the institution of punishment, typically either a retributive or utilitarian perspective is adopted. Broadly speaking, a retributive perspective focuses on the just, fair, and proportionate allocation of deserved punishment ('just deserts'), while the utilitarian perspectives encompass notions of prevention, such as deterrence (specific and general),[25] rehabilitation, and incapacitation. While no clear lines can be drawn between these theories of punishment – indeed each can be argued to play a greater or lesser role within the various institutions of punishment – some patterns can be observed. Although the utilitarian preventive purpose, as argued by Castellano and Gould (2007: 81–82), makes up an important part of the penal system, it has widely been accepted that recent theories of punishment (and sentencing) in countries such as the US and UK are dominated by the notion of 'just deserts', and that the preventive purpose of punishment has been diminished. Von Hirsch and Ashworth (2005: 3), two of the most prominent, leading proponents of desert theory, have affirmed the contemporary dominance of retribution over prevention-based rationales for punishment at sentencing:

> In the first two-thirds of the 20th century, the idea of proportionate sentencing was largely invisible: sentencing policy was supposed to be shaped principally by crime-prevention concerns of rehabilitation, deterrence and incapacitation. When the 'desert model' emerged in the mid-1970s, it swiftly gained much influence.

Moreover, Ashworth and Zedner (2010) contend that any 'preventive function' resulting from a criminal sentence is subsidiary or coincidental to the punishment imposed for the wrongdoing. One explanation given for these developments is that there were increasing indications that many of the utilitarian assumptions and functions of imprisonment (rehabilitation and correction) were failing, and therefore the primary basis left for imprisonment simply became desert-based punishment (O'Malley 1992: 257; Anleu 1998: 22).[26] While institutions of punishment may have historically grown out of a desire to reform those incarcerated,[27] as this 'rehabilitative ideal' deflated, we were left to question the other key purposes of punishment, namely, desert-based or preventive detention. O'Malley (1992: 265) argues that this may represent a form of 'politics of failure', serving to justify the punitive state:

> [T]he 'politics of failure' provide a technical gloss to justify punitiveness. If correction and deterrence do not work, then sanctions based on these ideas must be swept away. What is left for the offender but punishment, *retribution* and *incapacitation*? (Emphasis added)

This principle of incapacitation provides the justification for the use of preventive detention, discussed in Section 3.1.1, where the central claim is that rehabilitative and retributivist theories alone fall short of adequately controlling crime: 'If you can't change people, you certainly can control them' (O'Leary 1987: 9). Tadros (2007: 658) maintains that the state has two obligations: first, to deliver retributive justice, and second to ensure security from crime (so-called 'criminal security'). This security from crime reinforces the control of 'those you can't change', as a legitimate preventive function of the state. Thus, another way to conceptualise the competing rationales of punishment is either as 'desert theory', rendering proportionality as the key component of sentencing, or as crime control, rendering prevention as the key component. Even during the period of dominance of the just desert model of punishment,[28] the ascendancy of crime control clearly persisted in upholding preventive ideals and competing strategies to retribution (Garland 2001).

Robinson (2001: 1441) contends that these competing rationales cannot be balanced: '[T]he traditional principles of incapacitation and desert conflict; they inevitably distribute liability and punishment differently. To advance one, the system must sacrifice the other.' The incapacitation principle attempts to identify either a potential future *or* past wrong, where either present facts or demonstrated dangerousness provide the grounds for attributing liability. By contrast, the desert principle attempts to identify only past wrong, where the facts indicate blameworthiness (moral culpability), which provides the grounds for attributing liability. A more detailed examination of these competing rationales of punishment is outside the scope of this brief section. However, it is important to note that even within the specific field of retribution and desert theory, there are differing claims, for example, about the expressive purpose of punishment. A comparison of the works of theorists such as von Hirsch, Ashworth, and Duff demonstrates that the latter places far greater emphasis on the communicative purpose of retributive punishment than either of the others.[29] This communicative purpose of state coercive intervention could also be blurred by a preventive ideology where the message might change from 'if you obey the law your liberty is secure' to 'your liberty is secure so long as you don't appear likely to be dangerous in the future' (Foote and Frankel 1970: 54).

What is important to note here is that punishment can carry two general potential purposes: a retributive purpose or a preventive purpose (Castellano and Gould 2007). Assuming for a moment that a preventive ideology has regained some ground from a period dominated by retribution (based on the above observations of a potentially prevailing preventive state), a number of questions arise. What role is there for retribution in a state governed by broad ideological principles of prevention? Can the dual demands of retribution and prevention be reconciled under one measure (such as a preventive order)? And above all, must there be a trade-off between the different rationales of punishment? That is, does retribution have to diminish in order for a preventive state to exist (as claimed by Robinson above)? In responding to these questions about the role of prevention within retributive punishment, it seems that three key rival propositions arise: first, they are simply irreconcilable purposes; second, an early form of retribution or pre-punishment can occur; and third, prevention can be justified post hoc and thus combined with retributive punishment at sentencing. The first proposition suggests that whenever a preventive purpose is claimed, retribution cannot exist at all. This is currently the most widely accepted proposition. As the discussion above has shown, coercive restrictions on liberty that are backed by a preventive purpose are not given proper attention – they are preventive orders and thus can be construed as *not* constituting punishment and retribution. This proposition is clearly problematic because it ignores the punitive aspect of preventive measures and in so doing denies those subject to such measures proper due process protections (or comparable safeguards). However, the second and third propositions require deeper consideration.

3.4.2.1 Prevention as retributive pre-punishment

The second proposition is that a form of early retribution or pre-punishment is justified based on a temporal shift from post- to pre-crime, where punishment can occur prior to the criminal act. New (1995) makes the claim that it is at least theoretically possible to extend the criminal standard of beyond reasonable doubt to pre-punishment, as it exists for post-punishment. That is, if we can be confident in our predictions with a given (high) level of certainty, beyond all reasonable doubt, then whether the punishment comes temporally prior to or after the act is, he argues, peripheral and unimportant. Furthermore, early pre-punishment has the benefit of preventing any criminal harm from occurring. However, there are a number of apparent difficulties with this logic. First, it is questionable whether the inherent *doubt* entailed in predicting future harmful action renders impossible the determination of an issue beyond reasonable doubt. That is, the intrinsic uncertainty of the future could constitute grounds for a judge to have sufficient doubt (at the criminal standard).

In addition, Smilansky (1994: 52) contends that it does not allow free will of the potential future offender to make a 'last-minute moral improvement'. Similarly, von Hirsch (1971: 743) claimed that even if predictions about an individual's likelihood of committing a crime in the future could be completely and accurately determined, it would be insupportable on moral grounds as it removes the choice (and freedom) of an individual. Despite these moral objections, it can equally be argued that it is immoral to resolve to wait knowingly for an offence to occur in order to allow for any 'last-minute' change in decision. Statman (1997: 131–132) argues that what distinguishes those criminal acts that do *not* eventuate from those that are committed is in fact often merely 'moral luck', and consequently 'moral desert' or blameworthiness is the cause of the demonstrated 'bad character'. That is, whether or not an act is actually committed is inconsequential, as it is often based on conditions outside the control of the individual – the punishable constant is the intention which reflects culpability. Statman (1997: 134) also points to the Talmudic logic that to prevent someone from becoming guilty, it is necessary to punish them while still innocent. Nonetheless, he emphasises in his conclusion that this is only a theoretical exercise, and that '[p]ost-punishment is the only decent institution of punishment available to us' (Statman 1997: 134).

While this pre-punishment discussion is broadly philosophical, the important point is that in some circumstances, it is at least conceivable that there might be sufficiently strong evidence for the state to intervene by employing coercion, before matters worsen. Determining when such state intervention should occur is obviously more problematic, but investigations into these boundaries may be important to gain a better understanding of the limits of the preventive state. Such early intervention may be even more desirable or defensible for only particular subcategories of crime control, such as serious crime control where arguably '[i]n the case of serious harm, conventional punishment occurs too late' (Zedner 2007a: 174). This is certainly an important question for this book with its focus on the SCPO. That is to say, should a situation

ıg serious crime and harm be considered a more defensible basis
y coercive state intervention strategies?

3.4.2.2 *Prevention as part of post-conviction retribution sentencing*

The final proposition is that retributive and preventive goals are not necessarily mutually exclusive or conflicting. Ashworth and Zedner (2011: 281) argue that the two are not separable: if a crime is serious enough to merit punishment, it necessarily follows that it should be prevented. Thus, it is important to consider the role of retribution when using preventive measures at sentencing. It is arguably more defensible to use preventive measures post-conviction (as part of sentencing), where there has already been an apparent 'past wrong'.

> [I]t is impossible to 'punish dangerousness'. To 'punish' is 'to cause (a person) to undergo pain, loss, or suffering for a crime or wrong-doing' – therefore, punishment can only exist in relation to a past wrong. (Robinson 2001: 1432)

Preventive orders at sentencing (or 'criminal preventive orders') could be viewed as combining the preventive aspiration with retributive punishment, so that punishing dangerousness is not done in isolation but in relation to a past wrong. For example, when using preventive orders at sentencing, the conditions and restrictions imposed might also satisfy the requirements of desert or retribution. This could provide an additional and beneficial dimension to preventive orders if they are incorporated into sentencing options. In what has been described in the UK as an 'imprisonment binge', punishment and deserts are increasingly being dealt with by way of custodial sentences (Castellano and Gould 2007: 82). Preventive orders and other non-custodial sentences might have the potential to reduce this 'binge' by restricting liberty as an initial alternative to immediate deprivation. However, whether the essential requirements of retribution can be adequately satisfied by ordering restrictions on liberty requires closer analysis.

At least conceptually, the substantial restrictions which can be placed on liberty as part of a preventive order arguably impose burdens that could patently satisfy the retributivist demand for desert. For example, it has been argued that the application of a preventive order on an individual can be an 'extraordinarily invasive measure' which carries 'grave burdens' (Zedner 2007a: 175).[30] The restrictions of a preventive order, like any other non-custodial penalty, could therefore clearly imbue burdens that would satisfy retributivists. The true appeal of retributive theories is the intrinsic value of ensuring the necessity and proportionality of sentences. Feeley and Simon (1992: 450) observed that the discourses of a new penology (namely, risk and actuarial justice) have tended to replace these aspects of 'retributive judgment'. However, these notions of necessity and proportionality are essential to ensuring a balance between liberty and security.[31] Such crucial elements of justice should arguably not be exclusive to retributive punishment, but remain central to all sentencing policy (including preventive orders). These two principles are germane to all measures (whether having a punitive or preventive purpose) to ensure that state coercive restrictions on liberty are weighed fairly against (1) necessity, the need for the measure, where without the restrictions there would be a significant probability of reoffending; and (2) proportionality, where restrictions are made appropriately, relative to the original consummate harm caused and with any other components of the sentence. These two key criteria should be equally applicable to preventive orders at sentencing. While there may be some significant benefit in embracing a preventive strategy at sentencing – allowing an initial step back from the mainstream punitive approach – such changes should not be permitted to create new coercive measures by disposing of the important principles of retribution and protections of the criminal process.

Castellano and Gould (2007: 85) provide examples of the problems that result from overlooking these important principles: '[W]ithout a proper emphasis on proportionality and basic fairness, the demands of crime control have allowed us to impose life sentences on marijuana smokers.' One of the central obstacles to applying retributive principles to restrain the burdens of preventive measures at sentencing is that they are often not classified as penalties, and therefore cannot be weighed up against other punitive options at sentencing (Ashworth 2005: 335–337). That is, an important qualification for the proper, proportionate use of preventive orders at sentencing is to recognise that any imposed (preventive) restrictions also potentially have a punitive dimension, and, as such, they should be proportionally considered at sentencing and assessed together with custodial or non-custodial penalties. By following retributive principles when issuing these preventive orders at sentencing, it could ensure that where breach occurs any ensuing sanctions are also made proportionate to the original consummate harm.

Dershowitz (1970: 25) states that there are two focal questions for criminal justice: (1) 'Did he do it?', the 'punishment-deterrent strategy'; and (2) 'Will he do it?', the 'prediction-prevention strategy'. He contends that both of these questions have featured in all societies, each society usually favouring one over the other (though not neglecting the other) (Dershowitz 1970: 25). Based on these strategies and the arguments made above, it can be extrapolated that a judge could ask two essential questions at sentencing: first, 'what coercive measures are necessary and proportionate to serve just and fair deserts?' (the retributive element); and second, 'what coercive measures are necessary and proportionate to provide just and fair protections for preventing future, repeat harm based on the defendant's demonstrated capacity to inflict harm?' (the preventive element). In answering these questions at sentencing, the appropriate intervention(s) (sentence) would consist of the provision of assistance (positive requirements) as much as negative prohibitions, in order to most effectively ensure no continued future harm. It might often be thought that in delivering an appropriate response for retribution, the preventive element is already satisfied (or vice versa). That is, retribution (the resulting punishment) may sometimes (but not always) provide satisfactory prevention (be it specific deterrence, incapacitation, or rehabilitation among others), whereas the preventive element, which almost always manifests itself as restrictions on liberty, may be an adequate (necessary and proportionate) response to criminal behaviour – thereby avoiding the more extreme recourse to (perhaps disproportionate) deprivations of liberty.

Although historically the general notion of prevention has long been in the minds of decision-makers – prevention is the ideal and 'better than the cure' – principles of (criminal) justice have provided protections and controls which guard against excessive coercive state action. The gradual percolation of the preventive ideal has found new methods and justifications, which can now be seen to challenge the shape and foundations of criminal justice. The disparate discipline of criminology has noted a change in criminal justice, through varied observations of 'new penology', regulation, risk, and security (see below). However, it is argued that rather than being viewed as largely heterogeneous subject areas, these should all be seen as being driven by the same mechanism: the desire to prevent. This is addressed in the next and final section of this chapter.

3.5   The preventive state: Encompassing new conceptions of criminal justice

It is widely acknowledged that the last 30 years or so have witnessed a considerable shift in the way in which crime is governed, in which prevention has become a defining logic. This preventive turn has been associated with a new discourse of urban safety concerned with security, order and prevention, through risk-reduction, harm-minimisation and loss-prediction. (Crawford 2007: 69)

The logic of prevention has produced various new states of governance which are changing the nature and shape of justice and crime control. This preventive philosophy has a central role – one which is often not distinctly recognised – within other criminological discourses. This final section maps out a number of core concepts in contemporary criminal justice: protection, pre-emption, precaution, threats, dangerousness, security, regulation, and risk. While the criminological lexicon has expanded to include all of these new conceptions, precisely how these concepts interconnect remains somewhat obscure. This section examines how they might be arranged conceptually and whether there is any broad agreement in the literature about the interplay of these facets of modern crime policy. It is argued that a preventive ideology is the common or shared constant standing behind many of these concepts, which propels (and justifies) the growth of new coercive measures such as preventive orders. The analysis also produces a number of spectra or continua to help conceptualise various degrees of prevention, harm, certainty, and risk, and highlights the trend towards new (earlier) points of state intervention.

3.5.1 Prevention and security

The first notable phenomenon is the interplay between prevention and security. Security has emerged in criminological discourses as the umbrella concept influencing the development of new crime policy.

> In a post-crime society there are crimes, offenders and victims, crime control, policing, investigation, trial, and punishment . . . in a pre-crime society, there is calculation, risk, and uncertainty, surveillance, precaution, prudentialism, moral hazard, prevention, and, arching over all these, there is the pursuit of security. (Zedner 2007b: 262)

While often overlooked or simply assumed, the notion of prevention holds a central position in the state's 'pursuit of security' (Zedner 2007b: 262). Bentham (1843: Part I, Chapter II) argued that, among the distinct objectives of law, 'security is the only one which necessarily embraces the future'. However, Tadros (2007: 662) makes an important distinction regarding the role of prevention in the pursuit of security – he argues that it is not always the case that the state is trying to predict future offending: 'The ambition in this respect is not primarily forward-looking rather than responsive. It invites us to investigate what the state can do to protect its citizens and others from future criminal offending.' As an objective of law, security can be based on legal reason (for example, conviction for a past criminal offence) and respond through preventive action. In this way, security is not necessarily *predicting* crime, but rather creating a form of post-crime preventive action or protection, only *after* a criminal act has occurred. Here, the notion of prevention can be employed to conceptualise two forms of security, where 'legal security' is a *responsive* preventive action, distinct from other purely preventive actions (namely, 'private security' such as guards, CCTV, alarms, etc.). This might also distinguish between preventive orders at sentencing in the Crown Court (focused on security) and those more purely civil preventive orders in the High Court.[32]

Clearly the theme of *protection* also runs parallel to prevention and security. Tadros (2007: 680) argues that the state has an apparent obligation to protect its citizens from 'illness and disease', 'invasion', and 'environmental disaster'. The goals of protection, prevention, and security together function as the central mechanism to legitimise and substantiate state intervention (see Figure 3.2).

The apparatus of state crime control functions through a process of three key overlapping objectives. Together these concepts drive a

Figure 3.2   The interplay between prevention, security, and protection

broadly similar goal of preventing future harms, and serve to justify state intervention. The machinery of prevention includes pre-emptive and precautionary state action. However, some discernible distinctions can also be made between these concepts (see Section 3.5.2). The essential role of prevention and security in the state's agenda of protection is demonstrated by the breakdown in Figure 3.3.

As shown in Figure 3.3, at its broadest conception the protective function can denote either the protection of a state's land and territory or the protection of its citizenry. The protection of land or territory primarily refers to wartime policies, which is beyond the scope of this study of domestic crime policy formulation. Nonetheless, it can be noted in passing that a preventive ideology often also guides wartime decision-making, perhaps best exemplified by the pre-emptive action taken by the Bush administration in the Iraq war (Dershowitz 2006: 164; Cole and Lobel 2007). The protection of a state's citizens – politically reframed in the UK as 'public protection' – is achieved through security.

Loader and Walker (2004: 226) state that a distinction can be made between 'subjective security' and 'objective security' (see Figure 3.3). The subjective dimension is 'our sense of feeling safe' (or 'reassurance function'), while the objective dimension is the actual provision of substantive security measures (see also Ashworth and Zedner 2010: 67). This provision of protection, or substantive security, is delivered both by the state and through private sector involvement. Private sector provision of

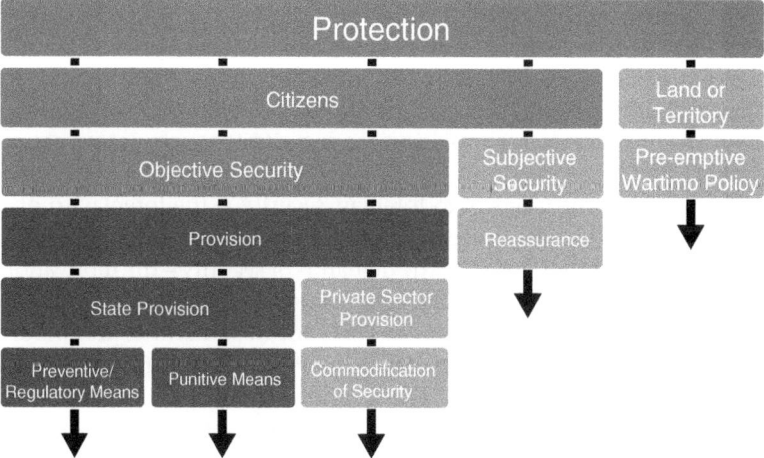

Figure 3.3 Protection agenda

security has been the subject of intense analysis in the security literature in relation to the increased use of CCTV, particularly in the UK, and the more general commodification of security (Loader 1997). This private provision of security is not (or is less) concerned with traditional roles of policing, investigation, and prosecution – that is, 'serving the criminal process' – but rather is primarily aimed at loss reduction (Zedner 2007b: 263). This has a number of potential social and economic ramifications based on the affordability of self-provision, for example, the provision of unequal levels of private security owing to the unequal distribution of economic wealth (that is, private security is clearly dependent on personal wealth; see Thumala, Goold and Loader 2011: 298).

However, Crawford (2006: 471) maintains that the 'state remains an anchoring role in the provision of security' (see also Loader and Walker 2007: 192–193). This provision is distributed by the legislature's enactment of powers through both the criminal law ('punitive means') and other preventive action ('preventive and regulatory means') (see bottom of Figure 3.3). The criminal trial is therefore the process where the state attempts to seek punitive means to sanction one or more individuals, in order to provide security and protection of its broader citizenry (the public). In fact, Tadros (2007: 658–659) conceptualises this state provision of security through preventive state intervention in the criminal law as 'criminal security'. In securing the environment of its citizenry, it logically follows that the state itself is part of this environment. This highlights the importance of structures like due process protections, which ensure the security of citizens *from* the state. Lastly, it is within the state provision of security that the new preventive order model exists. Figure 3.3 shows that 'preventive means' (and regulatory means) emerge as a strand of measures that run parallel to those of the punitive state. Therefore, the new preventive orders in the UK have a similar disposition to the criminal law and criminal punishment in that they create provision for security through state coercive intervention.

If romance is the foreplay to foreplay, security is the foreplay to prevention. However, we can see that the reverse is also true. Conceivably, notions of prevention usher in the demands of security – the motivation of the state to secure its citizenry (and territory) is driven by its desire to prevent future occurrences of harm. This control of 'harm' is profoundly linked to the concept of risk, which provides grounds for preventive intervention, as there are indications of more remote harms or threats. These degrees of preventive intervention, an important part of the preventive framework, are expounded in the next subsection.

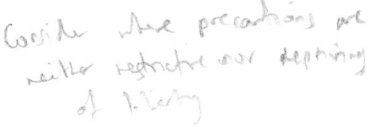

3.5.2 Prevention and risk

Risk plays a central role in the preventive paradigm; if preventio harm and future crime is to occur, then (1) 'risky' individuals must first be assessed and (2) measures are required to manage the identified 'risky' patterns of behaviour that are deemed conducive to crime. Many risk-based procedures have been criticised for not adequately and effectively addressing the latter component of *managing* risk (Hebenton and Seddon 2009: 352). Notwithstanding these questions of efficacy, Feeley and Simon (1992: 452) proclaim the dominance of managerialist techniques of a new penology:

> [T]he new penology is markedly less concerned with responsibility, fault, moral sensibility, diagnosis, or intervention and treatment of the individual offender. Rather, it is concerned with techniques to identify, classify, and manage groupings sorted by dangerousness.

In such a 'risk society',[33] the danger is that we might undermine the core infrastructure of 'old penology', such as replacing guilt with risk, to be the 'key predicate for liberty deprivation' (Janus 2004: 31). When formulating policies based on risk and prevention, the point at which the state can intervene to deprive or restrict liberty through the use of coercive measures shifts temporally to an earlier juncture. As depicted in Figure 3.2, the machinery of prevention also involves both 'precaution' and 'pre-emption'. These three concepts can be delineated further on a continuum relating to the level of certainty for state intervention (from precaution to pre-emption through to prevention). They represent different degrees of intervention that can occur in relation to the level of certainty, risk, and harm presented. Figure 3.4 presents a continuum to depict this relationship between the degrees of state preventive intervention and their levels of certainty and risk.

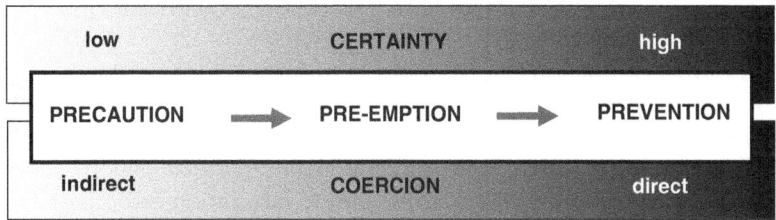

Figure 3.4 The continuum of preventive state interventions

State precautionary measures can be considered as indirectly coercive and lower on the spectrum of certainty and risk (see Figure 3.4). They are generally manifested as 'safety' measures relating to, for example, occupational safety, medical, or environmental contingencies (Hebenton and Seddon 2009: 346). Figure 3.4 also shows that pre-emptive and preventive interventions are often more directly coercive to achieve their preventive goals. The potential hazard of taking more *direct coercive action* on an individual at the lower end of the scale, towards pre-emption and precaution, is that an unjustified intervention could be made (and thus a potential violation of an individuals' rights), as there is a lower degree of certainty about the actual risk of harm. Accordingly, Stern and Wiener (2006) postulate that further down the spectrum towards precaution it is more likely that a state intervention will register 'false positives'. That is, if the level of certainty is lowered then more errors are likely to be made about the actual risk of harm. Two contemporary examples of pre-emptive intervention that resulted in false positives demonstrate these perils. One relates to pre-emptive intervention in wartime, where one of the greatest examples of a false positive occurred when the US forcefully entered Iraq based on risk assessments regarding the alleged production of weapons of mass destruction (WMDs). Assessing the risk, a senior law enforcement official reportedly advised the White House that WMDs would certainly be found, describing the level of certainty as a 'slam-dunk' (Stern and Wiener 2006: 408). Another example of false positives relates to terrorism policy, where Cole (2004: 1753) demonstrates that the preventive detention of terrorists in the US, after 9/11, 'has been spectacularly unsuccessful': 5,000 people were detained; of those, zero were associated with Al Qaeda; three of them were charged; two were acquitted; and only one was convicted. Finally, the continuum in Figure 3.4 can provide some level of differentiation in the preventive order model where, for example, SCPOs issued at sentencing have a higher level of the certainty about risk of harm because an individual has already been convicted of consummated criminal harm, whereas those civil preventive orders (issued in the High Court) are closer to being 'pre-emptive orders'.

A further distinction can be drawn between the degree of harm and the level of certainty and risk, particularly between pre-emptive and preventive measures. That is, while preventive measures are based on 'known risks' (consummated criminal harm, post-conviction), pre-emptive and precautionary measures aim to take action earlier in relation to more remote harms. Hebenton and Seddon (2009: 346) argue that this makes us 'riskophobes', ever trying to remedy lesser harms.

Accordingly, Dershowitz (1970: 26) maintains that we make a 'decision to authorize state intervention at one point, rather than another, along the continuum of predicted danger to consummated harm'. This identifies another important continuum, depicted in Figure 3.5, which integrates degrees of risk, harm, and certainty.

The latter two degrees of harm – *inchoate harm* and *consummate harm* – are addressed by the criminal law. Individuals who commit, attempt to commit, or facilitate the commission of a crime are deemed sufficiently blameworthy and are dealt with under established criminal law and procedure. While inchoate harms are shown to be situated higher up the spectrum, the dominance of a preventive ideology has arguably also resulted in the expansion of the category of inchoate offences to include lesser harms. For example, McSherry (2009: 141–143) has argued that the boundaries of inchoate liability have expanded to include both *preparatory acts* and *possession offences*.[34] Therefore, Ashworth and Zedner (2011: 288–289) posit that '[t]hese tendencies suggest a transition from inchoate liability to risk-based liability'.

There is significant debate in the literature regarding the lower degrees of harm, particularly whether or not 'risk' itself could be considered sufficient harm to justify intervention (Finkelstein 2003; Bergelson 2009; Renzo 2010: 274). Powell (2012) makes several important distinctions between risk of harm (propensity or dangerousness) and threats. She argues that with *threats*, there is a 'negative occurrence' which is 'imminent or anticipated', whereas with *risks*, there is only the 'probability or chance' that a negative occurrence will occur (Powell 2012: 16). For example, high-risk investments are insecure (returning to the broader concept of security) because of the high likelihood of chance or probability negatively affecting the result – but this cannot be deemed a threat (Powell 2012: 16). Moreover, Powell (2012: 15–16) also emphasises that one cannot threaten oneself, but one *can* create risks for oneself – thus they are operationally different. Powell (2012: 17) therefore concludes

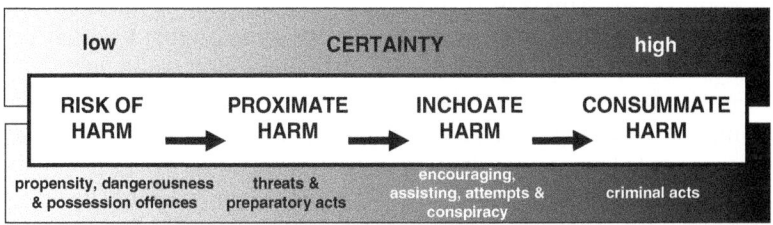

Figure 3.5   The continuum of degrees of harm and certainty

that threats are 'intrinsically bad', whereas risk is only bad if negative consequences eventuate. Nonetheless, Finkelstein (2003: 963) contends that 'risk of harm' could also be a predicate condition for blameworthiness, as mere 'luck' is the difference between harmful behaviour that causes no eventual harm and that which does cause actual consummate harm. This contention is supported by the claim that harm, based on 'moral wrongdoing', is a sufficient requirement for liability, both in civil torts and criminal law (Finkelstein 2003: 964). Both Finkelstein (2003) and Powell (2012) provide grounds upon which blameworthiness or liability might be attributed to lesser degrees of harm. Finkelstein (2003: 987) provides two instances where risk could constitute harm, that is, 'a basis for punishing risky behavior that does not result in outcome harm'. The examples she provides are reckless driving, where it is argued that dangerous driving is harmful even if no crash follows, and similarly Russian roulette:

If a death results, the surviving players can be prosecuted for manslaughter. But what if no one dies? Arguably, the law should punish the players, not simply to deter adolescents from playing extremely dangerous games, but because the same culpable risk that justifies a manslaughter conviction in the case in which someone dies should also justify a conviction for risk creation where no actual harm results. (Finkelstein 2003: 987–988)

However, Hebenton and Seddon (2009: 346) contend that any attempt by the state to respond to lower degrees of harm through the criminal law should be resisted. Such endeavours to deal with these levels of harm through law can have a destructive side effect: 'the deployment of law against law in order to erode, eliminate or circumvent laws or legal procedures that are perceived to get in the way of the pre-emption of harms' (Hebenton and Seddon 2009: 346). As discussed earlier, Ericson (2007: 24) condemned this erosion of due process protections as a form of 'counter-law'. This counter-law was argued to 'erode or eliminate traditional standards, principles, and procedures of criminal law that get in the way of preempting imagined sources of harm' (Ericson 2007: 24).

Finally, the use of civil preventive orders shifts state intervention along the continuum in Figure 3.5 away from actual criminal acts (consummate harm) towards targeting dangerousness or remote harms. An important empirical question for this book – posed in the introductory chapter – is whether there was a distinct policy decision made to change the point of intervention, through the development of new preventive measures.[35] In addition, the continua developed above, which represent degrees of risk and harm, are valuable in discriminating among the vast range of preventive orders. For example, Travel Restriction Orders, Football Banning Orders, and Exclusion Orders are used to address the risk of harm only; whereas Control Orders (for suspected terrorists) and Restraining Orders (for example, for stalkers) dealt specifically with threats or imminent potential for harm. A number of preventive orders, including the SCPO and ASBO, can currently be utilised across the entire spectrum of harm, including at the more serious end of the spectrum for both consummate offences and inchoate offences as part of sentencing. In fact, to date, the SCPO has only been used post-conviction.[36] This post-conviction application has been examined far less in the literature on preventive orders (the focus has generally remained on civil preventive orders on application in the High Court); however, it is equally important to examine this emerging non-custodial option at sentencing. It is particularly important because this sentencing practice persists in placing an offender on the harm spectrum. That is, after a punishment is served for a consummate harm (at the higher end of the harm spectrum), the imposition of a preventive order returns an offender to a 'risk of harm' status (at the lower end of the harm spectrum), a classification of dangerousness, or having the propensity to reoffend.

This cycle is also particularly notable in other preventive practices such as the IPP, where after a sentence has been served for a consummated harm, instead of being released, inmates continue to be detained based on their dangerousness or renewed risk of harm. Whether this imposes too much control over individuals so that they become 'stuck' within this cycle of state control and coercion, or whether this is a welcomed development that continues to protect against dangerous offenders is a subject that is yet unresolved (see Slobogin 2005). Indeed this is a central consideration when appraising a potential system of preventive justice. To develop these structures into a thorough preventive justice framework would require further determinations to be made regarding the appropriate principles, such as those developed in criminal law, not least the key questions of responsibility and intention (Steiker 1998: 791).[37] Slobogin (2005: 40), a committed consequentialist, takes some initial steps in this direction when advocating a just system of prevention:

> A preventive regime that is limited to interventions after *non-accidental, unjustified harmful acts*, and that engages in competent risk assessment and risk management, might well be superior to the current system of criminal justice, or to any system of criminal justice based primarily on desert, deterrence, or ethical philosophy. (Emphasis added)

Other conditions might also be important to ensure procedural justice, for example, requirements that a jury of peers determine the 'non-accidental, unjustified harm', or that a judge should 'be involved in monitoring risk assessment and risk management' (Slobogin 2005: 42). This is a major project, and one which would need significant input from practitioners about the practicality of this radically new system of justice.

3.5.3 Prevention and regulation

Finally, it is worth a brief examination of the many parallels and overlapping observations between the discourses on prevention presented above and the literature on the regulatory state and regulatory justice.[38] It has already been noted, at the end of Chapter 2, that regulatory developments in organised crime control are underpinned by a pre hoc, or preventive, endeavour. However, there is a fundamental paradox in the discourse on regulation, which makes the development of a comprehensive preventive framework more pertinent to the current examination of preventive orders. That is, regulation is widely held to connote, and largely signify, the divestment of state coercive intervention:

> The regulatory state is a tag widely adopted by political scientists to describe the withdrawal of the state from the active delivery of services ('rowing') to their direction ('steering'), a withdrawal prompted by the proposition that states govern more effectively at a distance. (Ashworth and Zedner 2008: 38)

It is apparent from the analysis thus far that preventive orders in the UK present a strong investment of the state, utilising its authority to use coercive powers over individuals. This clearly contrasts with the regulatory aims of 'governing at a distance' outside the criminal law, with the explicit function of 'rowing'. Nonetheless, there are some important points of intersection between these two bodies of literature worthy of brief consideration.

First, the concept of 'counter-law' is also employed to discuss regulatory measures. For example, both Corrado (1996) and more recently Crawford (2009) argue that the limitations on regulatory measures are ambiguous and, as such, they can be used to circumvent the protections offered by the criminal law.

> And so we might reply to the court: you have sidestepped the issue by calling it 'regulation'; you can't make imprisoning the innocent acceptable just by calling it regulation. (Corrado 1996: 781)

Crawford (2009: 3) argues that these regulatory measures 'lower the threshold of intervention', which has also clearly been examined above in respect of the preventive state, through the analyses of various spectrums and continuums of harm, risk, certainty, and coercion. In addition, regulatory and preventive policies share a baseline utilitarian philosophy. While notions of prevention purport to protect and secure against wrongdoing rather than necessarily punish it, Ayres and Braithwaite (1992: 35) similarly defend a more general theory of regulation, arguing that compliance, through negotiation and regulation, is more effective than criminal punishment. Nonetheless, Braithwaite (2002: 19) admits that 'persuasion will normally only be more effective than punishment in securing compliance when the persuasion is backed up by punishment', which is clearly more pertinent to the structure of the preventive order model, where punishment is a consequence of any breach of the terms of an order.

The three central components of regulation – goal, monitoring, and realignment – are also useful in portraying the process sought by the use of preventive orders (Hood, Scott, James, et al. 1999). For example, the *goal* of preventive orders is to reduce (or prevent) more remote harms; the *monitoring* occurs through state agencies such as police, local authorities, probation, and parole; and the *realignment* component is triggered if one of the conditions of the order is breached, where severe criminal punishment can be imposed (such as imprisonment). We can distinguish here between preventive orders and the criminal law. The criminal law generally does not attempt, as its goal, to prevent remote harms;[39] rather, its focus is on actual or consummate harmful acts which have occurred in the past (demonstrated in Figure 3.5).[40] However, the key variance is that the criminal law does not engage in the function of monitoring. For the preventive order model, notions of regulation raise considerable questions as to the effectiveness of coordinating the monitoring component, which is carried out by numerous government agencies including those involving financial, immigration, customs, police, intelligence, and probation services. This concern is magnified given the simultaneous decline in government spending and cuts in resources for the probation service (the principle agency responsible for monitoring the orders) during the same period that preventive orders have spread across the crime control agenda.[41] That is, if the probation service is encumbered by its current remit to monitor post-release prisoners, the demands of various preventive orders are likely to seriously and negatively impede its ability to appropriately address all aspects of its roles.

Finally, two specific points can be made concerning the relevance of regulation in potentially defending the SCPO as an exceptional case when compared to other preventive orders. First, a case can be made for using preventive orders for 'serious crime' as exceptional, given that for this category of criminal behaviour individuals are monitored by intelligence agencies. In contrast, the continued monitoring of other types of (less serious) offences is less common practice. Second, as the regulatory framework is originally designed to respond to powerful corporations and businesses, Crawford (2006: 470) questions the problems that might arise in applying such a framework to control the behaviour of young people through ASBOs. However, the SCPO application procedure is different from other orders such as the ASBO, where a higher authority is required (directors of law enforcement and intelligence agencies, rather than local authorities) to begin the process. Furthermore, if the assumption can be upheld that serious criminal organisations operate like businesses trading in illicit goods/activities, then arguably it could be more relevant to view the SCPO through a regulatory framework.

The function of civil preventive orders can be (and has been) interpreted through various existing frameworks, including regulation, security, and risk. Each of these frameworks has shaped largely independent discourses about the changing nature of criminal justice. However, the changes noted in these discourses all corroborate a single trend: the state's direct use of coercive measures, to intervene and prevent lesser degrees of harm. A preventive purpose is the common denominator – new methods to restrict and deprive liberty are being justified in the name of prevention. Therefore, it has been argued throughout this chapter that policy-making and policy-makers are in a 'state' (mind set) of prevention which is reshaping the criminal justice system. While a preventive ideology is not new to criminal justice, it has become a pervasive influence in 21st-century crime control, and has demonstrable potential to skew the founding principles of criminal law and punishment. The development of a presiding preventive justice framework is clearly a priority; however, this is not the aim of this book. Rather the aim is explanatory – to explain the promulgation of the array of preventive measures and, in particular, the proliferation of the preventive order model. The next chapter develops a theoretical framework to examine the dynamics of incremental transfer and the spread of ideas during the policy-making process.

4
Policy Transfer and Everyday Policy-Making

We have established two key propositions thus far. First, that the SCPO is a novel measure for serious and organised crime control, in that no such civil–criminal hybrid statutory instrument has been previously used to regulate or control the behaviour of individuals engaging in serious or organised criminal behaviour. The second proposition is that this novel measure falls within a relatively new framework of civil preventive orders, which regulate or control other diverse types of criminal behaviour. This immediately presents some important research questions, such as how far did other preventive orders influence the development of the SCPO? Moreover, how does the mechanism of transfer operate in practice (who and what is involved, and when does it occur)? Some normative questions also arise about whether measures used to respond to one area of crime control can or should be adopted to respond to other quite distinct sets of criminal behaviour. What are the implications of generating policy responses through such transfer procedures?

The second half of this chapter addresses these questions by developing a policy transfer framework. The main contention is that during the early gestation period of policy-making, 'policy transfer' is a common, or central, feature of policy formulation. Furthermore, policy transfer, as a mechanism of everyday policy-making, produces innovation when existing measures in one policy domain are carried over into another. An overlapping body of literature encompassing theories of transfer, diffusion, convergence, and lesson-drawing is assessed in relation to more standard policy cycles and other classical theories of policy-making. Although these transfer models are more commonly applied to understand cases of international or cross-jurisdictional policy influence, the chapter explores the applicability of these models to cases of domestic

transfer – that is, across distinct areas of crime control within one jurisdiction rather than the policy influence between countries, states, or
jurisdictions.

This chapter begins by demarcating the processes of criminal justice
policy and 'statute law' making. Statute law should be distinguished
here from common law, or 'judge-made' law. While the process of making judge-made law also engages in transfer – in fact, it is in principle
based on transfer through the process of creating binding precedents
and argument by analogy – the focus in this book is on statute law-
making, where it is argued that policy precedents are also set, though
more informally, and are often not explicit. It examines past criminal
justice policy research and points to a significant gap in the field of
criminology to engage in analysis that attempts to understand how
policy and legislation are made – both analysis of the general structures of statute law-making as well as examination of specific instances
of policy creation at the level of process and decision-making. Given
that researchers and academics in criminal justice are often the first to
criticise new crime policies, such as preventive measures, it is surprising
that few have questioned how they are made. The legislative process is
outlined, drawing on research and knowledge in the political sciences,
particularly on the state actors involved in formulation and decision-
making, as well as classical distinctions in theories of policy-making,
namely, rationalism and incrementalism.

4.1   The criminologist as policy analyst

In a period of rapid policy-making in criminal justice, it is increasingly
important to understand the process of policy development. While
political scientists have developed various competing theories and models to explain processes of public policy-making (many are discussed
throughout this chapter), relatively little research has applied these tools
to understand change in crime policy. The most notable exception here
is Paul Rock (1995, 1998, 2004), who has extensively explored the developments in policy related to victims within the criminal justice system.
However, Rock's contribution in this area falls into Jones and Newburn's
(2002: 179) account of being primarily *descriptive*, rather than engaging
in an analysis of the process:

> [W]e still know very little about how penal policy comes to be the
> way it is. Much of the work on penal policy making to date has been
> primarily descriptive, and, although often making plausible claims

about the sources of influence over policy outcomes, these are rarely based upon systematic analysis of the process of policy formulation.

In their later work, Jones and Newburn (2007) identify two limitations with existing, current criminal justice policy research: first, policy analysts and political scientists have not tended to focus their research on the domains of criminal justice and crime control. Second, criminal justice scholars generally focus on the *impact* of criminal justice policy rather than its *origins* or processes that have occurred. Others such as Ismaili (2006: 255)[1] have made the same observation:

> [C]riminologists have tended to focus their empirical research on the effects of policies rather than on their origins . . . political science, the discipline most often engaged in studies of the policy process, has largely neglected the field of crime control.

Lord Rippon (1992: 2), in a report in Hansard on *The Legislative Process*, states that the 'process and product – are interrelated . . . many complaints are of defects which appear to result from failures in the process by which that legislation was made'. The importance of this link between policy substance and process has been largely neglected. This focus by criminologists on the product (effect and impact) of policy rather than the process which leads to policy outcomes might be for several reasons.

First, there is unresolved tension among political scientists about the utility (or disutility) of the 'policy sciences', which might in turn have deterred criminologists from adopting such contentious models of policy-making as a framework for analysis:

> Policy analysis is not an exact science. It involves trying to understand and explain events in situations in which we never have complete information about what happened and why it happened, and our interpretations are influenced by our frames of reference and our ideologies. (Hill 2014: 160)

However, as Ismaili (2006: 267) postulates, for 'truly policy-orientated criminology to advance, it is vital that this process be explored in all of its complexity'.

A second reason might be that criminologists who engage in policy research seem simply or implicitly to adopt a 'top-down' perspective of policy-making, where decisions are taken by politicians and the administration, and action that flows from such decisions is carried out by the civil service machinery. This is explained by Richards and Smith (2002: 4) as the exemplar Westminster model where there is 'executive dominance of the legislature':

> Implicit within this model is a particular view of the nature of power in the British political system. Power is regarded as sealed within the domain of Westminster. It is an elitist, hierarchical, top-down view, in which politics is a zero-sum game with the Prime Minister dominating ministers, ministers dominating civil servants, or central government dominating local government. (Richards and Smith 2002: 4)

This top-down perspective places the sole focus (and responsibility) for new policy measures on the politicians of the day: 'Criminal justice decision making is governed by the exercise of political power' (Garrison 2009: 11). This in turn has led to explanations for shifts in criminal justice policy as relating to public opinion, penal populism, and the politicisation of crime – all of which work on the assumption of a rational model for policy-making, wherein political actors have the ability to actively influence policy in a particular direction. However, Rock (1995: 1) maintains that there is a need to 'concentrate on the everyday policy-making that is stirred less by big events in the outside world than by the commonplace internal processes of bureaucracy itself'. The impact of 'big events' is an attractive segue for criminologists to enter into discussion and, at times, superficial analysis of policy decision-making in criminal justice. Loader and Sparks (2011: 13) stated that this might reduce criminology 'to a marginal place within a shrill, populist penal culture'. The simplification of a complex process often depicts a dystopian view in criminology of an authoritarian or draconian government with a desire to intrude on the civil liberties of its citizens. This is not to say that the outcomes of new policy and law that impact upon the rights of individuals should not be the subject of objection and critique. Rather, this underlying assumption about the process which leads to such policies – merely as the work of authoritarian decision-makers – is questionable and deserves further exploration.

The importance of 'everyday policy-making' (Rock 1995) within the bureaucratic structures of the civil service should not be overlooked. Rock's (1995: 3) focus on the internal processes of bureaucracy in criminal justice policy-making emphasises the impact that a few individuals in the Home Office can make through bottom-up (civil servants to ministers) decision-making. Moreover, in another rare empirical study into the operation of law-making in the Home Office, Page (2003: 674) concluded that the 'exemplar' top-down notions of policy-making – where politicians take the lead in developing the shape of legislation – do not accurately reflect the legislative process in the UK: 'Officials are given responsibility for developing legislation. . . . The idea that the politician is the author of legislation confuses constitutional formality with empirical reality.' It is argued by Richards and Smith (2002: 200) that this also reflects a broader transformation over the last century from 'government' to 'governance', moving away from government as it was in the 1950s (following a centralised top-down approach to decision-making) towards a dispersed multi-layered form of governance. These new conditions under which we govern and make policy might have consequently provided greater opportunity for new forms of decision-making such as policy transfer. However, the questioning of a top-down rational model is not new. Lindblom (1959, 1979) proposed an early alternative theory to the rational models which were dominant, arguing that policy change occurs through incremental decision-making. Lindblom's work is examined in greater detail below; however, it is important to foreshadow that an incrementalist perspective could provide alternative explanations to the rise in punitiveness, expansion of criminal law, and the development and spread of new preventive measures which are under examination in this book.

A final reason for the lack of empirical research by criminologists in this area might be a more practical one: the difficultly of identifying decision-makers and sources of data for analysis.

> The central presumption is that Whitehall knows best, and decisions can be made in secret through the complex interactions of officials and ministers . . . the much more complex reality of policy-making was hidden by the ethos of secrecy. (Richards and Smith 2002: 201)

This secret or 'private' practice might appear to be an incongruous stage of the process of 'public' policy-making. However, these backstage interactions should not deter researchers from probing through empirical enquiry. Ismaili (2006: 261) argues that it is a small policy community – a 'constellation of forces' – that develops public policy. At its broadest conception, a *policy community* would include any group or individual with an interest in the specific policy on the agenda, not only civil servants and ministers, but also a range of interest groups, professional organisations, academics, individuals, and media (Rush 1993: 76). However, Pross (1986: 98–100) terms this latter group the 'attentive public' who have a less direct role in policy formulation than the primary subdivision of the policy community: the 'subgovernment'.

> The subgovernment is composed of government agencies and institutionalized associations that actually make policy within the sector. . . . It normally consists of a very small group of people who work at the core of the policy community. (Ismaili 2006: 263)

To better engage in criminal justice policy analysis, criminologists can (and arguably should) identify members of this subgovernment as part of a rigorous methodological enquiry. The specific policy community and subgovernment for the SCPO is identified in Chapter 5, to determine the key decision-makers and potential agents of transfer.[2] These individuals are an essential source of knowledge regarding the early stages of policy formulation, and the genesis of the SCPO and other preventive orders. As such, they constitute the population of individuals sampled and interviewed in the second part of this book. However, the broader structures of the legislative process, classical theories of policy-making, and the further delineation of the constituents of a policy community first require further examination.

4.2   The legislative process

Numerous critics have flayed the legislative process for, inter alia, deficient consultation, poor drafting, ineffective parliamentary scrutiny, and overly hasty proceedings (Menard 1953; Rush 1993: 77; Garrett 1998: 688). In addition, policy- and law-making appear to be evolving into a less prescriptive process.

> The organization and politics of criminal justice policy making are currently in flux. One source of change has been a partial turning away from the once standard processes of internal consultation, from committee meetings, briefings and circulating files, towards procedures that are more fragmentary, centrifugal and loosely bounded. (Rock 1995: 2)

Nonetheless, Page (2003: 653) identifies three basic analytical stages of law-making: 'deciding the policy; producing the clauses of the bill; and handling the parliamentary process'. Each of these three stages, *gestation*, *drafting*, and *parliamentary scrutiny/approval* are briefly examined in turn, in order to establish the routine activities of the key actors involved. More detailed analysis is provided for this first period of policy gestation where it is argued that the opportunity for policy transfer primarily arises. The latter two stages are more formal and procedural, when policy decisions have occurred, and action is taken to develop the ideas into legislative form.

4.2.1   The gestation period: Early formulation of policy

While there is no precise timeframe for the gestation period of law-making, there are a few discernible formal components which mark this important initial stage. One important official procedure is the production of government papers by departments. The production of Green and White Papers marks the occasion when public policy becomes 'public'. White Papers have long been the end product of the gestation period. Shortly after the introduction of the idea of Green Papers in 1967, Pemberton (1969, cited in Zander 2004: 9) maintained the distinction: 'White Papers announce firm government policy for implementation [while] Green Papers announce tentative proposals for discussion'. However, Zander (2004: 10) argues that this distinction is (in practice) 'at best over-simplified', whereby White Papers frequently foster consultation and amendments, and Green Papers can often broadcast a firm policy direction. Jordan (1977: 30) therefore concludes that 'under close examination they often tend to merge to a uniform grey' (see also Zander 2004: 10). Yet the government's publication of either a Green or White Paper marks a significant phase in the early gestation period of policy-making: that is, when 'private' discussions among decision-makers about new policy direction become 'public'. This implies that a significant part of the early gestation period is unknown to the public, as '[t]he system of decision-making is secret' (Richards and Smith 2002: 200). At this stage, policy transfer might have already occurred as clearly the decision to proceed has already been made prior to the time of a written public declaration of a new policy. Therefore much of the work of policy transfer might be considered part of an under-researched yet important phase of gestation – the 'private public policy process'.

While not all policy eventuates in legislation, all legislation flows from an intricate and fluid policy process. Lord Rippon (1992: 6–7) contends that gestation is an influential stage: 'The origins of any policy which requires legislation strongly influences the conduct of the various stages of the legislative process.' Similarly, Rock (1995: 1) argues:

A number of small structures and processes animate the very core of the routine politics of criminal justice. They have such a marked effect on the formulation of policy in its opening stages, the stages before legislation and implementation, that they explain much of its character. They deserve attention.

However, while the opening stages of policy-making play a crucial role – ideas are generated and promoted onto the agenda – it is also apparent that these stages are not easily delineated. Zander (2004: 8) maintains that at the earliest 'gestation period' (the period before entering into drafting), the relevant government department has some flexibility as to how to proceed. For example, the sources it draws on to generate policy ideas and who (or whether) it consults are far less prescribed than in the latter stages of the law-making process (Zander 2004: 8). It is perhaps precisely this lack of a rational, structured approach at this early stage that presents an opportunity for policy transfer to occur (either intentionally or inadvertently).

A large body of literature prescribes a rational policy-making model to explain the nature of the proceedings at this early gestation period. The early proponents of rationalism, Harold Lasswell, Herbert Simon, and David Easton,[3] attempted to define and examine the distinct character of policy-making. The underlying assumption of the rational model is a reasoned problem-solving approach to policy-making:

> According to such a rational model, any decision-making should be based on a comprehensive analysis of problems and goals, followed by an inclusive collection and analysis of information and a search for the best alternative to achieve these goals. (Jann and Wegrich 2007: 44)

Simon (1956) also propounded a corresponding theory of 'bounded rationality', which argued that individual decision-makers experience particular limitations (finite time, information, and personal cognition) that affect their ability to make (absolute) free rational choices. Thus, a decision-maker's selection is less focused on an optimal outcome (the 'best alternative') and more on one that would *suffice* as a *satisfactory* alternative, so-called 'satisficing' (Simon 1956: 136). These classical theories of the rational or linear policy-making process have generally led to the formation of conceptual models divided into various stages of a policy continuum or cycle. While variations of this policy cycle exist, the core components are agenda-setting, formulation, decision-making, implementation, and evaluation (Howlett and Ramesh 2003: 13).

The gestation period of law-making encompasses these first three stages (agenda-setting, formulation, and decision-making), before the draft bill is put before parliament. Policy formulation is thus a central stage in the gestation period, where policy-makers must develop a 'course of action' based on the set agenda, and guide decision-makers in their process of selection (Howlett and Ramesh 2003: 143).

However, Jann and Wegrich (2007: 48) maintain that these stages are not discrete: '[A] clear-cut separation between formulation and decision-making is very often impossible.' This observation has significant merit, as clearly various aspects of decision-making take place throughout the entirety of the policy-making process (for example, the decision to set the agenda, the decision when to implement, and the decision how to evaluate). Furthermore, Jann and Wegrich (2007: 56–57) claim that 'the policy cycle framework ignores the role of knowledge, ideas and learning in the policy process as influential independent variables affecting all stages of the policy process'. This criticism overlooks the utility of the policy cycle as a heuristic framework, rather than assuming it to be a reflection of a single empirical reality. That is, the benefit of adopting a rational policy framework lies in creating a conceptual instrument for research enquiry:

> Studying regime interactions within different stages of the policy cycle thus enables researchers to reveal not only a static 'snapshot' of the policy-making process in particular areas of government activity, but also the *dynamics* of policy stability and policy change. (Emphasis in original; Howlett et al. 2009: 88)

Accordingly, the case study focus in this book, on particular interactions during policy formulation, permits the examination and analysis of the dynamics of policy change including policy transfer. Once the agenda is set to 'do something' about a particular crime problem, policy transfer can occur to facilitate the process of policy formulation and decision-making. In a rational search for alternatives, policy transfer is a process of selecting ideas, or existing measures, for adoption from distinctly different areas of crime policy. As is shown at the end of this chapter, policy transfer models can therefore be conceptually built into the rational model, or theory, of policy-making.

This account of policy change, however, assumes an underlying rational process where decision-makers knowingly engage in policy transfer. Lindblom's incrementalist model posits an alternative theory of policy-making to the dominant 'rational-comprehensive' model. Rather than a comprehensive search for the most appropriate alternative solution to a problem, decision-makers select from a small sample of familiar solutions – those which are only marginally different from the status quo (Lindblom 1959: 84). This process is one of 'disjointed incrementalism' or 'muddling through', which depicts a more fluid process where marginal changes to existing policy occur via gradual steps (Lindblom 1959; Braybrooke and Lindblom 1963: 81–82). In addition, incrementalist approaches generally imply a static policy-making process. That is, while rationalism suggests a progressive and enlightened process, giving due weight and consideration to potential responses and alternative responses, incrementalism illustrates the inherent: 'pro-inertia and anti-innovation forces prevalent in all human organisations, administrative and policy-making' (Smith and May 2014: 166). Smith and May (2014: 166) maintain that this incremental process consequently creates 'major barriers to policy innovation'. However, arguably, incremental change could actually facilitate policy innovation, provided that the incremental changes occur alongside policy transfer. The important distinction here is that gradual steps can also take place *across* policy domains, and where policy is transferred, policy innovation is the result. This represents a form of transfer while 'muddling through'. For example, it is arguable that through policy transfer from the ASBO and other preventive orders, the SCPO was developed as an innovative response to organised crime control. While policy-making might generally be considered evolutionary rather than revolutionary, revolutionary policy change could therefore perhaps occur by way of transfer.

Therefore, two specific alternative hypotheses arise: whether policy is knowingly transferred via a considered decision (rationalism), or unknowingly transferred while muddling through (incrementalism). One way to distinguish on any practical basis between rationalism and incrementalism is as follows: the rationalist model is normative (what procedures ought to be) while the incrementalist model is explanatory (the way procedures are reflected in actual practice) (Smith and May 2014: 171–172). However, both these approaches can be viewed as instrumental, providing the foundations for a more detailed theory of the dimensions of policy transfer. The recognition of transfer as a (common) mechanism for policy formulation, and policy innovation, should not be underestimated. As Lindblom (1959: 88) argued: '[B]y becoming more conscious of their practice of this method, administrators might practice it with more skill and know when to extend or constrict its use.'[4]

4.2.2 Drafting and handling

The gestation period comes to a close soon after a White Paper is published and the drafting begins. Drafting is an 'iterative process, involving counsel, legal advisers, policy civil servants and ministers' (Page 2003: 665). The mode of production can be summarised as a set of formal interactions between key actors:

> The policy civil servants give instructions to the relevant solicitors in their department, and the solicitors send their instructions to Parliamentary Counsel (PC). The draft will be passed backwards and forwards between these three groups – generally termed 'toing and froing' by the officials . . . the brief given to the solicitor, which will be used to write the instructions to PC, will have been submitted to the minister for clearance, and any substantial changes in the policy will have to be cleared with the minister along the way. (Page 2003: 661)

Therefore, instructions to Parliamentary Counsel – compiled by departmental civil servants and legal advisors – mark the beginnings of the drafting period (Zander 2004). Based on data gathered from interviews with legal advisors, Page (2003: 661) found that these instructions included a great amount of detail on the intention behind the bill and the decision-making process. These instructions are an important documentary source when assessing the origins of policy. In addition, at this stage of drafting, it is important to analyse the role of policy transfer occurring between lawyers (both departmental legal advisors and PC). Given that the statutory provisions of a number of preventive orders are similar, it is important to examine the occurrence of transfer as a more direct result of legal administration, that is, drafting to adhere to a convention of consistency across different statutes.

While the drafting of clauses continues throughout the parliamentary process, as amendments are made during debate in both houses (Commons and Lords), the beginning of the parliamentary period – the stage of handling a bill through the parliamentary process – is indicated by a bill's clearance by Cabinet Legislative Programme (LP) Committee (Zander 2004: 11–12). Once approved by LP, a bill is officially given a place in the parliamentary session. After a bill reaches Parliament, with policy proposals now formalised into clauses, it moves through several stages of scrutiny in each house (see also Figure A.1 in Appendix 'B').[5] Most bills are first introduced in the House of Commons; however, some begin in the House of Lords. The strategic reasons for a government to initiate a bill in the House of Lords are unclear; however, it is likely to be for bills of larger size or complexity, or alternatively just a matter of convenience regarding timetabling (Lord Rippon 1992: 8; Zander 2004: 13). Page (2003: 670) argues that it is rare that bills will *not* get through the parliamentary process, as one civil servant he interviewed stated:

> The more normal [case] is that concessions and compromises are made which placate concerns but at the same time protect key policies. This is a balancing act and the role of the official is to advise on where ground can be given . . . to relieve pressure with minimum damage.

While there might indeed be some room for negotiation on the final shape of policy, the process of policy transfer is less likely to occur at this final stage since policy ideas are already well established: 'By the time that this Cabinet sub-committee has approved the project for inclusion in the legislative programme, most of the policy will already have been developed' (Zander 2004: 7).

Despite this, parliamentary debates still provide a useful secondary source of data indicating the origins of policy. Hansard records indicate where existing policies or measures were used in argumentation during debates to justify the acceptance of new similar policy measures in another domain. This presents a proposition that 'policy precedents' can be used to facilitate the policy transfer process. That is, with the acceptance of a single policy measure – particularly a controversial measure, such as the ASBO – there is a broader potential implication for future (less foreseeable) proliferation, spread, and transfer to occur. The passing of an act affirms not only the policy measures contained in the bill but also the principles behind it. This means that with the passage of one policy measure, a precedent is set for subsequent similar measures to be more easily developed (as matters of principle have already been accepted). The process of policy transfer is advanced by the precedent set by existing measures, which might diminish the requirement for a demonstration of practical need for a new measure to be enacted into legislation.

4.2.3   Policy actors and a policy community

Finally, it is important to identify the various actors involved in formulating policy during the legislative process, to determine the potential agents of transfer. Hill (2014: 8) contends that

> it becomes less plausible to speak of locating the 'real' policy-makers. Policy-making, like 'power', appears as a dynamic yet diffused element

in the relations between public actors and the world on which they act.

This depiction of power is reinforced by Foucault's (1980: 154) postulation that '[p]ower is not something that is acquired, seized, or shared, something that one holds on to or allows to slip away; power is exercised from innumerable points'. The implication of this statement is that identifying a single decision-maker as responsible for policy-making (or indeed policy transfer) is unachievable since an immeasurable number of contributions are made. That is, there is an apparent group dynamic to policy formulation and decision-making where influence comes from many points. Policy subsystems are the dominant unit of analysis for studying those involved at the stage of policy formulation. Howlett and Ramesh (2003: 148) state:

> Unlike agenda-setting, where members of the entire policy universe theoretically can be involved in policy deliberations and actions, in policy formulation the relevant actors are usually restricted to members of policy subsystems.

These subsystems have been conceived variously as policy networks, policy regimes, iron triangles, epistemic communities, and policy communities – however, the distinction between these competing conceptions is often nebulous (Howlett and Ramesh 2003: 148). One simple explanation for this is that they are similar concepts which have derived from diverse academic fields. For example, the concept of 'policy community' is derived from political sciences, whereas the notion of 'policy networks' has sprung from organisational theory (Homeshaw 1995: 521). It has already been established above that the 'subgovernment' of a policy community encompasses the key influential players in a process of ideas and policy generation, whereas other actors of the broader policy community such as the 'attentive public' have a more amorphous role in formulation (Pross 1986: 98–100; Howlett and Ramesh 2003: 147–148). The influential actors in the policy community's subgovernment can be broadly divided into two core groups: ministers and civil servants.

> [T]he old policy-administration distinction: politicians do the policy – resolve or generate conflict and set out the broad strategic vision – and the administrators have the dull detailed work needed to give effect to the grand design. (Page 2003: 673)

However, as discussed above, there is some debate about the direction, role, and relative contribution of these two groups of actors in policy formulation and law-making. One dominant view of the process might be best characterised as the *Yes Minister!* scenario:[6]

> Departments were at the core of the policy process, and therefore had a considerable impact on outcomes. . . . In certain departments, for example the Home Office, it appeared that officials effectively ran the department, and ministers were seen as obstacles to its smooth running. (Richards and Smith 2002: 61)

However, it has also been argued that this depiction should not be overstated:

> [W]e must avoid exaggerating the bureaucracy's role. The political executive is ultimately responsible for all policies, an authority it does assert at times. High-profile political issues are also more likely to involve higher levels of executive control. Executive control is also likely to be higher if the bureaucracy consistently opposes a policy option preferred by politicians. (Howlett et al. 2009: 67)

Despite this, it is also apparent that this identification of responsibility and accountability does not automatically equate to a leading influence on policy formulation. For example, it has been argued that the process is designed to 'appear' to operate in this manner: 'Decisions must always seem to flow down from those who are accountable, not rise fully formed from obscure officials below' (Rock 1995: 5). One interpretation of this design would be to conclude that ministers often become the scapegoats for a decision-making process in which they play a lesser role.

> Individual Ministers are ultimately responsible for the wording of the bills they present to Parliament, but it is rare for Ministers to insist on a form of words against the advice of Parliamentary Counsel. (Lord Rippon 1992: 7)

In a democratically driven public policy process, it might simply be accepted that the system under which decisions are taken is 'closed, secretive, and elitist', and that the political decision-makers who oversee the process should be held accountable for any occurrence of policy failure (Richards and Smith 2002: 200). However, this too quickly (and easily) attributes blame without questioning the workings of the formulation process as potentially contributing to the failure which has occurred.

> [M]inisterial control over the process is not guaranteed. Ministers typically know little about the law they are bringing in until they receive the submissions and briefings that their officials give them. Perhaps the biggest danger for democracy is not a civil service putting forward proposals which a minister feels forced to accept, but rather that ministers do not notice or fully appreciate what is being proposed in their name although they have the political authority to change it and a civil service which bends over backwards to accommodate them and keep them informed and briefed. (Page 2003: 673)

There is also a danger here that the civil service machinery pushes forward even controversial proposals, believing that a political authority will moderate excess (be it an individual minister or the structures of the parliamentary process).[7] Nonetheless, it is among these complex interactions between ministers, civil servants, and other members of the subgovernment where policy transfer takes place.

In terms of crime policy formulation, this subgovernment would typically include the following key actors: Home Secretary (most senior minister in the Home Office) and other ministers of state for the home department; Permanent Secretary (head civil servant in the Home Office) and other senior civil servants in the Home Office; directors of other relevant criminal justice departments and public bodies (for example, Ministry of Justice, Probation and Parole, HM Revenue and Customs, or SOCA); the Crown Prosecution Service; and the Association of Chief Police Officers, among others. The involvement of each of these actors in the subgovernment clearly varies depending on the policy under examination. For example, the Permanent Secretary's role has been observed to be increasingly managerial rather than being directly involved in policy issues (see Richards and Smith 2002: 222). It is also important to note that the Prime Minister could at times be included in a subgovernment:

> It can be argued that prime ministers have become increasingly proactive in policy-making and that they have had clearer policy visions. It is also true that Prime Ministers are less dependent on departments for advice and have, through the expanded policy unit, a source of independent policy advice that greatly increases policy-making capacity. (Richards and Smith 2002: 224)

Finally, less attention has been paid to another key group of civil servants who are intimately involved in policy development at each of the periods of the legislative process: departmental bill-teams. The bill-team plays a significant role in the organisation and development of policy and legislation, championing ideas onto both the political and legislative agendas (Page 2003: 656–657). Departments create either a 'policy' bill-team or a 'handling' bill-team: the former is engaged in each of the three periods discussed above (gestation, drafting, and parliamentary), while the latter is concerned only with 'stewarding' the bill through the final parliamentary period (Zander 2004: 7). The number of members on a bill-team can vary depending on the size and complexity of the bill; however, teams will typically include: a 'head', the official charged with oversight of the entire bill (often also referred to as a 'handler'); a 'policy lead', the official who takes responsibility for particular aspects of policy in the bill;[8] and at least one 'legal advisor' (see also Page 2003: 654–655; Zander 2004: 7). These officials in the bill-team are also usually from the lower ranks of the civil service (Page 2003: 653).

Therefore, civil servants (including members of a bill-team) and ministers of state are central to a policy community's subgovernment, which encompasses the key individuals who determine a policy's content. As a consequence, these individuals are the potential agents of transfer. It has also been argued above that policy transfer primarily occurs early at gestation; however, how and why policy is transferred has not yet been fully explained. The full extent of the varied dimensions of the process of transfer requires detailed analysis and prescription. This task forms the final section of this chapter, in which a more detailed policy transfer framework is constructed.

4.3   Developing a policy transfer framework

Pure innovation in any area of public policy-making is rare. The use of borrowing, copying, and amending policy from one area to another by policy-makers seems commonplace (Burke 2011). Jones and Newburn (2007) explored the role of policy transfer (the exportation of policies from the US to the UK) in three areas of criminal justice policy: privatisation of prisons, mandatory sentencing, and zero-tolerance policing. Despite these observations, the procedure for, and extent of, policy transfer is often not obvious to those outside the policy-making process (and perhaps not even to those within). Indeed similarity in policy between two entities does not necessarily lead to the immediate conclusion that transfer has occurred. For example, Garland (2001) has observed the convergence of policies in crime control between the US and U[...] generally, arguing that similar political structures and similar pr[...] have resulted in convergent crime control measures.[9] Conseq[...], Dolowitz and Marsh (2000: 21) asserted that there is invariably a cen- tral empirical question about transfer during the policy-making process: 'When we are analyzing policy change we always need to ask the ques- tion: Is policy transfer involved?'.

A number of important theoretical concepts, such as lesson-drawing, diffusion, convergence, and organisational theory, have been employed to understand the perceived growth in processes of transfer as a central factor in affecting change. The application and utility of these concepts for interpreting the emergence of the SCPO in the UK are explored in turn below. While the differences between these concepts are high- lighted, the discussion primarily demonstrates their apparent overlap. The concept of 'policy transfer' (Dolowitz and Marsh 1996, 2000) is proposed as a useful overall theoretical framework that engages and augments – but does not supersede – these other important concepts of cross-jurisdictional influence. This section concludes by refocusing this conceptual framework for the specific circumstances of domestic *intra*-departmental policy transfer. While the policy transfer literature is valuable, as it supplements more traditional models of policy-making, researchers who have employed this framework have focused exclusively on forms of cross-national transfer (see Stone 2004; Jones and Newburn 2007; Cairney 2009; Marsden and Stead 2011). It is maintained that this focus is unnecessarily restricted to international transfer and that these concepts are equally relevant to the understanding of the process of transfer across substantive areas of domestic policy.

4.3.1 Policy transfer

There are numerous concepts that have been used in different fields of study to understand the process of importing or exporting elements of policy from one place to another. In comparative politics and public pol- icy studies, the dominant concepts have emerged in the form of 'policy convergence' (Bennett 1991b), 'lesson-drawing' (Rose 1991), and 'policy diffusion' (Walker 1969). Other concurrent developments in organisa- tional theory and comparative law focus on similar concepts such as 'isomorphism' (to explain similarities in organisations) and 'legal trans- plants' (deliberate lifting of legal measures, processes, or institutions from one jurisdiction to another) (respectively, DiMaggio and Powell 1983; Watson 1974). The policy transfer framework, a relatively recent development conceived primarily in the work of Dolowitz and Marsh (1996, 2000), emerged with the objective of comprehensively framing the vast spectrum of possible dimensions of policy influence. Dolowitz and Marsh (1996: 344) define policy transfer as

> a process in which knowledge about policies, administrative arrangements, institutions, etc. in one time and/or place is used in the development of policies, administrative arrangements and institutions in another time and/or place.

Their framework captures the various other explanations and theories under one heuristic model, as well as adding some new dimensions of policy transfer (such as how uninformed, incomplete, or inappropriate policy transfer might result in policy failure). Dolowitz and Marsh (1996, 2000) perceived several shortcomings with existing concepts in their ability to appreciate the full range of possible ways in which knowledge about policies in one time or place is used in the development of another policy. Principally, it is argued that the convergence and diffusion literature (Bennett 1991b and Walker 1969 among others) diminishes or ignores the role of agents, while lesson-drawing (Rose 1991) focuses exclusively on voluntary transfer, thereby omitting coercive processes (Dolowitz and Marsh 2000: 3). The framework offered by Dolowitz and Marsh (1996, 2000) contains the following eight dimensions:

1. What is Transferred: policies (goals, content, or instruments), programmes, institutions, ideologies, ideas, attitudes, cultural values, or negative lessons?
2. Why Transfer: voluntary (lesson-drawing), coercive (direct imposition), or a mixture of both (lesson-drawing with pressure)?
3. Degree of Transfer: copying, emulation, mixtures, or inspiration.
4. Who is Involved in Transfer: elected officials, bureaucrats, civil servants, pressure groups, political parties, experts, policy entrepreneurs, consultants, think tanks, transnational corporations, and supranational institutions (for example, the European Union)?
5. Transfer Origin: past (policy history), within-a-nation (or 'domestic'), or cross-national.
6. How to Demonstrate Policy Transfer: media, reports (commissioned and uncommissioned), conferences, meetings/visits, and statements (written and verbal).
7. Constraints on Transfer: policy complexity, past policies, structural feasibility (ideology, cultural proximity, technology, economic, and bureaucratic), and language.
8. How Transfer Leads to Policy Failure: uninformed transfer, incomplete transfer, and inappropriate transfer.

Essentially, this framework classifies policy transfer into its elements based on basic interrogatives, for example, what, why, who, from where, and to what extent? These are refined into the eight themes which provide spectrums to guide researchers in developing an understanding of the various potential characteristics of policy transfer. Importantly, this framework guides the generation of questions that a researcher should consider when examining the transfer process. For example, in relation to the SCPO, Dolowitz and Marsh's (2000) classification of 'transfer origin' has already been discussed in previous chapters, and there appear to be two main potential origins of transfer: the first, from civil RICO measures ('cross-national'), and the second, from preventive orders in other areas of crime control in the UK ('within-a-nation') (point 5 above). Equally, these other dimensions (particularly points 1–4) can be applied to guide research and analysis in understanding the emergence of civil preventive orders in the field of organised crime control. Accordingly, based on these eight dimensions, the next subsection specifically outlines some preliminary hypotheses, questions, and tentative deductions about the genesis of the SCPO. These guide the empirical research and analysis in subsequent chapters in Part II of this book.

4.3.1.1 Application of this model to the serious crime prevention order

What is transferred? This theme probes the substance of a transfer. For the SCPO, it is necessary to determine whether there was a transfer of the statutory content of existing preventive orders ('instruments') or whether there was a transfer of attitudes and political beliefs about the utility of civil prevention as a beneficial method to be introduced to the organised crime control policy agenda.

Why transfer? Here Dolowitz and Marsh suggest a continuum (voluntary at one end and coercive at the other) that questions whether the shift to using civil preventive orders for organised crime control was pursued actively and voluntarily by policy-makers or whether other factors were at play. Furthermore, it raises the question as to why there was a decision to introduce this measure to deal with organised crime in 2007, if knowledge of civil methods as they were operating in the US RICO Act had existed since 1970. While there is no indication that an overarching foreign or supranational government has imposed or recommended the shift towards civil orders in the UK, coercive transfer could also be conceived of as occurring through systemic or institutional pressure from other areas of policy – a form of intra-departmental harmonisation.

Degree of transfer. This dimension also encompasses a continuum (from mere inspiration to direct copying) and generates questions regarding the extent of transfer. That is, has the content of other preventive orders (for example, terrorism Control Orders, ASBOs, or Civil RICO) been copied directly, or has there been substantial adaptation to the needs of the SCPO (for example, extending the application of orders to businesses rather than exclusively to individuals)? Alternatively, have there been various degrees of mixed transfer occurring simultaneously from different sources, for example, has the inspiration been drawn from civil RICO, while the substance of the SCPO been copied from domestic preventive orders in the UK?

Who is involved in transfer? While most of the actors listed by Dolowitz and Marsh (point 4 above) may have indeed influenced the formulation of the SCPO in different ways, it is important to consider who was most active, and in particular, which of these individuals (or networks) may have previously worked on other areas of policy-making (for example, terrorism policy, anti-social behaviour policy). Clearly, the recognition and identification of policy communities and subgovernments are fundamentally important here (discussed in Section 4.2.3).

Demonstrating policy transfer, constraints on transfer, and *policy failure.* The last three themes in the Dolowitz and Marsh model digress from the objective of characterising policy transfer. The *how to demonstrate policy transfer* theme merely catalogues resources that researchers can analyse to assess transfer. It has been demonstrated above that it is likely that transfer occurs early in the gestation period, where events are informal and part of a private policy process. Therefore, decision-makers who were involved in early informal discussions of policy formulation are the quintessential primary resource to determine the origins of policy. However, secondary documents, such as Green Papers, White Papers, Instructions to Parliamentary Counsel, and departmental consultation, also provide evidence about policy formulation and the role of transfer.

Finally, *constraints on transfer* and *how transfer leads to policy failure* raise important questions related to the 'transferability' of civil orders across a range of diverse areas of crime control, and the potential for such transfers to lead to 'inappropriate transfer' and thus policy failures. These two themes emphasise the potential perils of engaging in the transfer of a common policy solution for distinct problem areas.

This exploratory framework identifies some important questions that undoubtedly assist in examining the interdependence of criminal justice policies (that is, how policy-making in one domain can be influenced by the transfer of ideas and structures from another). However, the several other existing theories, mentioned above, that have attempted to explain policy influence, are also clearly identifiable in this transfer framework. For example, Dolowitz and Marsh's 'Degrees of Transfer' (point 3 above) clearly mirrors Rose's (1993: 30) description of the degrees of 'lesson-drawing' including *copying, emulation, making a hybrid, synthesis,* and *inspiration.* Similarly, Bennett (1991b: 218) contends that policy convergence refers to the transfer of policy *goals, content, instruments, outcomes,* and/or *styles,* which are obviously also present in the framework offered by Dolowitz and Marsh (point 1 above).

James and Lodge (2003: 190) have suggested that rather than developing and uniting prior concepts of lesson-drawing, convergence, and diffusion, the policy transfer framework has rendered each of these theories unintelligible:

> Rather than just a case of old wine in new bottles, the framework is an unpalatable cocktail of different types of beverage. The framework obscures differences between theories and might lead researchers who follow it to neglect the variety of theories that are available.

However, it is argued that this critique is misguided. The intentions of Dolowitz and Marsh were for this framework to be used as a heuristic device, whereby other concepts can also be employed to 'deepen our understanding of transfer' (Dolowitz 2000: 3; Dolowitz and Marsh 2000: 14). Accordingly, Radaelli (2000: 26) contends that the policy transfer framework is conceptual, and that it can be supplemented by other theories such as organisational theory, which assist in further explaining the mechanisms of transfer. Thus, researchers ought to go beyond the guiding framework that is posed by the eight themes of policy transfer posited by Dolowitz and Marsh above. For example, in the case of the SCPO, concepts of diffusion and lesson-drawing can enhance the explanation of the underlying mechanisms of transfer which occurred. These complementary theories require further examination.

4.3.2 Policy diffusion and 'policy isomorphism'

Diffusion theories have typically been employed to explain the process by which innovations travel between states within the US (Walker 1969; Strang and Meyer 1993). However, conceptually, this theory extends beyond these boundaries. According to Bennett (1991b: 220–221), diffusion refers to the successive adoption or spread of a policy innovation without intentional or conscious emulation. Simmons et al. (2008: 7) argue that this form of unconscious policy influence, even occurring between countries, is the result of conditioning: 'International policy diffusion occurs when government policy decisions in a given country are systematically conditioned by prior policy choices made in other countries.' This conception of unconscious policy transfer (or form of 'policy conditioning') is absent in Dolowitz and Marsh's framework. That is, Dolowitz and Marsh assume a baseline *intention* on behalf of policy decision-makers who engage in transfer, whereas diffusion models support the alternative hypothesis presented above about unknowingly transferring while muddling through. Diffusion conjures up images of a drop of ink in a glass of water, whereby the introduction of a novel substance or idea spreads rapidly. If applied to the situation of preventive orders in the UK, the implication is that once the model of a preventive order is introduced in one area of crime control (such as to control anti-social behaviour) the spread to other areas will rapidly follow. Furthermore, Berry and Berry (2007: 224) maintain that the diffusion of policy innovation is analogous to the developments in organisational theory, which go further towards explaining how and why diffusion might occur.

'Isomorphism' is a concept popularised by DiMaggio and Powell (1983) to assist in understanding the similarities and convergence of organisations and bureaucracies. DiMaggio and Powell (1983: 147) argued that contrary to conventional economic (Weberian) assumptions, homogeneity between organisations is not the result of competition and the demand for efficiency. Rather they contend that coercion, uncertainty, and constraint better explain convergence of organisational structures (DiMaggio and Powell 1983). In particular, three mechanisms are at play: *coercive isomorphism, mimetic processes*, and *normative pressures*.

Coercive isomorphism refers to pressures, intentional or unintentional, stemming from the dependence on another organisation. This pressure can be exerted by a more powerful organisation(s), or be a product of inadvertent adoption when conforming to norms or laws (DiMaggio and Powell 1983: 150). Mimetic processes are governed by the principle that uncertainty fosters imitation: '[W]hen goals are ambiguous, or when the environment creates symbolic uncertainty, organizations may model themselves on other organizations' (DiMaggio and Powell 1983: 151). Importantly, imitation in times of uncertainty does not need to be voluntary. Mimetic modelling, for example, could occur as a result of 'employee transfer' between organisations (DiMaggio and Powell 1983: 151). Finally, 'normative pressures' focus on the phenomenon of 'professionalisation'. Essentially this refers to the often shared or homogenous experiences and background such as systems of education or training of employees, which results in the development of shared concepts of legitimacy. This includes the continued sharing of information between 'professional networks' across different organisations (DiMaggio and Powell 1983).

Both Harmsen and Wilson (2000) and Radaelli (2000) have applied organisational theory to understand shared legitimacy and similarities in policy-making, or 'policy isomorphism'. Therefore, policy isomorphism can also be employed to understand the apparent transfer of preventive orders across numerous areas of crime control policy in the UK. Of particular importance are potential 'mimetic processes' in domestic formulation that might have led to the adoption of the SCPO. That is, as discussed at the beginning of this book, in formulating the SCA 2007, the government expressed a view of uncertainty regarding the measures that could be employed to deal with the identified 'gaps' in existing law enforcement tools to respond to organised crime. If organisational theory is applied to understand these circumstances of policy change, it might be argued that a mimetic process occurred, whereby there was significant uncertainty about appropriate new responses to organised crime, which led to a response being modelled on those in other policy domains. Moreover, this mimetic modelling may be the result of the more direct 'employee transfer' of policy-makers between divisions in the Home Office (for example, from divisions dealing with terrorism and anti-social behaviour to those responding to organised crime).

4.3.3 Policy convergence

It is also important to appreciate the broader theoretical concept of 'convergence', as there is an emerging perception that US and UK public policy are more convergent than divergent (Garland 2001; Jones and Newburn 2007). Jones and Newburn (2007: 23) suggest that convergence must be considered outside the framework of policy transfer that has been presented above: '[P]olicy transfer is not a necessary prerequisite for policy convergence.' That is to say, simply observing that two countries' or jurisdictions' policies are similar is not sufficient to conclude that policy transfer has occurred. Rather, convergence implies that similarities in policies and laws are able to develop independently (Deacon 1999, cited in Jones and Newburn 2007: 33). In specific regard to the UK and US, this may be owing to the presence of similar political models, similar problems, and/or similar cultural conditions (Garland 2001; Jones and Newburn 2007). Therefore, we cannot simply assume that the emergence of comparable policy responses means that one jurisdiction's policy has necessarily *influenced* another.

Perhaps the strongest case for convergence in criminal justice has been put forward by Garland (2001) in *The Culture of Control*. Garland (2001) suggests that the social, political, and cultural conditions of late modernity have produced corresponding and coexisting, yet largely mutually exclusive, problems of, and more importantly solutions to, social order across comparable, late modern societies (notably the US and the UK). A convergence framework appears to suggest that a focus on agency (the actors who make or influence policy) is less important than the larger structural factors to be considered. Consequently, many have argued that convergence theories transmit a 'deterministic flavour', suggesting the inevitability of policy development and change in a particular direction (Rose 1991; Edwards and Hughes 2005: 346; Jones and Newburn 2007: 7). Despite these critiques, convergence theory is important as it presents an anti-thesis to more conscious (though perhaps still coercive) policy transfer and lesson-drawing. In the context of the current study of policy transfer, convergence theory explains how the preventive order model could be formulated in the UK without direct transfer from civil orders in the US RICO Act – that is, the similar legal structures and common problems in the UK and US have led to a similar civil policy response. In line with this argument, for example, convergence theorists would explain evidence such as the UK government's stated consideration of RICO in the early consultation papers simply as a way to 'legitimate decisions already taken' (Bennett 1991a: 38).

4.3.4 Lesson-drawing

According to Rose (1991: 9), theories of convergence (and diffusion) imply 'technocratic determinism', which ignores situations where governments and policy-makers voluntarily engage in transfer. Consequently, Rose (1991) laid the foundation for policy learning and lesson-drawing. The process of lesson-drawing has three broad stages: searching for policies in other places; developing domestic policy; and 'prospective evaluation' of policy (Rose 1991). First, searching for policy, or 'scanning programmes elsewhere', refers to the process whereby policy-makers explore measures that are being employed in other cities, states, nations, or organisations to address a similar problem (Rose 1991: 19). Rose (1991: 28) argues that the search for lessons from abroad is prompted by dissatisfaction with current domestic policy, where policy-makers must then promptly satisfy the majority within the community of officials and experts, as well as the wider public, by developing a new alternative strategy. This clearly implies that policy-makers do not search for an *ideal* solution but rather one that *satisfies* both practical standards (of experts) and politically desirable standards (of officials and politicians) (Rose 1991: 24). Furthermore, Rose (1991: 13) asserts that 'policymakers do not have the time or capacity to search everywhere; they follow the line of least resistance'. This has the hallmarks of the abovementioned process of 'satisficing' and bounded rationality (Simon 1956: 136). Within the initial search stage, two key procedures occur: first, policymakers create a 'conceptual model' to assist in understanding the dynamics of policy operating in another place; and second, this model is compared with the domestic policy that is seeking change.

> The model should be accurate as description but its elements should be generic. . . . A model should contain the basic elements of a programme, but no more detail than is necessary to incorporate what is needed to be effective. (Rose 1991: 20)

The aim of creating these models of comparison is to provide a generalisable understanding of how policy addresses an issue in the exporter jurisdiction and how politically compatible this policy would be given the circumstances of the importer (or 'policy-maker's constituency') (Rose 1991: 20–21). It is also important to highlight that a lesson can be either positive or negative – just as a policy-maker might draw positively on policy solutions to similar problems in other jurisdictions, a 'negative lesson' is where policy-makers learn 'what not to do' (Rose 1991: 4). The US Boot Camps for young offenders is one such example of a failed experiment, where a negative lesson might be drawn.[10]

The second procedure in the process of lesson-drawing is to develop domestic policy based on the lessons from foreign measures (that is, the integration of exogenous measures). Rose (1991: 21–22) identifies five potential forms that lesson-drawing can take in shaping domestic policy: copying, emulation, hybridisation, synthesis, and inspiration. Copying is argued to be only possible in federal or unitary political systems, as to copy a policy would require the complete transfer of policy measures as they operate in the exporter jurisdiction, including the political, cultural, and historical circumstances (Rose 1991: 21). However, surely these circumstances could vary by state even in a unitary system. Therefore, emulation is more commonplace where programmes or policies must be adapted to suit the new domestic conditions. Hybridisation occurs when the policies of two places (importer and exporter) merge together, for example, the structure of an established importer policy with the innovative substance of the exporter policy (Rose 1991: 22). Synthesis is similar to hybridisation except that lessons are drawn from more than two different places, which results in the development of a policy that is novel and distinct from each of the original exporting jurisdictions (Rose 1991: 22). The fifth type of lesson that might be drawn relates to inspiration, which refers to the transfer of ideas without more structural or tangible elements of policy (Rose 1991: 22).

The final stage of the lesson-drawing process is *prospective evaluation* (Rose 1991: 23). This deductive process attempts to evaluate the potential suitability of a foreign policy:

> Prospective evaluation differs from conventional evaluation research. . . . Retrospective evaluation has the scholarly advantage of basing conclusions on empirical evidence. But for policymakers under pressure to act in conditions of uncertainty, it has the disadvantage of providing too much (or too little) knowledge too late. The demand of policy makers is for *ex ante* assessments that can be instrumentally useful in determining whether they should emulate programme A, adopt a hybrid of A and B, a synthesis of several different programmes, or lower their aspirations and accept that their present programme is the best that can be achieved. (Rose 1991: 23)

Therefore, lesson-drawing leads to the strong conclusion that lessons which are drawn from within a political structure will most likely be adopted (notionally supporting the idea of 'domestic transfer'). Rose (1993: 97) argues that '[t]he easiest place to search for lessons is within one's own country, for the preconditions for lesson-drawing are easily met'. This is owing to the fact that the conditions that surround policy-making favour policies that are from similar political systems; the knowledge can be easily located and the satisfaction of public, political, and expert actors are more easily met. Arguably, innovation transferred from another area of policy with similar conditions is preferable as it presents an incremental change rather than a radical one. However, Rose (1991: 25) also maintains that 'it is usually impractical and undesirable to think in terms of drawing lessons from one policy area to another, e.g. to run schools like the armed forces'. While this example of lesson-drawing from one department to another might raise significant questions about the appropriateness of some instances of 'domestic policy transfer', it only paints a partial picture. That is, this example only refers to *inter*-departmental forms of transfer (education and defence respectively) where the policy environment and conditions are patently heterogenous. The spread of preventive orders across diverse areas of crime control happened *intra*-departmentally where policy environments overlap, and therefore this concept of lesson-drawing may be more applicable for understanding the incremental policy change that occurred. Nonetheless, the implicit perils of transfer emphasised by Rose (1991: 25) remain a concern: that is, the success of the preventive order model in one area of crime control does not mean that it is necessarily desirable or practical for the distinct crime problems of another area or type of crime.

This discussion about the domestic policy-making process and the role of internal learning or transfer highlights a fundamental issue which requires further examination. That is, the question as to whether or not the policy transfer framework presented above (integrating other theories of lesson-drawing, diffusion, and convergence) can actually be applied to the circumstances of domestic, intra-departmental, policy change (James and Lodge 2003). Despite the *prima facie* evidence of a 'policy transfer' of preventive orders across areas of crime control in the UK, it is also clear that these theories are seldom employed to understand transfer from within a unitary political system. This issue needs to be addressed by exploring where policy transfer and other similar theories fit in relation to the more standard model of domestic policy-making.

4.3.5 Domestic policy transfer?

As shown above, studies of policy transfer, lesson-drawing, convergence, and diffusion have focused almost exclusively on the role of policy transfer between nation states. The origins of the SCPO present (on the surface) two potential sources of policy transfer: US civil RICO, and other UK preventive orders (ASBOs, Control Orders, etc.). The first source corresponds with mainstream research into policy transfer between a national exporter and importer; however, the latter source presents some problems that need to be addressed.

As suggested above, policy transfer occurs from one *time and/or place* to another *time and/or place* (Dolowitz and Marsh 1996). There is an underlying assumption in the policy transfer literature that transfer occurs between nations, that is, between the UK and another country (such as the US) rather than within UK domestic policy domains. This is reflected in the later development of the Dolowitz and Marsh (2000) model wherein there is a conceptual shift of policy transfer from speaking of 'from one *political system* to another' rather than *time and/or place* (Dolowitz 2000: 3). The exception to this more general application to international transfer is in the circumstances of federations such as the US or Australia, where transfer or diffusion of innovation within a nation (but between states) takes place (Walker 1969; Strang and Meyer 1993).

There are two apparent reasons for this exclusive focus on international or interstate transfer. First, these theories of policy transfer have largely emerged from the field of comparative politics and policy, which principally observed the similarities and differences between countries. The second reason is that the idea of 'domestic transfer' is already assumed in standard policy-making models (James and Lodge 2003: 181). In fact, James and Lodge (2003) used this second reason as grounds to criticise policy transfer frameworks, including cases of international transfer. They argue that these concepts of lesson-drawing and policy transfer are simply recreating elements of the 'wheel' (or policy-making 'cycle'!). However, it is argued that instead of disregarding the work done by policy transfer theorists, these models should be embraced as an intrinsic and routine part of everyday policy-making. Dolowitz and Marsh's (1996: 357) original conceptualisation referring to 'the process by which actors borrow policies developed in one setting to develop programmes and policies within another' has taken an unnecessarily narrow international focus, and has largely overlooked its applicability to the understanding of those important transfers that occur domestically. If transfer is recognised as having a common role in policy-making, the important implication is that we could develop systems that facilitate the process of policy transfer (international and domestic) which would minimise the occurrence of uninformed, incomplete, or inappropriate cases of transfer.

4.3.6 Rational policy-making cycles and the search for alternatives

Policy transfer, both domestic and cross-national, mirrors similar concepts in the standard or rational policy-making model. As discussed above in Section 4.2.1, the central conception of policy-making is that it operates as part of a cycle moving through stages of *agenda-setting, policy formulation, decision-making, policy implementation*, and *policy evaluation* (Howlett and Ramesh 2003: 13). This chapter has focused on the stage of policy formulation, as this is the stage where policy transfer is most likely to occur. In a more elaborate policy-making cycle, Althaus et al. (2007: 37) expand this stage of policy formulation as conceived in the Howlett and Ramesh (2003) model, proposing four more precise and defined sub-stages of formulation: *policy analysis, policy instruments, consultation*, and *coordination* (see Figure 4.1).

Figure 4.1 demonstrates that the preliminary stage of policy formulation is 'policy analysis' (Althaus et al. 2007). During this policy analysis stage, policy-makers engage in a 'search for alternatives', which explains the process whereby policy-makers use 'shortcuts' in formulating an

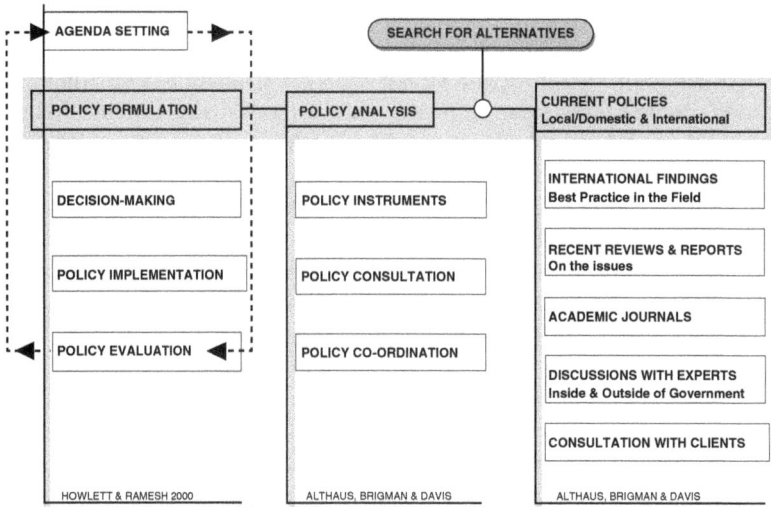

Figure 4.1 Standard policy-making models and searching to transfer

appropriate solution for a given problem (Althaus et al. 2007: 65). Althaus et al. (2007: 57) contend that this search represents the admission and recognition by policy-makers that they operate in a process of imperfect rationality; that is, political and time restraints impede complete analysis of all options and the creation of innovation is unrealistic. Indeed the process of searching and adopting a policy from another area of domestic policy could be understood as incremental change where 'an extension of familiar procedures to a new domain . . . minimizes search and analysis time' (Bridgman and Davis 2004: 53). As also highlighted in Figure 4.1 (right-hand column), Althaus et al. (2007: 65) delineate a list of places in which policy-makers commonly search:

- Current policies, locally and in other jurisdictions;
- International findings on best practice in the field;
- Recent reviews and reports on the issue;
- Academic journals;
- Discussions with experts within and outside government;
- Consultation with clients.

There are obvious parallels between this 'search' process and the process of policy transfer described in detail throughout this chapter. Specifically, the search for alternatives within 'current policies, *locally* and in *other jurisdictions'* is clearly analogous with the concept of policy transfer (both domestic and international, respectively). In this sense, the observation by James and Lodge (2003) is accurate in that the processes discussed in lesson-drawing and policy transfer can be linked to similar concepts already established in the standard policy-making model. However, their deduction that these frameworks are therefore indistinct overlooks the auxiliary benefits and contribution to be made by these theories in developing a more detailed understanding of the dynamics of transfer. Moreover, the search for alternatives in other areas of policy is only one dimension of searching in the standard policy-making model. Clearly, notions of policy transfer have expanded, and in the process augmented, the understanding of one (increasingly) important facet of conventional policy formulation. Yet in this process of expansion, the search for alternatives in 'current policies locally' (that is, domestically) has been overlooked.

The recent motivation to develop more comprehensive modes of thinking about transfer as a feature of policy-making might be attributed to technological changes that have facilitated global communication and borrowing from beyond national or institutional boundaries:

> While there is no denying that the process of policy transfer is not new, it nonetheless appears that over the past decade or so, as technological advances have made it easier and faster for policy-makers to communicate with each other, the occurrences of policy transfer have increased. (Dolowitz and Marsh 2000: 6)

The framework that has been developed in this chapter is clearly valuable in providing a more detailed understanding of this more recently identified aspect of policy formulation. The various theories that have been developed here (policy transfer, lesson-drawing, convergence, and diffusion) can be refocused to contribute to the broader practice of searching for alternatives in the context of domestic policy transfers.

In creating the SCPO, the UK government has implemented an innovative response to organised crime control. This chapter has suggested that the innovation of this measure can be considered the product of policy transfer during the stage of policy formulation. A policy transfer framework provides a schema to comprehend the proliferation of preventive orders in UK crime control, which has most recently been extended to respond to organised crime. This framework cannot provide conclusive proof regarding instances of transfer; rather it provides a space and method to derive important questions and hypotheses for empirical verification. Such a framework for policy transfer could also find application in explaining other subtle and gradual changes in criminal justice which have been detected theoretically but do not result from considered empirical analysis. For example, the notion of 'sleepwalking into a surveillance society' (Rhodes 2004) is one instance of an existing claim where ostensibly unconscious developments may be occurring but are not yet fully understood empirically. In the case of the SCPO, this chapter has emphasised a number of specific areas of enquiry. The most fundamental of these areas of enquiry involved an attempt to answer the question as to whether decision-makers knowingly attempted to create a new system of preventive justice by promoting the spread of preventive orders, or whether these developments were the serendipitous result of a slow percolation or symbiosis of ideas. The remaining chapters of this book (Part II) address these important issues, to empirically determine the extent to which policy transfer was involved in developing the SCPO.

Part II

5
Process-Tracing: Case Study and Method

The primary aim of this book is to explore and explain the nature of criminal justice policy development and decision-making, with a particular focus on how the preventive order model rapidly spread into criminal legislation. A case study approach has been adopted in the research design, to examine the genesis of one selected case of a preventive order, namely, the SCPO. This case study embodies a method of 'process-tracing' and has drawn on a diverse range of documentary sources and interviews conducted with 'elite' decision-makers. Past researchers who have employed a similar methodology, particularly elite interviewing, have often failed to reflect on their experience and the processes and issues involved (Berry 2002: 679; Duke 2002: 39; Smith 2006: 644). Consequently, this chapter provides a reflexive account of the case study approach undertaken, and the multiple methods of data collection and analysis that were employed. This chapter begins by providing the reasons for selecting the SCPO as a case study and then turns to some of the key considerations embedded in the design of the research. The chapter concludes with an outline of the two key methods employed – documentary analysis and semi-structured interviews – providing justification for their use, and an explanation of the various steps involved, including sampling and coding procedures.

5.1   Case selection: Why the SCPO?

There are several important reasons for selecting the SCPO as a case study to understand the spread of preventive orders. Principally, as argued in the previous chapters, it is apparent that the SCPO did not emerge naturally from past policy and legislative responses to organised crime. That is, it has been demonstrated that this civil preventive order was an entirely novel development on the UK organised crime control agenda. Given the *prima facie* similarities between the SCPO and other civil orders, this case study provides strong grounds to test the hypothesis that policy transfer is a dominant force in the policy-making and innovation process.

In addition, there are several other methodological reasons for selecting the SCPO over other preventive orders. Importantly, the SCPO is one of the more recent additions to the family of preventive orders to be enacted.[1] This is important for two reasons. First, the selection of a contemporary case assists in addressing one of the central methodological issues in case study research and other oral history research, namely, the reliability of the memory of interviewees (see Richards 1996: 200; Seldon 1996: 355; Davies 2001: 77; Tansey 2007: 767). Second, the SCPO has received little attention in the academic community. This analytical gap is somewhat peculiar given that this order is situated (in terms of severity of criminal behaviour) between two preceding civil preventive orders, the Control Order for terrorism and the ASBO, which have both received considerable scrutiny (for critiques of these other orders, see Zedner 2007a and Ramsay 2009a, 2009b).

Finally, this case selection is politically and historically significant. The SCA 2007, which embodies the SCPO, constitutes the last piece of criminal justice legislation implemented by the Blair government, and the 60th piece of legislation coming from the Home Office during this period (Brimelow 2007). The political context demarcates a defined period of time for investigation, wherein one of the earliest prototypes of the civil preventive order, the ASBO, was introduced in the *first* piece of criminal justice legislation by this government (the Crime and Disorder Act 1998). Moreover, Brimelow (2007) notes that '[t]here were only 48 pieces of Home Office legislation in the previous 100 years'. While the case study findings will not lead to complete explanatory and generalisable claims regarding this increase in criminal justice legislation, they will reveal important alternative causal mechanisms that have probative and inferential value (Bennett and Elman 2006: 458–459).

> Even when there are enough observations to allow statistical analysis, conducting in-depth case studies can still offer separate inferential advantages. Some of these advantages are highly complementary to quantitative approaches. For example, case studies can help determine whether correlations in statistical analyses are spurious or subject to problems of endogeneity. (Bennett and Elman 2006: 458)

Therefore, the case selection was based on its suitability for hypothesis testing about policy transfer, its methodological fitness, and its historical significance. The study of the genesis of the SCPO provides a 'contemporary historical' case, which seeks to understand the internal mechanisms of policy-making that permit a measure to migrate across different areas of crime policy. Such mechanisms demonstrate how repeated incremental policy change might have contributed to the pre-emptive turn in criminal justice.

5.2 The case study and process-tracing approach

Within social science research, the case study method received considerable early criticism concerning the reliability and generalisability of any research findings (see Flyvbjerg 2006). In particular, critics questioned the *external validity* and *consistency* of findings, meaning, respectively, the ability to extrapolate conclusions to broader phenomena by studying a single case, and the dependability of repeat testing (Berry 2002: 679). Questions about reliability and validity in research methods are correlated, but are not mutually determinative. That is, '[r]eliability is a necessary but not a sufficient condition of validity . . . [nonetheless] an indication of the quality of the information they provide' (Dorussen et al. 2005: 318). These concerns relate to intrinsic epistemological issues about the veracity and dependability of research findings; however, they are not exclusive to case study research. That is to say, there is no ideal method, as each has its benefits and shortcomings (Seldon 1996: 361). As Tansey (2007: 769) argues, 'methodological choices involve trade-offs, and how we evaluate those trade-offs and develop research designs on the basis of those evaluations will depend strongly on the assumptions we hold and the research aims we are seeking to pursue'. The only redress available for researchers is a rigorous research design and acknowledgement of the 'methodological, operational and interpretational problems involved' (Richards 1996: 200). These important concerns of reliability and validity are addressed throughout the more detailed discussions on research design and methods below.

More recently, the utility of the case study approach has been recognised, and is increasingly preferred, by social scientists (particularly in political science and in anthropology) (Hall 2004: 86). George and Bennett (2005: 5) provide one of the strongest defences for the case study approach, which they define as 'the detailed examination of an aspect of a historical episode to develop or test historical explanations that may be generalizable to other events'. They explain how the rise of statistical modelling and quantitative methods in the 1960s and 1970s led to a discrediting and decline of qualitative case studies in political science; however, recent recognition of their comparative advantage has led to the resurrection of this approach (George and Bennett 2005: 3–4). The perceived advantages of the case study approach include flexible research design, an enhanced capacity for theory testing and building, and the collection of multiple sources of data (Hall 2004: 86). These were notable assets in designing the current methodology to study the genesis of the SCPO: a flexible design, for example, enabled the extended examination of the origins of other earlier preventive orders, particularly the ASBO as the primary prototype; and theories of policy transfer were tested through the analysis of a range of documentary sources (public and departmental) and interview data.

Hall (2004: 83) contends that case study research should be undertaken under three key conditions: it must examine contemporary or recent events, have a 'real-world' setting, and employ multiple methods and sources. In particular, the mixed-method approach is a welcomed aspect of research design because it supports the central goal of triangulation. The logic and importance of triangulation is straightforward: with more methods and perspectives on a given social problem or enquiry, researchers can engage in a practice of cross-checking, thereby increasing the reliability and validity of findings, and compensating for limitations of a single method (statistical or otherwise) (George and Bennett 2005: 6). For example, the methodological problems with the interview method are well documented in the literature on oral histories (Williams 1980: 316). However, triangulation through a multi-method case study facilitates cross-referencing between the interview data and other archival or documentary sources (Davies 2001: 75).

> A complication exists in the combination of oral and archival evidence in compiling a qualitative developmental account. That is, the use of different standpoints for qualitative perception rather than quantitative measurement means that one not only sees the same thing from a different angle, one sees entirely different facets of that thing. Thus the point of view in one particular document may reveal entirely different features of some historical item from other documents, or of a witness or group of witnesses, and they in turn may provide information additional to that in the documentary record. (Davies 2001: 75)

Triangulation can also be augmented *within* a method such as interviewing, through careful sampling procedures and a comparison of parallactic responses (sampling procedures are discussed later in this chapter) (Davies 2001: 78). Tansey (2007: 766) contends that the interview method of data collection in case study research is underplayed because of academics (including George and Bennett [2005]) attributing the case study method to historians with a focus on archival and documentary analyses. Case study research is undoubtedly focused on providing historical accounts:

> The analysis of the role of ideas is a topic which is particularly suited to a historical approach. In place of simplistic and generalized theories about the impact of ideas, historical analysis of specific policy changes tends to be less clear-cut about when ideas actually influence and how they impact on policy-making. (Parsons 1995: 175)

The technique of 'process-tracing' has been promoted as the best way to examine the causal mechanisms involved in such complex cases of policy decision-making (Tansey 2007: 765, 771). Process-tracing permits researchers to study the micro-causal mechanisms of decision-making in their full context, through the extensive collection of data from a variety of sources (Tansey 2007: 765; Ruback 2010: 477).

> In process-tracing, the researcher examines histories, archival documents, interview transcripts, and other sources to see whether the causal process a theory hypothesizes or implies in a case is in fact evident in the sequence and values of the intervening variables in that case. . . . Process-tracing can perform a heuristic function as well, generating new variables or hypotheses on the basis of sequences of events observed inductively in case studies. (George and Bennett 2005: 6–7)

The role of (elite) interviewing in process-tracing should not be undervalued, as it permits researchers to 'move beyond written sources, and ask probing, theoretically driven questions of key participants in the events and processes of interest' (Tansey 2007: 771). A thorough process-tracing approach should necessarily combine all available sources. Collecting interview data fills the gaps in information unavailable elsewhere, and aids in interpreting documentation (Richards 1996: 200; Seldon 1996: 354–355). As Davies (2001: 75) argues, 'interview evidence can provide information additional to documentary materials, as well as corroborative information'. For example, in this book, key informant interviews were an essential resource for examining the policy decision-making that occurred since public documents (such as White and Green papers) only provided very partial information.

Process-tracing embodies a precise methodology for conducting theory-driven, historical, case study research, to assess empirically the specific policy change that occurred on the serious organised crime control policy agenda, which led to the introduction of the novel SCPO measure. The remainder of this chapter provides a detailed account of the methodology used for the empirical component of this book, including the procedures for data collection, sampling, coding, and analysis for each method.

5.3   Two methods of data collection

The two methods of data collection employed in the case study of the SCPO were documentary analysis and semi-structured interviews. Numerous sources of data formed the basis for this analysis including primary legislation, policy documents, parliamentary debates, and elite interviews conducted with key decision-makers. While the discussion below separates the two methods employed, it is worth noting that in the process of data collection they were often mutually dependent. For example, preliminary analysis of documentation helped to demarcate the population of policy decision-makers who were approached for an interview. Likewise, after conducting interviews with these decision-makers there was an opportunity to obtain further internal departmental documents that would not have been available before meeting inter-viewees personally. Other researchers have also observed the benefits of this interactive approach, which is central to the goals of triangulation and process-tracing that were discussed above:

> The methods were therefore interconnected with the documentary analysis informing the direction and focus of the interviews and pro-viding historical and contextual data, while the interviews influenced further analyses and explorations of the documents. (Duke 2002: 42–43)[2]

The procedures for data collection and analysis for each method are described in turn.

5.3.1   Documentary analysis

Documentary materials were gathered for two distinct areas of empirical analysis. Principally, an analysis of primary legislation (statute law) was undertaken to examine the detailed statutory provisions of a number of key preventive orders enacted over the last few decades. The analysis identifies a number of important trends within the preventive order model, observable across orders ranging from the Exclusion Order for offences on licensed premises, through to the ASBO, and later the SCPO (see Chapter 6). The second area of analysis drew on a range of departmental documents (public and internal) and parliamentary debates (Hansard) that record the stages of policy and legislative development of the SCPO. This secondary analysis was used to corroborate the results from the interviews conducted with elite decision-makers involved in formulating the SCPO (see Chapter 7). A description of the specific documentation and procedures used for each area of analysis is provided in the following three subsections.

5.3.1.1 Legislative trends and preventive orders

The analysis of primary legislation involved the examination of 20 preventive orders. The criteria for designating an order as 'preventive' were threefold: (1) it places prohibitions and/or restrictions on an individual or other entity,[3] (2) it seeks to prevent harm or risk of harm in relation to a specific offence category, and (3) breach of the order triggers (further) criminal action.[4] An order was only included if it complied with all three criteria. To identify and draw out potential preventive orders to test against these criteria, an initial systematic review of criminal justice and policing acts enacted over the last three decades was conducted using Halsbury's Laws of England[5] online through LexisNexis. Two central problems were experienced when conducting this review. First, while combined keyword searches such as 'order*', 'prohibit*', 'restrict*', and 'prevent*'[6] in criminal justice legislation produced a suitably small number of results ($n = 28$), it is clear that criminal offences (and orders that address them) are not confined to criminal justice and policing legislation. For example, criminal offences (and potential preventive orders) are also contained in family law and financial regulation legislation.[7] The second difficulty is related to the polysemic search terms employed. These key words (order, restrict, prohibit, and prevent) are frequently used in published legislation, and can hold a variety of meanings. As a result, this renders any broader, all inclusive, searches of all statute law in Halsbury's Laws of England ineffective because the number of results are too high ($n = 1000+$).

Consequently, an alternative selection procedure was developed to identify the potential preventive orders for inclusion in the analysis. This process was akin to the non-probability sampling technique of snowballing, commonly used in interviewing.[8] The deductive selection procedure occurred through the following steps. The process began with the selected case study of the SCPO in the SCA 2007. Then, through analyses of background documentary material on the 2007 Act, the author worked backwards to reveal any mention of previous orders that might have had an influence (for example, the Drinking Banning Order, and terrorism Control Order). This method of process-tracing was then repeated for each of these identified orders until no new orders were mentioned.

The background documentary materials primarily relied on were Blackstone's Guides and House of Commons' Library Research Papers, which provide summary material and commentary on the justifications and reasons for any given act of parliament. This selection technique, using reverse engineering, has the potential limitation of creating a narrowly focused sample of connected preventive orders that share similar characteristics (Tansey 2007: 770). However, as part of a process-tracing method, the objective of the legislative analysis was precisely to examine these homogenous features and identify key trends, in particular, showing how these specific shared characteristics (the substantive statutory provisions of each order) have expanded over time. The key statutory provisions examined included the following: to whom the order can apply; whether the order is granted post-conviction, on application, or if there is a procedure for both; the level of harmful behaviour required to obtain an order; who can apply for the order to be imposed; who the order is intended to protect; the duration of the order; the standard of proof and evidence that is required; and the potential duration of a sanction for breach. The final sample of the 19 preventive orders that preceded the SCPO, and which meet these criteria, is provided in Chapter 6 (Figure 6.1).

5.3.1.2 Policy and early legislative process: The serious crime bill 2006–2007

The second area of analysis focused on the earlier policy and legislative processes which led to the SCPO. A number of key documentary sources were used to assess the influences of existing preventive orders on the development of the SCPO. The principal purpose of this second area of documentary analysis was to verify information provided by interviewees (re-triangulation, discussed above). The range of documentation analysed incorporated the following policy sources retrieved from either the Home Office or SOCA:

- Internal departmental policy documents – consultation responses, departmental briefs or memos, and departmental Impact Assessments.
- Departmental instructions to Parliamentary Counsel.
- Official, publicly available, departmental papers pertaining to the SCPO or SCA 2007 – Green and White papers, and publicly released

reports from larger stakeholder groups such as the Law Commission, and non-governmental lobby organisations such as Liberty and Justice.

In addition, the analysis of parliamentary debates on the clauses concerning the SCPO in the Serious Crime Bill 2006–2007 was conducted, particularly the stages of 2nd Reading, Committee and Report. These debate transcripts were from both the House of Commons and the House of Lords, and taken from the archives of Hansard online.[9] Various other important items of documentation pertaining to the Serious Crime Bill 2006–2007 were also analysed, such as Joint Committee Reports, Select Committee Reports, House of Lords Library Notes, House of Commons Library Research Papers, pre-legislative scrutiny reports, Explanatory Notes, and Cabinet Legislative Consent Memoranda. In conducting the analysis, use was made of any available documentation that could provide support and insight into the origins of the SCPO.

While these documents provided a strong foundation to analyse the process involved in developing the SCPO, from policy gestation through to legislation, there are some notable limitations with these materials. One central problem relates to the extent of relevant, yet unavailable, departmental documentation. This is exemplified by the author's private correspondence with a senior policy official in the Home Office who wrote:

> I now attach all the relevant material I have been able to track down. . . . I am afraid that on a quick look it paints a rather partial picture. . . . This really is all I have been able to find. I would like to be able to say that the Home Office is a well-oiled machine in keeping records but I am afraid that in this instance (and I suspect others) it is not.

It is difficult to estimate the amount of informal documentary materials omitted in the analysis resulting from difficulties in access or poor record keeping.[10] Another potential problem with these documentary materials concerns the accuracy of the accounts which they provide. As Tansey (2007: 767) explains:

> [D]ocuments can still entail some inherent weaknesses of which the research must remain aware. In particular, documents can often be incomplete and present a misleading account. By presenting the official version of events, documents often conceal the informal processes and considerations that preceded decision-making.

Therefore, it is unknown whether the materials relied upon present an incomplete or biased account. This is where the multiple-method approach and triangulation become essential. Tansey (2007: 766) argues that 'process tracing frequently involves the analysis of political documents at the highest level of government, and the elite actors will often be critical sources of information about the political processes of interest'. Similarly, Davies (2001: 75) contends that departmental documents 'often tend to mask over the political process of debate and discussion and record only that which was or could be agreed upon'. Therefore, the results of this documentary analysis of the genesis of the SCPO, provided in Chapter 7, are presented to reinforce the findings from key interviews with the decision-makers involved. Chapter 5 has already established that domestic policy transfer is likely to occur at the earliest stage of policy gestation. A careful selection of interviews with elite decision-makers responsible for developing the SCPO provides invaluable testimony to corroborate and add to the reconstruction of the events during this gestation period, often undocumented and behind closed doors (Lilleker 2003: 208, 213; Tansey 2007: 766). Further justification for including elite interviews in this research design is provided in the last section of this chapter, along with the description of sampling strategy, instrument design, and other procedures carried out for this method. However, first it is necessary to explain the procedure used to sort and analyse the documentary content.

5.3.1.3   *Content analysis and coding procedure*

Yin (2003: 111) argues that it is critical to have a general analytical strategy for the examination of materials, and offers three such approaches, based on *theoretical propositions*, *rival explanations*, and *case descriptions*. Since Yin (2003: 114) claimed that the latter approach was less desirable,[11] the first two strategies were drawn on to examine the present case of the SCPO. Principally, a theoretical proposition strategy was employed, given the primary purpose of the documentary analysis was to look for evidence supporting concepts of policy transfer. Policy transfer was operationalised according to the framework already developed in Chapter 5 – based on the work of Dolowitz and Marsh (1996, 2000) – and this framework provided a foundation for deriving a number of theoretical propositions which anchored the coding scheme. This was achieved by creating an initial list of *a priori* categories, namely:

- What was transferred (for example, policy ideas or legal instruments);
- Why transfer occurred (for example, mimesis or serendipity);

- Degree of transfer (for example, copying, emulation, mixture, or inspiration);
- Who was involved in the transfer (for example, politicians, officials, or legal advisors);
- Transfer origin (for example, domestic or foreign policy influence).

These categories reflect the core set of questions inherent to the method of content analysis. That is, as Lasswell (1951; cited in Maxfield and Babbie 2005: 339) professed, content analysis aims to assess 'who says what, to whom, why, and to what extent and with what effect'. This method of analysis was utilised to organise the gathered documentary materials and interview transcripts. There are generally two identifiable types of content that are the focus of this method: manifest content and latent content (Aberbach and Rockman 2002: 675). Manifest content analysis focuses on an analytical process of counting the frequency of selected words or phrases (individual words or word clusters), whereas latent content analysis probes deeper into the meaning and context of the phenomena under examination (McBurney and White 2009: 234). McBurney and White (2009: 235) argue that it is important to engage with both types of content to increase the reliability of coding. In examining the case of the SCPO, it was important to analyse both manifest and latent content. Some elements of policy transfer could be measured by manifest content analysis (frequency counts): for example, how many times was the word 'ASBO' or 'Anti-Social Behaviour Order' mentioned in a given policy document or transcript (compared to other preventive orders)? This provides an indication of the most prominent and influential policy precedents. However, latent content analysis is also important to provide a richer qualitative account, for example, if the ASBO (or another order) was mentioned in relation to justification, argument, as a specific statutory prototype to be replicated, or in another context.

The qualitative analysis computer software NVivo 9 was employed to organise and code the data. Any evidence of policy transfer was assigned (coded) to these categories to facilitate subsequent processes of 'tabulation, interpretation, and analysis' (Crittenden and Hill 1971: 1073). It was also important to code any evidence pertaining to 'non-transfer' origins of the SCPO, in order to explore alternative hypotheses. This satisfies Yin's (2003: 112) second *rival explanation* strategy. This approach was fundamental to include in the overall analytic strategy, as alternative hypotheses offer a comparative perspective to evaluate the *extent* of policy transfer as a driving force in policy-making.

Finally, Crittenden and Hill (1971: 1073–1074) contended that coding structures should be 'objective or reproducible'. Two important procedures were taken when coding the data to enhance these measures of reliability. First, *inter-rater* reliability (objectivity) was addressed by employing two separate researchers to independently code overlapping portions of the data and compare coding schemes (Maxfield and Babbie 2005: 342).[12] Second, *intra-rater* reliability (reproducibility) was addressed by the primary researcher coding the data twice. Maxfield and Babbie (2005: 342) argued that, for this 'test–retest method', some time should elapse between the two attempts at coding by the same coder. Accordingly, the author maximised the time between the initial coding and the re-coding. This was easier for the documentary data, which were coded with a 12-month interval, before and after the interview fieldwork period. This also provided important auxiliary benefits in structuring the interview process – as Aberbach and Rockman (2002: 676) observed in their research:

> Using a systematic coding procedure not only allowed us to employ quantitative techniques in our later analysis, but also kept us from allowing the colorful interviewee or especially enjoyable story to dominate our view of the overall phenomena we were studying.

The explanation of the procedures and instruments employed in conducting these interviews are provided next.

5.3.2 Elite interviewing

Semi-structured interviews were conducted with 21 elite decision-makers who were central to the development of the SCPO, including Home Secretaries, Parliamentary Counsel, Ministers of State, Permanent Secretaries, and civil servants in the Home Office. The role of elite interviewing in this research, particularly regarding the multi-method approach, triangulation, and process-tracing, was discussed briefly above. This final section of the chapter provides a more thorough discussion of this method of data gathering. The purpose and procedures are outlined in five distinct subsections: definitions and justifications for elite interviewing; determining the population; sample characteristics and procedure; the design of the interview schedule; and ethical considerations.

5.3.2.1 *Definitions and justifications*

Since Lewis Dexter's (1970) seminal work on *Elite and Specialized Interviewing*, a niche body of literature has evolved to describe the purpose and procedures of this method. Historically a technique more familiar to the field of journalism, elite interviewing has become more common in academic research, particularly in the political sciences (Kezar 2003: 397). Most of this literature has focused on the methodological experience of researchers using this method, for example, reliability and validity issues (Berry 2002; Dorussen et al. 2005); gaining access (Duke 2002); sampling (Rivera et al. 2002); and specific interview techniques and procedures (Leech 2002). While these are valuable issues to address for all researchers (see below), there has been a more fundamental failure to distinguish between 'elite interviewing' and other more common 'non-elite' qualitative interviewing techniques (Richards 1996; Smith 2006).

In particular, Smith (2006: 648) makes a strong case for the overlapping issues experienced in 'elite' and 'non-elite' interviewing. Throughout her analysis of the elite interviewing method, Smith (2006: 648) provides examples of how the ethical concerns, power relations, and issues of gaining access are equally complex in other populations, providing an example of interviewing drug dealers from Puerto Rican neighbourhoods. Smith (2006: 652) concludes that 'there is little evidence to support the idea that any areas of concern relate *specifically* to interviewing "elites"' (emphasis in original). However, some distinctions can be made in terms of the *public* role of elites. First, elites have specialised knowledge about public policy and decision-making. That is, what makes individuals elite (such as judges, politicians, and senior civil servants) is that they are privy to, and participate in, discussions and decisions which *directly* affect the wider community of individuals:

> [T]he whole notion of an elite implies a group of individuals, who hold, or have held, a privileged position in society and, as such, as far as a political scientist is concerned, are likely to have had more influence on political outcomes than general members of the public. (Richards 1996: 199)

Other members of the community who can *indirectly* affect public affairs (such as drug dealers) might hold specialised knowledge, but they cannot be considered 'elite'. Second, elites are arguably more familiar with the interview setting because of their public role, and this may have implications for some aspects of interviewing (for example, obtaining 'informed consent', discussed in Section 5.3.2.5). Third, there is arguably heightened validity in elite interviewing since the public status of interviewees provides supplementary information about the population:

> Even when the goal is more broad generalisation, this is actually an area where small [population] elite interviewers have an advantage over researchers doing surveys of the mass public. . . . Unlike those doing survey research of the mass public, researchers using elite interviews actually know quite a bit about those who remain uninterviewed. (Goldstein 2002: 672)

Thus, a working definition of elite interviewing for the purposes of policy and political studies seems less problematic, that is, a small group of influential, and public, decision-makers:

> Elites can be loosely defined as those with close proximity to power or policymaking; the category would include all elected representatives, executive officers of organisations and senior state employees. Beyond the confines of politics the definitions could clearly be broadened out. (Lilleker 2003: 207)

Finally, elite interviewing can be employed with a number of separate goals in mind, such as gathering data on decision-maker behaviour, gaining access to further documentary materials, and/or adding a more in-depth qualitative context for events that have taken place (Goldstein 2002: 669). Therefore, this method possesses some unique opportunities for researchers that are not available through other methods. Given that Kezar (2003: 397) argues that elite interviews target knowledge of having 'participated in a certain situation' and 'try to understand the micro-politics of personal relationships', this method of data collection is particularly pertinent to the process-tracing method.

> Process tracing requires the collection of data concerning key political decision-making and activity, often at the highest political level, and elite interviews will frequently be a critical strategy for obtaining this required information. While their corroborative function should not be under-played, it is the additive role of elite interviews that is most relevant when considering their use in association with process tracing. Such interviews can allow the researcher to collect first hand testimony from direct participants and witnesses regarding critical events and processes. (Tansey 2007: 767)

As mentioned above, elite interviewing complements documentary analysis in process-tracing case studies by corroborating the findings, adding new information, and ultimately reconstructing events that occurred (Davies 2001: 75; Tansey 2007: 766). As Aberbach and Rockman (2002: 673) put it, it is used 'to help the investigator fill pieces of a puzzle or confirm the proper alignment of pieces already in place'. The gaps are particularly problematic in policy studies, as the process that occurs is hidden behind closed doors (Davies 2001: 74; Lilleker 2003: 213). Indeed, Davies (2001: 74) proposes that the 'British government is one of the most secretive democratic governments'. Therefore, gaining access to key decision-makers is likely to be a particularly fruitful source of information about policy development in the UK, where documentation might otherwise be hidden from the public. While discussions with elite decision-makers undoubtedly assist in process-tracing, the corollary problem is how to identify (and access) the population of those involved in any given case.

5.3.2.2 'Subgovernment': The population of decision-makers

A single criterion underpinned the derivation of the primary population of potential interviewees in this study: direct *involvement* in the development of the SCPO. Setting the parameters for this population required the initial casting of a broad net, followed by a methodical process of refinement. The initial capture group was based on a preliminary documentary analysis to ascertain a list of individuals believed to be in some way associated with the SCPO. This was based on 'positional criteria', that is, those who were identified as holding a position of decision-making power (or influence) in one of the departmental bodies/organisations associated with SCPO (namely, the Home Office, SOCA, Attorney General's department, ACPO, Serious Fraud Office, Crown Prosecutions Office, and Liberty).[13] Based on the names found in the documentary analysis,[14] 34 letters were sent out, asking individuals firstly, if they were involved in the development of the SCPO, and, secondly, if so, would they be willing to participate in a short interview (30–45 minutes). If participants indicated that they were *not* involved, a follow-up letter or phone call was made asking if they could suggest individuals who they believed might have been involved.

Any responses indicating non-involvement also began the process of refining the population through self-exclusion. The iterative process of refinement and exclusion continued throughout the interview fieldwork period based on 'reputational criteria', through referrals and a snowballing technique. Both positional and reputational criteria have long been used to identify those in the position of power: '[T]he reputational, combined with the positional, technique was very effective for locating leaders' (French 1969: 820). These techniques have been adopted more recently to aid elite interviewing sampling designs (Rivera et al. 2002: 683). The benefit of combining these two techniques in process-tracing is described by Tansey (2007: 771):

> In this way, researchers cannot only interview a set of political actors that their research objectives suggest will be highly relevant [positional criteria], but will also open their research to the possible inclusion of other influential players who may not be *ex ante* – that is, political actors who will only be identified by their peers through a process of sampling based on reputational criteria and snowball sampling.

The snowballing technique in elite interviewing can be direct or indirect. As with other non-elite interviewing that adopts a snowballing technique, individuals interviewed can *directly* refer a researcher to their colleagues or acquaintances, thereby helping the researcher to recruit other relevant participants. However, perhaps unique to elite interviewing, indirect means of recruitment can also occur by using the reputation of those already interviewed (Richards 1996: 202). For example, mentioning the names or titles of prominent individuals already interviewed can facilitate the process of gaining access to other interviewees of the subgovernment (indirect snowballing). The ethical issues associated with providing interviewee names to third parties as a form of recruitment are discussed below (see Subsection 5.3.2.5).

In addition, the referral process – asking 'who else was involved?' – played an important role in verifying and reinforcing the selected population, as names of interviewees were repeated (Tansey 2007: 770). Moreover, Duke (2002: 47) argues that this process yields important findings about some more qualitative attributes of the policy network:

> At the end of all interviews, I always asked respondents to provide names and contact details of others they thought were important for me to interview. This simple question generated very interesting data in its own right on who knew whom, who valued whom and who networked with whom. This technique enabled me to establish a fairly accurate picture of the membership and shape of the policy network and which members were considered to be major players.

A total of 53 letters were sent, including the initial 33 individuals identified in the documentary analysis and 20 based on referrals. There were four categories of responses: no response (n = 3); responded but refused (*n* = 6); responded and accepted (*n* = 18); and responded but not involved (*n* = 26). The response rate was high with only three individuals not responding.[15] The six who indicated that they were involved in the development of the SCPO, but would not interview, generally gave the reason of heavy diary pressures (though one respondent gave no specific reason).[16] The largest response category was non-involvement (50 per cent), which ranged from those stating that they were entirely uninvolved to those on the periphery (assisted in minor administrative or consultative ways, but uninvolved in any level of decision-making).

This process of refining the population – in particular, separation from the larger contingent of those uninvolved or on the periphery – can be understood conceptually as locating the subgovernment within a broader policy community (as argued in Chapter 5). A policy community can be extensive, with various actors contributing to policy development. However, it is the subgovernment of this broader community which encompasses the more influential decision-makers, those involved in a process of idea and policy generation (Howlett and Ramesh 2003). Rock (1995: 3) explains this dynamic:

> To be sure, the numbers of officials in attendance will swell as a piece of policy making becomes more urgent, complex, and immediate in its demands, as political alliances are sought and new boundaries are explored, but the formative early life of a policy can rarely be nurtured by more than a few people.

Accordingly, the sample size in elite interviewing will inevitably be smaller than broader probability samples of 'non-elites' (Richards 1996: 200). However, the smaller sample size is relative to the population of key decision-makers who were involved. Including the 3 non-responders, 27 people can be argued to comprise the subgovernment responsible for creating the SCPO. Therefore, the sample of 18 who responded and accepted an interview represents over 65 per cent of the subgovernment population. The characteristics of this sample and other sampling considerations are discussed next.

5.3.2.3 Sampling procedures

A total of 21 interviews were conducted as part of this research, of which 18 interviewees were taken from the subgovernment discussed above. Three other interviews were conducted with elite decision-makers involved in the development of other preventive orders that preceded the SCPO. The reasons for including these additional interviews were twofold. First, after several initial interviews were conducted, it was apparent that it was also important to understand more about the origins of earlier preventive order prototypes, in particular, the ASBO (one of the earliest examples). Perhaps more importantly, and relevant to the SCPO case study, it was important to inquire about any specific intentions to promote the use of earlier preventive orders to other areas of crime control. Such indications of any level of predetermination were crucial for addressing the components of a policy framework, such as why transfer occurred (Dolowitz and Marsh 1996, 2000).

The sample of 21 interviewees was taken from a population of 30 individuals privy to specific information about the development of the SCPO, which is unobtainable through any other method. While specific anonymity assurances were made to the interviewees regarding direct quotations – namely, that all direct quotations would be non-attributable – all participants consented to be (indirectly) identified as having participated in the study. Therefore, Figure 5.1 reveals the full subgovernment population (n = 30) of the key actors involved in developing the SCPO.

While the identities of a number of these actors will be identifiable to many readers, it is argued that anonymity is still preserved as those actually sampled from this list remain unknown to the reader (these ethical issues are discussed further in Subsection 5.3.2.5). Figure 5.1 also shows that these actors can be classified into six categories of decision-makers involved in developing the SCPO: those from the Prime Minister's Office (Number 10); political actors; senior civil servants in the Home Office; civil servants from the Home Office who worked on the bill-team; legal advisors; and various other 'directors'. The term 'directors' is used to refer to an assorted group of key decision-makers who were involved because of their position of authority, that is, members of senior management from various departments, organisations, agencies, or NGOs. These six categories are important as they are employed in Chapter 7 to reference the responses of interviewees in the presentation of the findings, without revealing their specific identities.

Goldstein (2002: 670) argues that 'in a perfect world, the sampling frame would be identical to the target population. At the very least, it should be a representative sample of the target population'. The sampling procedure employed in this book attempted to interview the complete target population of 30 elite decision-makers in the subgovernment. Richards (1996: 200) maintains that, with elite interviewing, sometimes unrepresentative sampling becomes an issue owing to low

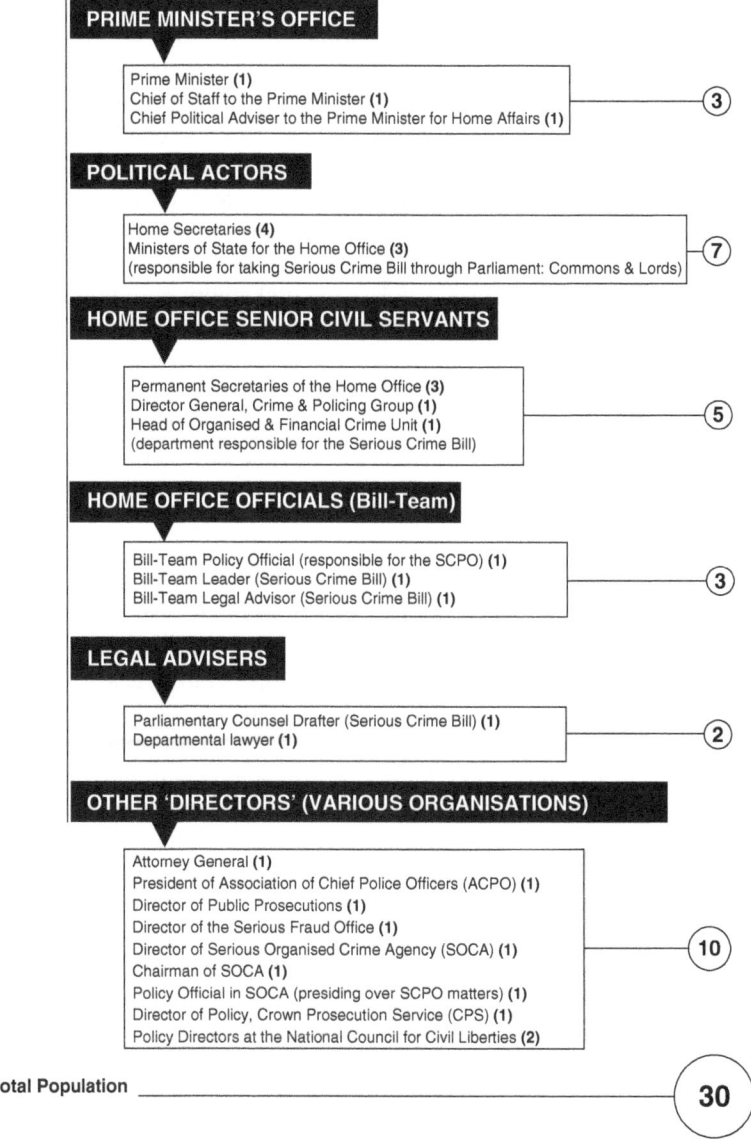

Figure 5.1 'Subgovernment' – the population of decision-makers

response rates and problems with access. However, in this study, the sample size was large relative to the population (65 per cent of the subgovernment), and at least one actor was interviewed from each of the six categories, representing a hierarchical range of elite decision-makers. Therefore, it is argued that this sample is indeed representative of the subgovernment population who formulated the SCPO.

As discussed above, both purposive (expert) and snowballing techniques were employed, meaning that a non-probability sampling method was used to recruit participants (Li and Walejko 2008: 281). Many qualitative researchers consider the probability sampling method superior to non-probability sampling (Tansey 2007: 768).

> Probability sampling provides a means of decreasing investigator- and respondent-associated biases, evaluating the reliability of estimates and the magnitude of the sampling error, and producing unbiased estimates that can be generalized to the target population. (Semaan et al. 2002: 214)

However, Tansey (2007: 765) contends that for process-tracing, a non-probability sampling technique is more appropriate. The goal of sampling in process-tracing is to target particular elite decision-makers involved in a given event or set of circumstances (Tansey 2007: 765). By contrast, the goal of probability sampling is random selection, which means that there is a chance that important decision-makers will be omitted (Tansey 2007: 771). Moreover, probability sampling and random selection are advocated by researchers wishing to ensure external validity, whereby 'the aim is to extrapolate broader generalizations from the sample to a wider range of respondents' (Tansey 2007: 769). However, elite interviewing, as part of a process-tracing method, does not aim to generalise to the broader population of decision-makers in all situations. Rather, the process of generalising takes an alternative form:

> Yet such suggestions rest on the assumption that the sample will be used as a source from which to generalise findings to the population, and this is not the case when process tracing is being pursued. In this situation, the aim is profoundly different, as scholars seek highly specific information about highly specific events and processes. Once such processes are reconstructed by the researcher, and findings about the relationships between the variables and causal mechanism are made, it may then be desirable to generalise about those processes to other cases. But in reconstructing that initial process, the aim of

collecting interview data is to obtain specific data to fill in a specific gap, and not to abstract to a wider population of interviewees. (Tansey 2007: 771)

Therefore, the dominant purpose of conducting the elite interviews is to rigorously assess the policy process under examination. Only after using multiple methods of data collection and analysis can deductions be made about any causal mechanism involved (for example, the role of policy transfer), and only then might broader generalisations be made regarding other cases of policy-making (Tansey 2007: 769).

5.3.2.4 The interview procedures and schedule

This subsection briefly examines the procedures undertaken in carrying out the elite interview and the design of the interview protocol, the instrument employed to guide this field research. There are a number of important procedural considerations and techniques for any researcher employing the elite interviewing method. Goldstein (2002: 669) states that, above all, it 'depends on getting in the door, getting access to your subject':

> A well-prepared personable researcher who would be able to control an open-ended and wide-ranging interview, while establishing a strong informal rapport with an elite respondent will never get to demonstrate his or her interviewing skills – or ability to decrease measurement error – if the meeting never takes place.

Duke (2002: 45) argues that '[g]aining access to elites can be problematic as they have the power to create barriers, shield themselves from scrutiny and resist the intrusiveness of social research'. A number of related strategies were used in the book's research to increase chances of access. Primarily, Duke (2002: 46) argues that the approach to elites should be personalised, rather than a more general participant information sheet. Accordingly, in this research, all correspondence was tailored to the specific circumstances of each interviewee. This included any links to background information about the interviewees,[17] for example, drawing on the interviewees' university or collegiate alumni networks,[18] meeting interviewees at public talks and events (informal access before formal access), drawing on personal reputation, or any other informal connections.[19] Similarly, Leech (2002: 666) states that researchers should '[a]ct as though it is natural that people would want to talk to you'. This became a more useful strategy in approaching interviewees once a few interviews had been conducted, as letters and email correspondence could then include statements such as the following:

> I have conducted interviews with Home Secretaries, Permanent Secretaries from the Home Office, and other senior civil servants. Your name has come up in this process, as having played an important role in . . . I would now like to have a short conversation with you.

Finally, a number of researchers using this method have discussed the importance of persistence and 'fending off' the 'gatekeepers', such as personal secretaries or assistants who might filter correspondence (Peabody et al. 1990: 451; Aberbach and Rockman 2002: 674; Duke 2002: 49). In particular, as mentioned above, given that the field research fell during a general election, it was necessary to be respectful of immediate political pressures, but diligently follow up interviewees at a later stage.

Another important procedural issue is related to the power relations between interviewer and interviewee. Richards (1996: 201) argues that 'by the very nature of elite interviews, it is the interviewee who has the power. They control the information the interviewer is trying to eke out.' Two procedures are important to alleviate this dynamic: (1) a semi-structured interview approach, and (2) conducting the interviews at a later stage of the research process to know the interviewee and material extremely well (Richards 1996: 201). The semi-structured approach undertaken in the research for this book was achieved by creating an interview schedule with a number of key themes, and a few tailored promptitude questions (discussed below concerning schedule design) (see also Berry 2002: 681). This allowed the author to take a more fluid approach, and control the direction of the interview across the central themes. While knowing the interviewee and material well was clearly important, there was a delicate balance in presenting this knowledge in the interview. As Ball (1992: 99–100) states, researchers must balance a display of 'knowledgeability' and 'naivety' throughout the interview. While demonstrating naivety raises concerns, as the interviewees are unlikely to 'suffer fools gladly', a demonstration of too much knowledge risks that interviewees will 'leave something out because they assume I already knew it' (respectively, Richards 1996: 201 and Leech 2002: 666). Leech (2002: 665) contends that this balance in elite interviewing represents a mix of two more familiar interviewing styles: a 'journalistic style tries to verbally pin the respondent down by appearing to know everything already . . . [while an] ethnographic style of interviewing instead tries to enter into the world of the respondent by appearing to know very little'. In the specific circumstances of interviews undertaken, the author attempted to achieve this balance by demonstrating a high level of knowledge around the general topic area, while professing little to no knowledge of the crucial dynamics of decision-making that occurred.[20] Many researchers have emphasised the benefits of a semi-structured interview schedule, particularly in allowing open-ended questions to be asked, which give both the space for interviewees to provide the most relevant (and unforeseeable) information and the interviewers an opportunity to probe deeper into the discrete (and most relevant) experiences of interviewees (Williams 1980: 305; Peabody et al. 1990: 451–452; Aberbach and Rockman 2002: 674; Berry 2002: 681; Duke 2002: 53; Rivera et al. 2002: 686). The interview schedule opened with some simple corroborative questions to build a basic level of rapport with the interviewee (Peabody et al. 1990: 453). The schedule was then divided into five other key themes or subject areas, each with a set of 'probe notes' (Richards 1996: 202; Berry 2002: 681). The five main themes were as follows: (1) events and circumstances leading to the SCPO; (2) the role of policy transfer in policy-making; (3) development of the broader preventive order model; (4) discussions about preventive justice and broader ideology in policy-making; and (5) the future of the preventive order model. A sample version of this interview schedule, including some examples of tailored probing questions, is provided in Appendix 'C'. Interview questions were systematically marked off as the interview was conducted, and priority questions were highlighted on the schedule in case of time constraints (Berry 2002: 681). This systematic process and themed schedule allowed the interviewer to confirm at the beginning of each interview the exact time allocated for the interview, satisfying the assertion of Peabody et al. (1990: 453) that '[t]he interview schedule should be designed so that it can be administered in 20–30 minutes if necessary'.

5.3.2.5   Ethical considerations

This final subsection briefly covers the ethical considerations in elite interviewing, and the extent of confidentiality and anonymity assurances given when conducting the research. In designing the field research component of this book, the author followed the University of Oxford Central University Researcher Ethics Committee (CUREC) Protocol Pro-forma for Elite Interviews. The author also gained CUREC approval before conducting the interviews.[21] The important confidentiality and anonymity assurances that were made to interviewees in the study require explanation.

The underlying standard used in the present research was 'non-attribution', and it was found that this term was familiar to the elites interviewed. Goldstein (2002: 671) argues that complications often arise in research in respect of the use of terms such as 'on the record' and 'off the record'. The non-attribution standard was explained in letters, and at the beginning of each interview, to mean that any information provided in the interview could be used or quoted by the interviewer so long as it did not directly identify the interviewee as the source (Goldstein 2002: 671). Any mention of names of third parties during discussions would also be anonymised.

The important emphasis here is on the *reporting* of any data collected in the interview process. The author made it clear that quotations would not be directly attributed in the publication of any results (including at final dissertation stage) without making prior contact with the interviewee to gain their written permission. This is also important regarding confidentiality, as participants were asked at the end of the interviews if they were happy to be mentioned as having participated in the research project, to give credence to the results, and to assist in recruiting other elites by trading on their reputation. This means that interviewees are *indirectly* mentioned as having participated in the study; however, the data that they provide are not *directly* attributable to them.

Despite gaining consent from all participants to waive their confidentiality as having participated in the research project, caution was still taken by not confirming the names of participants in the final sample. That is, in the description of procedures above, only the broader population of the subgovernment was prescribed in detail. This assists in the reporting of the results in the next chapters, and assuring that quotations remain non-attributable and anonymous. For example, in the presentation of results, quotations are attributed using a nebulous format, such as 'one Home Secretary stated that', 'two Permanent Secretaries in the Home Office agreed that', or 'Interviewee 3 believed that', and so on. Accordingly, it is argued that anonymity is sufficiently achieved, as it is not known which one out of several potential respondents is being referred to. Nonetheless, the reporting of results requires particular care so as not to include any other identifying information that could reveal the interviewees' identities.

Informed consent was given verbally, not in writing, which can be a particular concession in elite interviewing so long as the confidentiality is stated in the initial letter and is reiterated at the beginning of the interview. The ethical guidance followed provides the following rationale:

> In elite interviews it is often argued that requiring written consent is not appropriate. This is because it is held that this type of person understands the situation s/he is in and in granting an interview is implicitly giving informed consent. (CUREC Pro-forma, s.6)

This verbal consent was given by interviewees (and recorded) to indicate their understanding of the assurances being made and their willingness to participate. In addition, interviewees were given the opportunity to review the transcript of the interview dialogue to assess and check the veracity of the recording. However, no interviewees requested this opportunity post-interview.

The process-tracing method is particularly suited to examining the genesis of the SCPO. Through both documentary analyses and elite interviews, multiple perspectives are investigated to discover the origins of this new measure. It has been demonstrated how this method of process-tracing allows for theory testing, specifically the examination of policy transfer as a key mechanism in everyday policy-making. The reflexive, narrative approach taken in this chapter has provided a transparent account of the research design and methods, and the detail of various procedures undertaken.[22] The results and analyses of the empirical component of this book form the next two chapters.

6
The Proliferation of the Preventive Order Model

The analyses in this chapter and in the next (Chapter 7) aim to empirically test some of the key questions raised by the policy transfer framework developed in Chapter 4. These questions are worth restating here, as the subsequent analyses in the remaining chapters refer to these five dimensions of transfer repeatedly:

1. *What was Transferred*: policies (goals, content, or instruments), programmes, institutions, ideologies, ideas, attitudes, cultural values, or negative lessons?
2. *Why Transfer*: voluntary (lesson drawing), coercive (direct imposition), or a mixture of both (lesson drawing with pressure)?
3. *What was the Degree of Transfer*: copying, emulation, mixtures, or inspiration?
4. *Who is Involved in Transfer*: elected officials, bureaucrats, civil servants, pressure groups, political parties, experts, policy entrepreneurs, consultants, think tanks, transnational corporations, or supranational institutions (for example, the EU)?
5. *What was the Transfer Origin*: past (policy history), within-a-nation (or 'domestic'), or cross-national?

The purpose of the next two chapters is to provide any evidence that policy transfer occurred during the formulation of the SCPO. This chapter conducts an analysis of legislation that has influenced the shape and form of the SCPO. This legislative analysis in the current chapter is primarily concerned with the *origins of transfer*, namely, to provide rigorous substantiation that *domestic* policy transfer does indeed occur. While the major part of this analysis therefore focuses on domestic legislative transfer, we begin by briefly considering the potential influence of organised crime control legislation in the US, namely, the civil orders in the RICO Act 1970.

6.1   A civil order for organised crime control: The international context

There are two official documents that indicate the genesis of the SCPO. First, the Home Office White Paper, *One Step Ahead* (2004), initially highlighted the concerns regarding gaps in the capacity of law enforcement agencies to deal with organised crime (preceding the SOCPA 2005). This paper outlined the UK government's intentions to amalgamate a number of institutional and legislative powers (principally under the auspices of the SOCA and then the NCA [as discussed in Chapter 2]). Second, a consultation paper (Green Paper) entitled *New Powers Against Organised and Financial Crime* (2006a) was produced – preceding the SCA 2007 – wherein the government initially proposed the SCPO to address the gaps in the traditional procedures of criminal law that were identified in the White Paper (2004). This earlier White Paper (2004) plainly acknowledged the UK government's consideration of organised crime control legislation in the US:

> In recent years, there have been calls for the introduction of laws modelled on the USA's Racketeer Influenced and Corrupt Organisations (RICO) statutes. . . . Probably most powerful of all, the civil use of RICO legislation has been particularly effective in enabling courts to impose external control over racketeering influenced organisations like businesses, union branches and even pension funds. (Home Office, White Paper 2004: 40)

Notwithstanding this apparent endorsement of the powers in the RICO Act 1970, the White Paper (2004) concluded that these civil measures would not be incorporated in the UK government's new response to organised crime:

> The Government has carefully considered the case for RICO style legislation to be introduced here. We are not convinced of the need at this stage. . . . Civil RICO is less relevant in the UK, as we do not face the same difficulties of organised crime infiltration of legitimate institutions as the US. (Home Office, White Paper 2004: 40)

Contrary to these conclusions of the White Paper (2004), two years later the Green Paper (2006a) stated that, in formulating the SCPO measure, the government was strongly influenced by the use of civil orders in the US:

> These orders against organisations draw on US experience on Civil RICO (Racketeer Influenced and Corrupt Organisations). Civil RICO is an exceptionally broad power. . . . From 1970, the Teamsters Union had had over 340 officers convicted for mafia related crimes, but these prosecutions altered nothing in the mafia domination of parts of the union, as convicted individuals were simply replaced. Only when civil measures began to be taken to introduce court ordered administrators into particularly corrupt 'locals' (union branches) did the threat of mafia influence begin to be tackled effectively. (Home Office, Green Paper 2006a: 34–35)

A civil order according to the RICO Act 1970 contains three preventative and restrictive powers which can be imposed by district courts of the US: (1) 'ordering any person to divest himself [sic] of any interest, direct or indirect, in any enterprise'; (2) 'imposing reasonable restrictions on the future activities or investments of any person'; or (3) 'ordering dissolution or reorganization of any enterprise, making due provision for the rights of innocent persons' (s.1964(a)). Clearly the civil orders and powers in the RICO Act bear some resemblance to the SCPO, namely, the ability to prevent or restrain an individual or business, and the potential for dissolution (or winding up) of an organisation or enterprise. However, there are also some important differences. Specifically, the RICO Act has a particular focus on 'enterprise' and a 'pattern of racketeering activity', while the SCPO could conceivably be imposed on an individual who has engaged in non-enterprise criminal activity for the first time (that is, no 'pattern' is necessary). In addition, while non-compliance with (or breach of) an SCPO constitutes a strict liability criminal offence, Civil RICO has no such statutory provision, besides the standard court powers in relation to contempt.

Therefore, the SCPO, a civil order used to respond to organised crime in the UK, can be seen to be substantively distinct from the civil powers used in the US to respond to the same category of crimes. At most, this might reflect peripheral policy transfer of the 'ideology' or 'attitudes' to using civil measures for organised crime control (*what is transferred*). This 'inspiration' (*degree of transfer*) from abroad is discussed further in ter 8. However, clearly cross-jurisdictional policy transfer (from the ~~ ~~ the UK) does not provide a complete picture of the emergence of the SCPO. It is necessary to look to internal domestic policy transfer as having a potentially greater influence.

6.2 Ordering the prevention of crime: The domestic context

The formulation of the SCPO is part of a palpable trend in developing preventive orders across a range of crime control policy areas in the UK. As acknowledged in the Green Paper (2006a: 29), the use of preventive orders in UK crime control policy can be traced to earlier orders such as the Football Banning Order (Football Spectators Act 1989), though public debate on the use of such orders intensified approximately a decade later with the introduction of the ASBO, under the Crime and Disorder Act 1998. While the ASBO has attracted most public and academic attention, the Crime and Disorder Act 1998 concurrently introduced several other types of preventive orders, such as the Sex Offender Order. Moreover, since the enactment of the 1998 Act, preventive orders have developed rapidly across other distinct areas of crime policy and legislation: for example, the Sexual Offences Prevention Order (SOPO; Sex Offences Act 2003); Non-Molestation Order (Domestic Violence, Crime and Victims Act 2004); and terrorism Control Order (Prevention of Terrorism Act 2005) among others (examined below). The vast array of preventive orders that preceded the SCPO clearly requires more detailed analysis.

Prior to the examination of these legislative precursors to the SCPO, a more detailed statement should be made about the criteria for inclusion in the analysis to determine what constitutes a 'preventive order'. The three core criteria for such orders, discussed in earlier chapters, are elaborated here. First, the order places prohibitions and/or restrictions on an individual or other entity. The inclusion of 'other entity' in this set of criteria is directly related to the SCPO and its applicability to companies and organisations under section 30 of the SCA 2007. Second, the order is designed to prevent harm or risk of harm in relation to a *specific offence category*. This is an important criterion as it excludes numerous civil remedies and injunctions which do not have a particular offence category at the core, even if breach of such preventive injunctions can result in criminal penalties through contempt of court. Examples of such remedies include prohibition orders in relation to public assemblies (Criminal Justice and Public Order Act 1994, s.70[1]);

anti-social behaviour injunctions (Housing Act 1996, ss.152 and 153); and residence orders (Family Law Act 1996, s.33). Third, breach of the terms of an order constitutes a *new* criminal offence. This excludes the number of community orders that can be made under the Powers of Criminal Courts (Sentencing) Act 2000, such as the Supervision Order (s.63), Drug Treatment and Testing Order (s.52), and Action Plan Order (s.69), in respect of which breach of such orders does not constitute a new offence. That is, on breach of a community order, a summons might be issued for the arrest of the individual; however, this generally results in revocation of the order where the offender is dealt with for the original offence (under Schedules 3, 5, 7, or 8). For example, on breach of a supervision order the 'court may deal with him [sic], for the offence in respect of which the supervision order was made, in any way in which it could have dealt with him for that offence if it had not made the order' (Schedule 7 ss.2(4)). These ancillary orders which can be issued as part of sentencing do not target a specific offence category, and are thus also excluded by the second criterion.

These criteria are not intended to ignore or repeat the contributions by Andrew Ashworth and Lucia Zedner (2010: 61–65), who map out the broader category of 'preventive measures', or those of Peter Ramsay (2009a: 110), who provides the essential criteria for 'civil' preventive orders. The set of criteria outlined above is not restricted to the 'civil' preventive order model, though this is a category to which the SCPO can be attributed. The focus here is on identifying numerous trends over time in the preventive order model more generally, including those used in criminal proceedings to respond to a particular offence category, where breach of the order itself constitutes an offence.[2] It is argued that the expansion of the application process to civil procedure is only one (albeit a major) trend that has occurred in the preventive order model – another is the expansive trend across most categories of crime policy (these and other trends are examined in Section 6.4). The preventive orders in the UK which fit the above criteria and preceded the SCPO are listed in Figure 6.1, in chronological order in relation to their respective Acts of Parliament.

There are 20 different preventive orders included in the analysis that span several diverse categories of criminality. Figure 6.1 demonstrates at least one preventive order embodied in a major criminal justice act almost every year during the decade leading up to the enactment of the SCPO in 2007. There is some repetition and duplication in this list, as various earlier preventive orders were superseded or significantly amended by another order. For example, there are three football-related

PREVENTIVE ORDER	OFFENCE/CONDUCT CATEGORY	LEGISLATIVE ACT
Exclusion Order	Offences on licensed premises	Licensed Premises (Exclusion of Certain Persons) Act 1980
Exclusion Order (or Domestic Football Banning Order*)	Football-related offences [Domestic only]	Public Order Act 1986
Disqualification Order	Misconduct or offences by a director of a company	Company Directors Disqualification Act 1986
Disqualification Order	Driving and Road Traffic Offences	Road Traffic Act 1988
Restriction Order (or International Football Banning Order*)	Football-related offences	Football Spectators Act 1989
Non-Molestation Order	Harassment or molestation	Family Law Act 1996
Restraining Order	Harassment or putting people in fear of violence	Protection from Harassment Act 1997
Anti-Social Behaviour Order	Harassment, alarm or distress	Crime and Disorder Act 1998
Sex Offender Order	Sexual Offences (or risk of sexual re-offending)	Crime and Disorder Act 1998
Banning Order	Football-related offences or violence and disorder (domestic or international matches)	Football (Disorder) Act 2000
Disqualification Order	Sexual Offences (or risk of sexual re-offending)	Criminal Justice and Court Services Act 2000
Travel Restriction Order	Drug trafficking offences	Criminal Justice and Police Act 2001
Sexual Offences Prevention Order	Sexual offences	Sexual Offences Act 2003
Foreign Travel Order	Sexual offences	Sexual Offences Act 2003
Risk of Sexual Harm Order	Risk of sexual offences	Sexual Offences Act 2003
(New) Restraining Order	Domestic Violence	Domestic Violence, Crime and Victims Act 2004
Control Order	Risk of terrorism or inchoate terrorism offences	Prevention of Terrorism Act 2005
Financial Reporting Order	Theft and fraud related offences	Serious Organised Crime and Police Act 2005
Drinking Banning Order	Disorderly conduct under the influence of alcohol	Violent Crime Reduction Act 2006
Serious Crime Prevention Order	Involvement or facilitation of serious or 'organised' crime	Serious Crime Act 2007

*These orders were renamed under the Football (Offences and Disorder) Act 1999

Figure 6.1   Chronological list of preventive orders in the UK

preventive orders listed, only one of which currently has effect – the Banning Order under the Football (Disorder) Act 2000. Similarly, the Sex Offender Order (1998 Act) was amended by the Sexual Offences Prevention Order (2003 Act), the Exclusion Order [Licensed Premises] (1980 Act) was made redundant by the Drinking Banning Order (2006 Act), and the Restraining Order (1996 Act) was amended by the 2004 Act. These amendments to preventive orders in one category of crime policy are important to include in the analysis, as they emphasise the gradual expansion of the substantive terms for application, effect, and use.

Broadly speaking, Figure 6.1 shows that there are five categories of crime policy in which preventive orders are used to prevent future offences or related harms: alcohol-related violence, football-related violence, anti-social behaviour (including harassment), sexual offences (including molestation), and 'serious and organised crime' and terrorism (including drug trafficking and serious financial crimes).[3] Given the wide ranges of prohibitions that can be made within the 20 preventive orders, these broad categories capture most criminal conduct in the UK (both actual offences and related harmful behaviour). However, the potential scope for new preventive orders to be created should not be underestimated, particularly in dealing with 'harmful' conduct. Since embarking on this study of the SCPO at the end of 2007, additional preventive orders have been legislated that potentially fit the criteria above, for example, the Violent Offender Order,[4] the Terrorism Prevention and Investigation Measure (TPIM)[5] which replaced the terrorism Control Order, and the Gang-Related Violence Injunction.[6] Nevertheless, the examination of the key statutory provisions of each of these 20 orders, in the next section, is divided into these five key categories of crime policy. This examination highlights the modifications that have been made to the preventive order model over the past three decades.

6.3   Subtle precedents: Broadening the statutory provisions of the preventive order model

As an initial stage of identifying the substantive trends across the preventive order model, it is necessary to provide a description of the central statutory provisions of each order.[7] This section probes several substantive statutory provisions of each order, educed from seven questions:

1. To whom does the order apply?
2. Can the order be applied post- or pre-conviction (or both)?
3. Who can apply for the order to be imposed?

4. Who does the order intend to protect?
5. What is the effect and duration of the order?
6. What is the behaviour or conduct which the order seeks to prevent?
7. What is the potential sanction for breach?

Each preventive order listed in Figure 6.1 is compared with the orders that preceded it, across these seven provisions. In particular, the analysis identifies any discernible changes to the preventive order model over time, no matter how small an alteration. Such trends are often quantifiable, such as increases or decreases in the length of duration that an order can be applied, or the custodial sanctions for breach. In addition, qualitative trends are identified concerning the broadening or narrowing of the model's scope, function, and purpose (such as the subject of an order, the applicant authority to obtain an order, or the procedure of application). These changes that occurred to the statutory provisions of each order are examined by distinct category of crime policy. The examination of these provisions illustrates a clear broadening of the nature and scope of the preventive order model.

6.3.1 Alcohol-related violence

The Exclusion Order, Licensed Premises (Exclusion of Certain Persons) Act 1980, is the earliest identifiable statutory model of a preventive order. An Exclusion Order could be imposed on individuals 'convicted of an offence on licensed premises' (s.1(1)). Therefore, only a judge or magistrate could apply the order *post-conviction* (thus no civil application procedure). The duration of the order had to be 'not less than three months or more than two years' (s.1(3)), and if breached resulted in 'a fine . . . imprisonment for a term not exceeding one month or both' (s.2(1)).

This was made redundant by the enactment of the Drinking Banning Order under the Violent Crime Reduction Act 2006. The revised Drinking Banning Order added the potential for positive requirements to be made, for example, to ensure attendance at an 'approved course' (s.2). These orders could also be applied either on individuals convicted of an offence (s.6) or through civil procedure for individuals accused of 'criminal or disorderly conduct while under the influence of alcohol' (s.3(2)(a)). An application through civil complaint can be made by a 'chief officer of police', 'the Chief Constable of a British Transport Police Force', or 'a local authority' (s.14(1)). The duration of an order must be 'not less than two months and not more than two years' (s.2(1)), and though breach of an order constitutes an offence under section 11(1), it is punishable only on summary conviction by a fine (s.11(2)).

6.3.2 Football-related violence

The Exclusion Order, later renamed the Domestic Football Banning Order,[8] Public Order Act 1986, could be applied on individuals convicted of an offence 'connected with football' (s.31). Therefore, only a judge, post-conviction, could apply the order (again, no civil application procedure).[9] The order aimed to prevent further 'violence or disorder' at prescribed domestic football matches (s.30(2)). The duration of the order was required to be no less than three months (s.32(2)) and no upper limit was specified, though after one year the offender was able to make an application to terminate the order (s.33). Breach constituted an offence, punishable summarily resulting in a fine, or no more than one month imprisonment, or both (s.32(3)).

Similarly, the Restriction Order, later renamed the International Football Banning Order,[10] Football Spectators Act 1989, could be imposed on individuals convicted of 'a relevant offence' [football-related] (s.15(1)). Again, only a judge or magistrate could apply the order, post-conviction.[11] The order aimed to prevent 'violence or disorder' (s.15(2)) at prescribed foreign football matches by adding a positive requirement on the offender 'to report to a police station on the occasion of the designated football matches' (s.14(4)). The duration of an order also became statutorily prescribed as five years for an offence involving imprisonment and otherwise two years (s.16(1)). Breach constituted an offence 'on summary conviction to imprisonment for a term not exceeding one month or to a fine . . . or to both' (s.16(5)).

The Banning Order, Football (Disorder) Act 2000, amended both the Exclusion Order (domestic football) and the Restriction Order (international football), making various new changes to the statutory provisions of these two earlier orders. In Schedule 1 of the 2000 Act, new provisions were established to be inserted into section 14 of the Football Spectators Act 1989. First, the Banning Order joined the category of preventive orders allowing application to be made on civil complaint (s.14B) as well as on criminal conviction (s.14A). A civil application could be made by 'the chief officer of police for the area in which the person resides or appears to reside' (s.14(B)(1)). More important, however, is that such a complaint can be made against any individual who has 'at any time caused or contributed to any violence or disorder in the United Kingdom or elsewhere' (s.14B), where '"violence" and "disorder" are not limited to violence or disorder in connection with football' (s.14C(3)). In addition, both the statutory duration and sanction for breach are increased when compared to previous football-related preventive orders. The duration of an order can be 10 years (maximum) and 3 years (minimum), where conviction results in a term of imprisonment; 5 years (maximum) and 3 years (minimum), where conviction *does not* result in imprisonment; and 3 years (maximum) and 2 years (minimum), if issued through civil procedure (s.14F). Breach constitutes an offence punishable on summary conviction only, for the benchmark sanction of six months imprisonment and/or a fine (s.14J(2)).

6.3.3   Anti-social behaviour and harassment

The Restraining Order, Protection from Harassment Act 1997, was the first preventive order to provide two distinct statutory procedures for obtaining orders, both post-conviction *and* on civil application by a plaintiff in the High Court (predating both drinking and football banning orders discussed above). A Restraining Order could be imposed on individuals 'convicted of an offence under section 2 or 4' (s.5(1)), which are respectively the 'offence of harassment' and 'putting people in fear of violence'. This addressed harassment that was *actual* (consummated harm) and *apprehended* (more remote harm), which was viewed by some as revelational 'because it allows an injunction to be granted where past harassment cannot be proved' (Leng et al. 1998: 8). Therefore, an application can be made either by a plaintiff to the High or County Court, or by a judge as part of sentencing. Prosecutors can also informally remind the court of this power (Lawson-Cruttenden and Addison 1997: 45–46). The purpose of the order is 'protecting the victim/applicant of the offence, or any other person mentioned in the order' (s.5(2)), and the order 'may have effect for a specified period or until further order' (s.5(3)). This order was also one of the first to have a more lengthy maximum punishment for breach (setting a precedent for subsequent orders regarding the statutory provisions for breach). Breach constituted an either-way offence punishable for up to six months imprisonment on summary conviction, or five years for indictment on conviction (s.5(6)). Section 3(7) of the 1997 Act made an important statutory distinction, stating clearly that contempt of court powers should not be used on breach, as breach itself constitutes an offence. Finally, the Restraining Order was later amended under the Domestic Violence, Crime and Victims Act 2004.[12] These amendments in the 2004 Act further broadened the provision of the Restraining Order where application could also be made on conviction of *any crime* (that is, not only those originally

specified in the 1997 Act) (s.12(1)), or on an individual acqui
offence (s.12(1)).

Despite the considerable attention it has attracted, it is re
to find that the ASBO, Crime and Disorder Act 1998, introduced only
one novel substantive change compared to its predecessors.[13] The
ASBO was the first preventive order to allow application to be made by
members of the local executive authority, that is, '"relevant authority"
means the council for the local government area or any chief officer
of police' (s.1(1)). These orders can be applied on an individual of at
least 10 years of age who has 'caused or was likely to cause harassment,
alarm or distress to one or more persons not of the same household as
himself' (s.1(1)(a)). This modification to the preventive order model
also marks an important shift in civil procedure, where the application is made by a public authority to protect the *general* public, rather
than an application made by an individual to protect herself/himself
or another *specific* person. In its original legislated form, the statutory
provision regarding application for an ASBO was through civil proceedings only; however, the Police Reform Act 2002 (s.61) extended
the powers by allowing the ASBO to also be imposed post-conviction
(a criminal ASBO, so-called 'CRASBO').[14] The duration of an ASBO must
be 'not less than two years . . . [and as] specified in the order or until
further order' (s.1(7)). Breach constitutes an offence subject to a maximum imprisonment term of six months on summary conviction and
five years on indictment and/or a fine (s.1(10)).

6.3.4 Sexual offences and molestation

The Non-Molestation Order, Family Law Act 1996, was one of the
first preventive orders to be applicable *only* through civil procedure.
Therefore, the standard of proof and evidence is strictly civil, under Part II
of the Magistrates' Court Act 1980, and there was no procedure for an
order to be applied as part of sentencing. The Non-Molestation Order
could be applied on individuals if either a (civil) complaint is made by a
person 'who is associated with the respondent' (s.42(2)(a)), or if during
Family Court hearings a judge at any time deems it necessary for the
benefit of any party, and particularly a child (s.42(2)(b)). The duration of
this order is wide-ranging, 'for a specified period or until further order'
(s.42(7)). Breach was not initially an offence in the 1996 Act.[15] However,
the Domestic Violence, Crime and Victims Act 2004 (s.1) amended the
Family Law Act 1996, so as to criminalise breach of a Non-Molestation
Order. The inserted section 42A(5) states that the offence of breach is
punishable on conviction on indictment for a 5-year maximum term

of imprisonment or a fine, or both; and on summary conviction an increased 12 month imprisonment or a fine, or both.

Conversely, the Sex Offender Order, Crime and Disorder Act 1998 targeted those individuals *convicted* of a sexual offence under the Sex Offenders Act 1997. While principally applied post-conviction, additional provisions were made for several cases where a conviction recorded in the UK was not required: (1) those found *not* guilty by reason of insanity, (2) after a police caution relating to a sexual offence, or (3) those individuals who have committed a sexual offence in a foreign jurisdiction (s.3(1)). The SOPO, Sexual Offences Act 2003, amended the Sex Offender Order to extend the statutory provision for full application procedures including civil complaint. An SOPO could be applied in circumstances where individuals were convicted of a sexual offence; individuals were found not guilty of such an offence by reason of insanity; or individuals had 'acted in such a way as to give reasonable cause to believe that it is necessary for such an order to be made' (s.104). In the latter circumstance, the reasonable cause and application must be both determined and made by a chief police officer. The duration is the same as the prior Sex Offender Order, that is, a period no less than five years or until further order (s.107(1)). Breach provisions also remained unchanged, constituting an offence subject to a maximum term of imprisonment of six months on summary conviction and five years on indictment, and/or a fine (s.113).

Three other preventive orders fall into this category of conduct, each related to the prevention of sexual offences against children. While these three orders present no new developments to the preventive order model, they are worth brief description as they reflect the consistency with, and continuity of, the statutory provisions analysed thus far. A Disqualification Order, Criminal Justice and Court Services Act 2000, could be applied on individuals convicted of an 'offence against a child' (s.26). The prosecution must apply for an order as an auxiliary measure to a given sentence, in order to prohibit a convicted offender from working with children (s.30(1)).[16] A Foreign Travel Order, Sexual Offences Act 2003, could similarly be applied on individuals convicted (including in a foreign jurisdiction), cautioned, or found not guilty by reason of insanity in relation to a sexual offence (s.116), if a chief officer of police makes an application (s.114). Such orders place restriction on travel outside the UK in order to 'protect children generally or any child from serious sexual harm from the defendant outside the United Kingdom' (s.114(3)).[17] Finally, a Risk of Sexual Harm Order (RSHO), Sexual Offences Act 2003, could be imposed when there is 'reasonable cause to believe' that, on two or more occasions, an individual has been involved in activities that risk sexual harm to a child or children (s.123).[18] An application could only be made via civil complaint by a chief officer of police (though individuals previously convicted of sexual offences would likely provide the reasonable cause necessary for issuing an order).[19]

6.3.5 Serious crimes (financial crime, organised crime, and terrorism)

The Disqualification Order, Company Directors Disqualification Act 1986, could be obtained for directors of companies (on application only by the Secretary of State) who are deemed by the court to be incapable or fraudulent in respect of their duties. Section 1(4) states that '[a] disqualification order may be made on grounds which are or include matters *other than criminal convictions*, notwithstanding that the person in respect of whom it is to be made may be criminally liable in respect of those matters' (emphasis added). This Disqualification Order, enacted as early as 1986, is therefore likely to be the earliest statutory example of a preventive order available through civil law proceedings. Separate statutory provisions are made in the 1986 Act in relation to various conduct, such as conviction of an indictable offence (s.2), persistent breach of company regulations (s.3), fraudulent activity during 'winding up' of a company (s.4), repeated summary convictions (s.5), or being unfit to act in relation to an insolvent company (s.6). The statutory duration of this order is one of the longest specified by the legislature, though it differs somewhat depending on the type of conduct – generally somewhere between a maximum period of 5 and 15 years (although section 6(4), *unfit directors of insolvent companies*, also states a minimum requirement of 2 years). Breach of an order constitutes an offence subject to a maximum imprisonment term of six months on summary conviction and two years on indictment and/ or a fine (s.13).

The Travel Restriction Order, Criminal Justice and Police Act 2001, can be applied to individuals convicted of a serious 'drug-trafficking offence', and who have served a term of imprisonment of at least four years (s.33(1)). This order, which restricts travel outside the UK, therefore adds an interesting dimension, where restrictions are statutorily required to begin *only* after release from custody (s.33(3)). The duration of an order must be for no less than two years (s.33(3)(b)), and breach constitutes an offence subject to a maximum imprisonment term of six months on summary conviction and five years on indictment and/or a fine (s.36).

Unlike all of the preventive orders above, the Financial Reporting Order, Serious Organised Crime and Police Act 2005, *only* makes provision for *positive* requirements (not prohibitions), that is, a requirement to do something rather than desist from doing something.[20] This order requires individuals convicted of offences related to serious theft or fraud, as listed in section 76(3), to make regular reports to the court as to the particulars of his or her financial activities (s.79). The duration of an order must be no more than five years (s.76(6)), and breach is a summary offence punishable for a maximum term of imprisonment of '51 weeks' and/or a fine (s.79(10)).

The Control Order,[21] Prevention of Terrorism Act 2005, was made for the purpose of 'protecting members of the public from a risk of terrorism' (s.1(1)) and *only* on application by the Secretary of State based on reasonable grounds for suspicion (s.2(1)). The procedure for obtaining this type of preventive order was therefore strictly civil and not applicable post-conviction.[22] A Control Order could be imposed on an individual 'involved' in terrorism-related activity. Such 'involvement' was defined in section 1(9) of the 2005 Act as '(a) the commission, preparation or instigation of acts of terrorism; (b) conduct which *facilitates* the commission, preparation or instigation of such acts, or which is intended to do so; (c) conduct which gives *encouragement* to the commission, preparation or instigation of such acts, or which is intended to do so; (d) conduct which gives support or *assistance* to individuals who are known or believed to be involved in terrorism-related activity' (emphasis added). This broad definition of conduct as 'involvement' marked a substantive expansion of the preventive order model (which has correspondingly been adopted for the SCPO – see below). The duration of a non-derogating order was 12 months (s.2(4)(a)) and for a derogating order six months (s.4(8)); however, both types of orders could be 'renewed on one or more occasions' (respectively, s.2(4)(b) and ss.10, 11, & 12). Breach constituted an offence subject to a maximum imprisonment term of 12 months on summary conviction[23] and five years on indictment and/or a fine (s.113).

The Serious Crime Prevention Order, SCA 2007, clearly reflects the number of statutory provisions that have evolved over the last three decades through amendments to, and adaptation of, the preventive order model across the orders dissected above. The SCPO also makes provision for yet another substantive expansion, allowing the orders to be applied to companies and organisations (in addition to individuals) who have been involved in serious crime. An SCPO can be obtained at sentence where an individual has been convicted of an offence of involvement in serious crime (s.1); or as a result of an application made to the High Court by either the Director of Public Prosecutions, the Director of Revenue and Customs Prosecutions, or the Director of the Serious Fraud Office, where individuals or companies are deemed to be 'involved' in serious criminal activity (s.8). This order can contain any 'prohibitions, restrictions or *requirements*' (s.1(3)) (emphasis added); thus, both negative and positive directions can be made. The duration of an order must be no more than 5 years (s.16(2)) and breach constitutes an offence under section 25(1), where the maximum imprisonment term is 12 months on summary conviction and 5 years on indictment and/or a fine (s.25). On breach, the court also has powers of forfeiture (s.26), and specifically in relation to a company or organisation, powers of liquidation (s.27–29).

Finally, one order listed in Figure 6.1 has not yet been outlined. The Driving Disqualification Order, Road Traffic Act 1988, is an anomaly as it does not fit into one of the five categories of conduct assessed above. However, it does satisfy the three criteria to be a preventive order (preventive, specific offence in mind, and breach is criminal offence), and therefore requires brief consideration to complete the analysis. Disqualification Orders [Driving] can be imposed on individuals convicted of a 'driving offence' as specified in the 1988 Act.[24] Disqualification, namely the revocation of an individual's driving licence, can therefore only be imposed post-conviction as part of sentencing. The duration of such an order typically carries a mandatory minimum of 12 months unless 'special reasons' are accepted by the court (Ashworth 2005: 335). Breach of an order, either driving without a licence or obtaining a licence while disqualified, constitutes an offence under section 103(1)(b) of the 1988 Act. The penalties for breach are listed in Schedule 2 of another act, the Road Traffic Offenders Act 1988, where on summary conviction an imprisonment term of up to 6 months and/or a fine can be issued.

This account of each of the 20 preventive orders in the UK presents some remarkable trends, which are worthy of further exploration. Through incremental reforms, the legislature has created a panoply of preventive orders across multiple areas of crime control. The gradual spread of this technique has permeated the criminal justice policy environment, as an instrument to prevent a substantial range of criminal harms. More importantly, however, are the other gradual shifts that have occurred in relation to the scope and breadth of the statutory provisions contained in these preventive orders. These important trends are discussed in turn.

6.4   Key trends: Broadening the scope of preventive orders

There are a number of trends observable across the 20 preventive orders examined so far. It is argued that these trends, on the whole, have generated increasingly broad-reaching statutory provisions across numerous orders, so much so that the SCPO is situated at one end of the spectrum, far away from the initial prototypical preventive order (for example, compared to the Exclusion Order [Licensed Premises] introduced in 1980). This is *not* to suggest that law and policy should not evolve – to be sure, one size certainly does not fit all. However, without comprehensive awareness and aggregate scrutiny of perhaps seemingly unrelated areas of policy, such gradual shifts can lead to radical departures from the original purpose and intention of similar procedures. This echoes Steiker's (1998: 778) concern about the potential dangers of treating new measures as *sui generis* (considered in Chapter 3, Section 3.2). This is an important aspect of incremental policy change, which is discussed further in the concluding chapter (Chapter 8).

A number of trends are examined in turn to demonstrate the nature and extent of the developments, which provide the foundations for the provisions of the SCPO. Based on its provisions, the SCPO is an extremely wide-reaching state power, even when compared to the more controversial and debated preventive orders (such as the ASBO and Control Order).

6.4.1   Trend 1: Criminal to civil procedure

As shown in Chapter 3, the most widely noted, discussed, and criticised trend that has occurred in the preventive order model is the broadening of its application procedure. Early preventive orders, such as the Exclusion Order [Licensed Premises] and Restriction Order, were only imposed on individuals post-conviction, as part of sentencing (criminal procedure). One exception was the Disqualification Order for company directors, which could be imposed within civil procedure only. Some consider this to be a cornerstone of the 'civil' preventive order model where it has set a 'precedent for subsequent use of the technique' (Lord Steyn, *Clingham and McCann*, 2002: para. 17). Since the mid-1990s, preventive orders such as the Non-Molestation Order and Restraining Order have increasingly allowed application both post-conviction as part of sentencing (criminal procedure) *and* on application to a judge through civil procedure. This is clearly demonstrated in the examination above where past preventive orders within a category of crime policy were replaced by a new preventive order to provide the additional procedure for applications to also be made on civil complaint. For example, for football-related harm, the Exclusion Order and Restriction Order were replaced by the civil Banning Order. Similarly, many subsequent preventive orders which were developed in distinct areas of crime control policy began procedurally as post-conviction only – such as the Sex Offender Order, Restraining Order, Disqualification Order (working with children), and Travel Restriction Order (drug trafficking) – but then later were either amended or replaced by newer preventive orders which afforded application through civil procedure (respectively, the SOPO, Restraining Order (amended), RSHO, and SCPO). As stated above, the ASBO reversed this trend where application was initially only through civil procedure, but was soon after extended to allow post-conviction procedures.[25] Nonetheless, the majority of these orders have gradually developed over time to allow the application of the preventive order model in both civil and criminal procedure.

Two preventive orders, namely, the Control Order and Risk of Sexual Harm Order (RSHO), have unique characteristics in that they do *not* follow this trend, providing *only* for civil application, not post-conviction.[26] Arguably this distinction is superficial in the case of the Control Order, as consummated harm was actually included in the criteria for 'involvement in terrorism', which determined whether an order could be imposed. That is, a Control Order was imposed after the actual commission of an act of terrorism under section 1(9)(a): 'the commission, preparation or instigation of acts of terrorism'. Clearly, where sufficient evidence of the commission of a relevant act existed, the offender would have been likely to be prosecuted, not placed on a Control Order (however, this argument could equally be made for other preventive orders at sentencing, where individuals have already been prosecuted). In addition, those convicted of a sexual offence against a child would either provide the 'reasonable cause to believe' an RSHO is necessary, or alternatively a SOPO (under the same 2003 Act) could be applied. Nonetheless, a separate application would still need to be made under these proceedings, rather than a preventive order being obtainable as part of sentencing for the specific offence.

6.4.2   Trend 2: Consummate to remote harms

A related expansive trend involves the conduct necessary to trigger a preventive order. A comparison of earlier and later examples of the preventive order model shows that later orders are being imposed based on judicial satisfaction of less inculpatory conduct. Early preventive orders (such as the Exclusion Order [Licensed Premises], the Disqualification Order [Driving], and the Sex Offender Order) could only be imposed post-conviction and therefore an offence (consummated harm) had first to be proven before an order could be imposed. As the civil application procedure became commonplace, the threshold to grant an order broadened to more remote harms; for example, an offence only need be *allegedly* committed (such as with the Non-Molestation Order and Restraining Order). This requirement was further broadened under the ASBO, whereby the allegation no longer had to be in relation to a criminal offence. Rather a mere act of nuisance would be sufficient, specifically one which is 'likely to cause harassment, alarm or distress' (1998 Act s.1(1)(a)). Similarly, the Football Banning Order expanded this requirement particularly when compared with the former football-related preventive orders, which could only be applied on convicted 'football hooligans'. The Football Banning Order broadened the requirement so that orders could be imposed on individuals who had 'at any time caused or contributed to any violence or disorder' where this conduct was no longer 'limited to violence or disorder in connection with football' (2000 Act s.14B and s.14C(3)).

The Control Order was even more widely drawn in that the required conduct was 'involvement in terrorism-related activity',[27] where such 'activities' included not only the commission or instigation of such acts (consummate harms) but also those which were 'preparatory' (remote harms). Moreover, the 'involvement' criterion included the act of 'facilitation' (s.1(9)(b)), 'encouragement' (s.1(9)(c)), and 'support' (s.1(9)(d)), which indicates that these orders were even targeting conduct prior to preparation. While McSherry (2009: 142) has argued (though in relation to expanding inchoate offences in the criminal law) that stronger controls to address more remote harms should be viewed as exceptional and exclusive to terrorism, given the seriousness of this offence category, the SCPO has also subsequently appropriated these statutory provisions. The requirement in relation to the conduct necessary to obtain an SCPO embraces this broad definition of involvement – and arguably goes further. Section 2 of the SCA 2007 states that involvement includes not only the facilitation of the commission of a serious crime, but also if the individual has 'conducted himself in a way that was likely to facilitate the commission by himself or another person of a serious offence (whether or not such an offence was committed)'. This definition clearly encapsulates more remote harms – conduct prior to preparation but 'likely to facilitate' – far from an offence (consummated harm) being committed. Again, the SCPO is positioned at the extreme end of this broadening trend to allow earlier state intervention to address more remote harms.

6.4.3 Trend 3: Specific to general protective purpose

A third broadening trend visible across preventive orders is the shift from a very specific to a more general protective focus. Early preventive orders had a more specific and defined population identified as in need of protection, for example, the Exclusion Order [Licensed Premises] focused on 'specified licenced premises' (1980 Act s.1) and the Exclusion Order [Football] and Restriction Order focused on 'designated football matches' (respectively, 1986 Act s.30(2); and 1989 Act s.15(3)). Similarly, many preventive orders were made to protect specific individuals named in the order, such as with the Non-Molestation Order and Restraining Order. However, with the enactment of the Crime and Disorder Act 1998 a broader protective purpose was proffered, whereby the specified goal of the ASBO is to 'protect persons in the local government area' (s.1(1)(b)) and that of the Sex Offender Order is to 'protect the public from serious harm' (s.2(1)(b)). Numerous preventive orders have since followed suit, adopting the more general goal and mantra of 'public protection' (including the Control Order, Travel Restriction Order, Financial Reporting Order, and SCPO). This particular expansion is also exemplified *within* the specific categories of crime policy that were assessed, for example, the Exclusion Order's protective focus shifted from specified licenced premises to protecting all persons in the public, under the Drinking Banning Order (2006 Act, s.1(2)).

6.4.4 Three final trends: Companies, duration, and penalty

There are three final trends which can be considered as evidence of the broadening scope and effect of the preventive order model in the UK: the use against companies, the indeterminate duration of orders, and the increased penalty for breach. First, an expansive trend is apparent where the preventive order model has broadened its provision concerning the subject of an order, from an *individual* to a *group* of individuals. This is evidenced by Section 5(4) of the SCA 2007, which makes provision for an SCPO to be also applied on 'bodies corporate, partnerships and unincorporated associations'. Second, while the length of duration that preventive orders can be applied has seen a less linear expansion, compared to other statutory provisions discussed above, there has unquestionably been a measurable extension. The

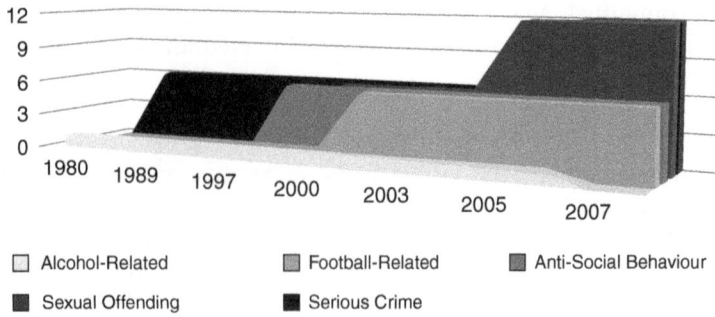

Figure 6.2   Maximum summary custodial sentences by offence category

preventive order model has shifted from being applied with a specified statutory upper limit (for example, the Disqualification Order
[Company Directors] and Exclusion Order [Licensed Premises]) to
being left to judicial specification, or being made indefinitely or 'until
further order'.[28] Even for preventive orders that have maintained a
statutory upper limit, for example, the Control Order and the SCPO,
statutory provisions were made for renewal of an order *without* restriction on the number of occasions when such an order can be renewed
(respectively, 2005 Act s.2(4)(b) and 2007 Act s.16(5) & (6)). Third, the
statutory criminal sanctions for breach of a preventive order have seen
an increase since the initial conception under the Licensed Premises
(Exclusion of Certain Persons) Act 1980 with the Exclusion Order.
While breach on indictment shows a more varied pattern of penalties,
there was an apparent increase in the maximum imprisonment terms
for breach on summary conviction (depicted in Figure 6.2).

While early preventive orders had a maximum imprisonment term
of one to three months, this penalty dramatically increased under the
Protection from Harassment Act 1997 for Restraining Orders to six
months imprisonment on summary conviction and five years on indictment. This has generally become the norm for subsequent preventive
orders.[29] Yet another increase occurred to the maximum imprisonment
term for summary convictions to 12 months, under the Control Order
and the SCPO. This increase might be argued to reflect the greater seriousness of these categories of conduct. However, if this reasoning is
correct, this indicates a development in the preventive order model to
include an element of proportionality: where sanctions are proportional
to the seriousness of harms, rather than being explicable as punishment
for defiance of the law.

6.4.5 Narrowing trends?

Finally, there are two further substantive trends which represent a potential *narrowing* of the scope of the preventive order model. First, the applicant authority for obtaining a preventive order through civil proceedings has heightened over time. The analysis shows that the application for preventive orders has shifted from being made on complaint by individual plaintiffs (for example, the Non-Molestation Order and Restraining Order) to applications made by local authorities (the ASBO and Drinking Banning Order), then by police (the Banning Order [Football] and RSHO) to prosecutors (the Disqualification Order [Working with Children]), and more recently to the Secretary of State or the Directors of Public Prosecution, Revenue and Customs Prosecutions, and the Serious Fraud Office (the Control Order and the SCPO, respectively). Since the civil law has traditionally been concerned with matters between two private parties, this trend to increase the role of the state as a party indicates a more general shift in civil procedure. While this might present a narrowing trend concerning the specific application authority in the preventive order model, it also clearly indicates an expansive trend in state regulation and control.

The heightened civil standard of proof, established in the case of *Clingham and McCann* [2002] in relation to the ASBO (discussed in Chapter 3), indicates the second trend regarding a narrowing of the scope of the 'civil' preventive order model. That is, compared to earlier preventive orders, such as the Non-Molestation Order where the standard of proof and evidence was strictly civil under Part II of the Magistrates' Court Act 1980, a higher level of proof is now necessary to obtain a preventive order (thus a narrower application). However, while the decision in *Clingham and McCann* [2002] is 'likely' to apply to subsequent civil preventive orders (such as the SCPO), it is important to note that the provisions of these orders have not formally (or statutorily) stipulated this requirement. For example, the Explanatory Notes for the SCA 2007 (para. 122) state that 'the same principle is *likely* to apply in relation to applications for serious crime prevention orders' (emphasis added). However, such a criminal standard (or even mention of a heightened standard) is *not* statutorily enshrined in the 2007 Act, where Section 35 clearly states that

(1) Proceedings before the High Court in relation to serious crime prevention orders are civil proceedings.

(2) One consequence of this is that the standard of proof to be applied by the court in such proceedings is the civil standard of proof.

This hesitancy by legislators to make proper provision to statutorily narrow this aspect of the civil preventive order model is perplexing. This concern was also expressed by Lord Lloyd of Berwick in debating the SCPO clause in the Serious Crime Bill 2006–2007 (column 668):

> If the standard of proof is going to be the criminal standard, as it should be, let us call it just that. . . . [T]he criminal standard of proof should be applied because of the extraordinary width of the definition of being involved in serious crime contained in Clause 2(1)(c). I have never seen anything like that provision in a criminal or quasi-criminal statute. I am very doubtful whether it would pass the test of legal certainty.[30]

Moreover, the difficulties with a heightened standard, rather than a statutory criminal standard, are also expressed by Sir Rhys Davies QC, Recorder in the *McCann* Appeal to the Crown Court:

> [I]n reality it is difficult to establish reliable gradations between a heightened civil standard commensurate with seriousness and implications of proving the requirements, and the criminal standard. (Davies, cited in Plowden and Kerrigan 2002: 243)

Similarly, in a study observing civil hearings in the Magistrates' Court for Football Banning Orders, James and Pearson (2006: 522) concluded that in numerous cases a 'mere lip service' was being paid to the test requiring the heightened standard.

Much of the attention of academics and practitioners has been focused on the specific expansion of the preventive order model that makes provision for applications through civil procedure. Despite attempts by the judiciary to narrow the scope of civil application (with a heightened standard of proof), the legislature continues to resist formal recognition of the criminal standard when formulating new preventive orders. While civil application is undeniably a contentious revision of the preventive order model, the analysis in this chapter has demonstrated that it has overshadowed other important expansive trends. The preventive order model has evolved into an instrument that has an extensive scope regarding whom it can be applied to, who it intends to protect, for how long it may have effect, and the severity of sanctions for breach. The analysis has also demonstrated that the SCPO, as a recent variant of this model, consequently contains some of the broadest-reaching provisions of the family of preventive orders.

Most importantly, however, the analysis in this chapter has left no doubt as to the connection between the SCPO and other preventive orders, as their provisions, taken together, demonstrate a clear shared nature, purpose, and effect. While it may not have derived from past policy attempts to prevent serious criminal activity, the SCPO is firmly grounded within this particular strand of domestic preventive measures (a clear indication of its 'transfer origin'). This substantiates an expansive trend that is at the core of this book – the expansion of the preventive order model to many diverse areas of crime control policy. This gives weighty evidence to support the thesis that domestic policy transfer occurred in the development of the SCPO. That is to say, the number, and extent of similarity, of the statutory provisions clearly indicates domestic policy transfer.

While this transfer origin appears clear, the other main dimensions of transfer require further analysis. The legislative analysis in this chapter has shown that it has been the legal instruments (complete provisions) that have been transferred from other preventive orders in the UK, although 'policy ideas' from the US about the use of civil remedies for organised crime control might have had some influence (regarding 'what is transferred'). The 'degree of transfer' is therefore likely to be a mixture of 'inspiration' from civil RICO and 'emulation' of the statutory provisions of other preventive orders. Dolowitz and Marsh's distinction between emulation and more direct 'copying' is applicable here where the provisions of preceding preventive orders required substantial adaptation to fit the conditions of the new arena of organised crime control. It is also important to note that it is emulation, not copying, that has permitted the incremental reformulation of the preventive order model (for example, in the case of the SCPO, the adaption for organised crime control resulted in the expansion of application to organisations and entities). These various expansive trends shown in the analysis could be perceived as a gradual process of pushing boundaries and up-tariffing – where this would suggest that calculated actions were taken by decision-makers to direct the broader goals of policy change – or alternatively a more osmotic process of policy transfer. Therefore, it is also particularly important to examine 'why transfer occurred' and 'who was involved'. The next chapter goes on to address these dimensions of policy transfer, by providing the results of the analysis of early policy documents and interviews with the key decision-makers who were involved in developing the SCPO.

7
Policy Analysis: Elite Interviews and Early Policy Documents

In the introduction to this book, two key questions were posed for empirical analysis: first, what was the nature and extent of the role played by preceding preventive orders in the formulation of the SCPO? And second, did decision-makers knowingly formulate the SCPO and other preventive orders as part of a broader goal to foster an alternative system of preventive justice? While the previous chapter demonstrated the true extent of similarity between the SCPO and pre-existing variants of the preventive order model, a number of questions remain about the function of transfer: for example, was there a decision made to transfer, and if so, by whom? When did transfer take place? Why did the transfer occur? The nature of policy transfer is explored in this chapter, as well as the extent to which decision-makers held broader preventive intentions to reform the criminal justice system. To address these questions, this chapter presents insights from the interviews conducted with key policy and decision-makers involved in developing the SCPO (responses of those sampled from the population of actors presented in Chapter 5, Section 5.3.2.3, Figure 5.1). Where relevant, this account is also supported by an analysis of policy documents from the Home Office and SOCA about the origins and use of the SCPO. In addition to addressing these two primary research questions, these sources of data provided some further general findings as a result of analyses of interviewees' accounts about the key stages in policy development, as well as documentation containing a description of the actual use of the SCPO in the UK (such as the current number of orders in place and the types of conditions currently imposed).[1] The purpose of this chapter is solely to present the results of the empirical analysis of the interviews and several key departmental policy documents. The implications of the findings are then discussed in greater detail in the final chapter of this book (Chapter 8), where conclusions and implications are drawn.

The first section of this chapter begins with a reconstructed time-line of policy development for the SCPO, based on the recollections[2] of interviewees and the dates of departmental papers and correspondence. This section also provides an account of the various stages of early development from the perspective of interviewees, which gives a unique insight into the environment and more general conditions under which policy decisions are made in the Home Office and the office of the Prime Minister (at 10 Downing Street, hereafter 'Number 10'). The second section then provides detailed findings about, and any evidence of, policy transfer that occurred during the development of the SCPO. This is based on the specific dimensions of transfer established in earlier chapters: primarily, who participated in transfer, what was transferred, and why transfer occurred. Evidence of both direct and indirect forms of transfer is presented. The third section examines the evidence from the interviews of any broader intentions (or ideological agenda) behind the development of the preventive order model, to determine whether (and to what extent) policy-makers were attempting to create an alternative system of preventive justice.

7.1   Policy development timeline: The SCPO

The primary purpose of this chapter is to set out the story of policy development surrounding the SCPO. This section constructs a timeline to depict the most significant events in policy development and the time periods between each event. This identification of key events during the early stage of the legislative process is an important initial step in narrowing down where transfer might have occurred and who was involved. The timeline is accompanied by a description of the nature of the policy-making environment and of these early events, according to the decision-makers interviewed (that is, those on the front line). This account demonstrates that policy-making is a highly fluid, iterative, and unstructured process, which precedes the more formal, structured, and ritualistic parliamentary process (the second phase in the legislative process). In particular, this account and timeline show the significant time pressures that occur during policy development, which can in turn induce policy-makers to engage in policy transfer as a shortcut to innovation.

The impetus for the SCPO clearly arose from a search for new and innovative ways to deal with serious and organised crime in the UK, particularly new powers to accompany the establishment of a new agency SOCA, as this testimony reveals:

> Well I don't think [the SCPO] was an afterthought, I think it was an extension. I think when you've got the Serous Organised Crime Agency who are a body which is specifically designed for tackling organised criminality, they are bound to come up with ideas for more effective measures as part of their overall brief . . . there hadn't been a body out there in the past, which would have that sort of thinking and drive. (Senior civil servant, Home Office)

While the amalgamation of various agencies (National Crime Squad, National Criminal Intelligence Service, and customs) was in part a strategic development for law enforcement – to enhance efficiency, avoid investigative duplication, and limit unnecessary bureaucracy – it was also intended that the new agency be 'much more than the sum of its parts':

> [T]o explore innovative and lateral approaches to dealing with serious organised crime. Because the remit all the time was to deal with the harm caused by it, and the disruption and the prevention, rather than just the cops and robbers. (Senior management, SOCA).

Accordingly, the development of the SCPO overlapped with the formation of SOCA. The timeline in Figure 7.1 demonstrates the key events that occurred in developing both the SCPO and SOCA.

Figure 7.1 shows that in January 2004, the former Director-General of the British Security Service (MI5), Sir Stephen Lander, was commissioned by the Home Office to conduct a review of policing and customs in the UK, with the view to forming a new national agency. Two Home Office officials assisted Lander to conduct this review, which took approximately eight weeks, and together they produced an internal report for the Cabinet Secretary and the Home Secretary. Based on this review, in March 2004, the Home Office published a White Paper entitled 'One Step Ahead', in which it publicly announced, inter alia, the government's intention to form a new agency SOCA. Approximately five months later, on 13 August 2004, Lander accepted the position to Chair SOCA, and began work in the Home Office to establish the organisation. On 13 September 2004, Lander was joined by the former head of the National Crime Squad, Bill Hughes, who later became the Director-General of SOCA, and a 'programme team' (consisting

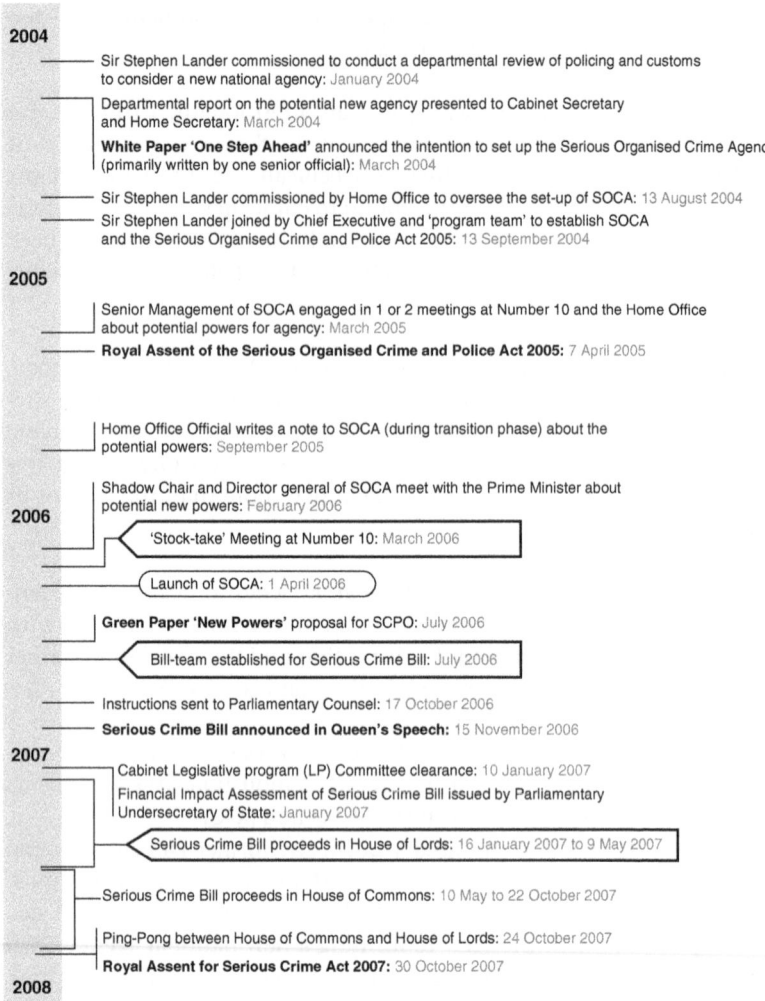

Figure 7.1   Development timeline – the SOCA and the SCPO

of several officials in the Home Office) that began to work on the duties and powers for SOCA to be enshrined in the Serious Organised Crime and Police Bill. Seven months later, on 7 April 2005, the Serious Organised Crime and Police Act 2005 was granted Royal Assent.

There was a 'transition phase' of approximately one year, prior to SOCA being launched on 1 April 2006. It was during this transition period that discussions about the SCPO are likely to have begun. As one senior Home Office official stated:

> I did a note in the Spring [March 2006] during the transition phase on some ideas about new powers, and sent it to [those] at SOCA . . . and you know, they were sort of interested but they said hold your horses a while because actually the big thing at the moment – back then – was actually setting up the organisation. Then almost immediately we were called in by Number 10 for some sort of potential, looking for some potential ideas and powers, and SOCA had built on some of the ideas that we had [in the note], and developed it, took it a bit further and developed some thoughts of their own.

A number of key policy-makers who were interviewed (Interviewees 1, 3, 4, 5, 7, and 21) agreed that it was during this meeting at Number 10 Downing Street, in early March 2006, that the idea for the SCPO was first conceived. Three of these interviewees described this meeting at Number 10 to be part of what was known as a 'stocktake meeting'. One staffer from Number 10 described these meetings thus:

> This policy was actually made in what we used to call stocktake meetings which is where you'd have . . . Tony Blair as the chair, the Home Secretary there, police chiefs, other junior ministers, other relevant senior civil servants from the Home Office, and our experts from Number 10. They would sit around and chew over these issues, the particular problems they were facing and what the possible solutions were.

At this stage, only a few individuals were involved in discussions about the potential new powers for SOCA: principally two ministers from the Home Office (including the Home Secretary), one senior Home Office official, the Prime Minister and his special advisor for home affairs, as well as two members of senior management from SOCA who were considered to be the 'policy customers'.[3] At this meeting, the senior Home Office official stated that there was a strong demand for new powers:

> We then had a process under Tony Blair, Number 10, they were looking for more powers and really it wouldn't be too much of an exaggeration to say that we were told, 'you need more powers and you've got the legislation and you better think of something to put in them'. . . . He [Blair] wanted more powers and wasn't taking no for an answer.

One interviewee from SOCA explained how this type of discussion, or vague policy direction, was not uncommon:

> [I]t's a thing that ministers really want to do, particularly prime ministers, 'what more powers do you need, just tell me what more powers you need, what else would you . . . you know, you just tell us'.

While initial discussions about potential new powers occurred in this meeting in March 2006, a month later at the launch of SOCA (1 April 2006) there was no mention of the SCPO. Rather, the Prime Minister announced four new powers upon which SOCA would rely: Queen's evidence, Financial Reporting Orders, Disclosure Notices, and multi-powers for police officers.[4] The senior Home Office official from this meeting (the same key official who authored the White Paper in 2004) was central to the initial policy direction for the development of new powers, and eventually, he wrote the consultation paper, 'New Powers Against Organised and Financial Crime', in July 2006. This was the first document to enunciate the idea of an 'organised crime prevention order'.

> Obviously as head of the unit, which is also the head of the sponsor unit for SOCA, I was probably fairly central to its early setting of strategic direction. I then sort of let the bill-team take many of the details forward – but no, many of the ideas in the various pieces of legislation was stuff that was generated from myself or with, or in collaboration with, SOCA. (Senior official, Home Office)

This formation of the bill-team marks a second stage of development, with a new set of actors influencing the shape of the SCPO. As depicted in the timeline in Figure 7.1, the bill-team was formed around the same time as the consultation paper (July 2006), when the new officials on this team continued to develop the SCPO and the other provisions of the Bill. One senior official explained that when a bill-team is formed, it is decided whether policy development is ongoing or if it is only the primary task of managing it through parliament that is required:

> It varies, bill-teams are set up in different ways. Sometimes they are managing, and they go out to other bits of the office for the policy, [however] on Serious Crime Prevention Orders, the bill-team also contained policy officials.

There were six core individuals on the Serious Crime Bill 2006–2007 team: two policy leads, two departmental lawyers, and two handlers (already defined in Chapter 4, Section 4.2.3). However, only two individuals were actually involved in the development of the SCPO, one policy lead and one legal advisor.[5] The two bill handlers (one senior official and one junior[6]) were far less involved in any policy development in the Bill; rather, they focused on the preparation of the Bill for the parliamentary stages:

> What happens is, they coordinate all the bills, look at how the amendments are going, and make sure – and from really high-powered strategic involvement to making sure that speaking notes are available when the amendments are all in order. Sort of really practical, right the way from that level, right the way to the top. (Minister, Home Office)

The additional policy lead and legal advisor worked on the other parts of the Bill, such as the clauses relating to data matching, encouraging and assisting crime, and the abolition of the Assets Recovery Agency. One Permanent Secretary described the process of forming a bill-team as usually one where positions are advertised internally on a full-time basis. Typically, bill-team members are selected based on their experience of working on other bill processes in the past rather than the more substantive expertise about the subject matter of the bill, because,

> in terms of substance, in terms of the real intellectual dimension if you like, for want of another phrase, well they can just press a button and get up the 10 officials who worked in a particular area. (Minister, Home Office)

This same minister described the fluid dynamic between the core bill-team and other officials:

> Now underneath [the bill-team] will be a whole series of policy officials in each policy directorate who'd be working specifically on the substance that goes to make up elements of that bill. So it's a bit like an American football team, you know, on one level the bill-team are the 11, 15, or whatever that are on the pitch, but there's a whole host of offence, defence, all around the specific areas.

However, two interviewees, an official and a Permanent Secretary, maintained that there is no strict formula for forming a bill-team, and it is often dependent on the size of the bill and the availability of officials. Another official described how this procedure created some difficulties in setting up the bill-team for the Serious Crime Bill 2006–2007, principally owing to time pressures:

> Well actually in this case we had a real struggle getting people [for the bill-team], because we'd come under such pressure from Number 10 to get something in place immediately. We'd been trying to do it through a managed move, and what actually happened in the end was that they ended up tapping people on the shoulder.

The bill-team lawyer also explained that this meant 'the bill-team wasn't actually put together until quite late' (July 2006), only six months prior to the introduction of the Serious Crime Bill 2006–2007 into parliament on 16 January 2007 (see Figure 7.1). Importantly, this may have limited the involvement of the bill-team in policy development. As Page (2003: 655) has observed, 'the teams which had the greatest involvement in policy development [are] the teams [that] were set up 11 and 10 months in advanced of the introduction of the bill into parliament'. However, one bill-team member interviewed stated that the relatively late formation of the bill-team simply resulted in policy development continuing during the parliamentary process:

> And because we did a lot of policy development, the policy development carried on while we were going through the house. That shouldn't normally be the case. You should normally be pretty much there, or thereabouts, when you introduce [the bill to the house]. But we weren't, because it was quite a rapid process.[7]

This intriguing admission highlights the empirical reality of the policy-making environment, which corresponds with Simon's (1956: 131) model of bounded rationality (discussed in Chapter 4), whereby a decision-maker's search for an innovative policy response is limited by the finite time allocated for policy development. A number of other interviewees (3, 7, 8, 15, and 17) also described the process of development for the Serious Crime Bill 2006–2007 as being under significant time pressure. This hurried policy environment (created by a ministerial demand for new powers) is also evident on two other occasions during policy development (in both cases diverging from 'standard procedure'). First, the timeline in Figure 7.1 shows that the departmental Instruction to Parliamentary Counsel were submitted on 17 October 2006, ... marked a third stage of policy development where legal actors begin to shape the policy into its statutory format. However, this was also the final date that the Home Office received responses to its consultation (Green) paper. The combination of these events suggests that the process of consultation became largely (or even wholly) inconsequential to policy development, as the instructions to Parliamentary Counsel were already drafted by the bill-team lawyers (signifying policy determination and intention to legislate) before the consultation period was complete. One simple explanation, offered by a senior official in the Home Office, was that the Green Paper was *less* about consultation and more akin to a White Paper that was announcing the government's intention for new powers:

> Well yes, we've got very slack in our definitions of white and green papers. . . . You could have described the Green Paper as a White Paper as well. . . . It used to be [more distinct], I can't remember the last time I've actually seen a governmental process where you have first a green paper and then you have a white paper. I just don't think it happens, because things are turning over so much more quickly, there just isn't time.

There is a real issue that arises from the lack of time given for the analysis of the responses to consultation and the consequent inability for such responses to have any impact at all on policy decision-making. As Jordan (1977: 30) remarked: 'What are Green or White but seldom Red (read)? The answer is, of course, governmental publications.' This might also be true of *responses to* government publications. The interviewees' disclosures about the time pressures involved in the decision-making process in respect of the SCPO and the lack of time allocated to incorporate feedback into the development of policy raise serious issues about the utility and purpose of the consultation process. For example, two interviewees (a minister and a Permanent Secretary) conceded that the purpose of consultation is not necessarily to receive input from the wider policy-making community on new law, but rather to identify any potential opposition that might impede the bill in parliament. As one Permanent Secretary described:

> If ministers wanted to pursue [a new idea], the next stage would then be to put out some kind of consultative document – fly a flag and see who shoots at it.

Similarly, the minister believed that the importance of consultation was less about enhancing or improving newly proposed law and policy, and more to identify 'what the reaction is going to be – who we think will support this and who we think will oppose it – and how are we going to handle that'. Therefore, one interviewee argued that a proper consultation process that allows genuine input into new policy would be most effective if it occurred *early* and outside the public domain:

> [O]nce something is made public, once it is in a bill, there is always – the politics comes into play and ministers don't like to back down basically. You know, it becomes just that much harder to try and influence something once it is, sort of, out there. So yes, it is important, as early as possible to be having those conversations with policy-makers. (Senior director)

The second anomaly indicating a hastened process in the case of the Serious Crime Bill 2006–2007 is that clearance was given by the Legislative Programme Committee several months after drafting had begun (as Figure 7.1 shows, this committee clearance was on 10 January 2007). This is despite the fact that one Permanent Secretary stated:

> You are not allowed to get parliamentary draftsmen working until you have got the sign off from the Legislation Committee. So it is quite late in the process that you are really sitting down to the hard work of trying to think how we would define it.

However, six days later, on 16 January 2007, the Serious Crime Bill 2006–2007 was introduced into the House of Lords. Clearly, most of the 'hard work' on defining policy had begun much earlier than the stage of Legislative Programme Committee approval.

Finally, the reasons interviewees gave for starting the Bill in the House of Lords rather than the House of Commons are of interest. Two reasons were given by those interviewed: one strategic and one practical. First, the House of Lords was perceived to be more rigorous in its critique and more prone to making legal amendments. Therefore, one official stated that it was preferred to begin proceedings in the Lords, especially given that amendments were expected as policy development was ongoing:

> We knew that the Lords weren't necessarily going to give it an easy ride. So actually, it wasn't necessarily a bad thing to let them have first crack at it. (Bill-team official, Home Office)

Second, one minister contended that it was actually less strategic and more to do with scheduling the parliamentary timetable:

> No, as far as I remember, it was purely practicalities. There were so many coming one way, from the Commons to the Lords, that something had to start the other way around . . . there were so many stacked up, again a bit like a sort of air traffic control, so many coming that way [Commons to Lords] that at least a few had to come that way [Lords to Commons].

The stages of policy development are less clearly defined, less strictly followed, and potentially contingent upon external demands (political and/or parliamentary), especially when compared to the later (more formal and ritualistic) stages of law-making, namely, the parliamentary process (as outlined in Chapter 4, Section 4.2.2: first reading, second reading, committee, report, and third reading; see also Figure A.1 in Appendix 'B'). However, there are several key events that set the parameters for the procedures involved in policy development.

In tracing the genesis of the SCPO, it is apparent that there were two points in time which mark the beginning and end of the early gestation period of policy-making: starting with the initial political support for an idea (during stock-take meeting at Number 10 about new powers) and ending with the introduction of the Bill into parliament. These two points demarcate the complete time period allocated to policy-makers to formulate new and innovative responses for the Bill, which was over approximately 10.5 months. Moreover, the timeline and account presented above exhibit three key stages of policy development during this period:

1. Development of initial ideas (ideation and policy direction);
2. Further development of policy content by the bill-team;
3. Final drafting of policy into clauses for the Bill.

In addition, at each of these three stages, different actors were involved (principally politicians, officials, and lawyers, respectively). This involvement of many and different actors at each stage of development meant that the time each actor was allocated to complete their duties was further shortened. While there was clearly some overlap, the time period at each stage was roughly equivalent: 4 months to develop the idea and strategic direction, from the meeting at Number 10 in March to formation of the bill-team in July; 3.5 months for development from the bill-team, from July to 17 October when Instructions to Parliamentary Counsel were submitted; and a further 3.5 months to draft the clauses of the Bill before parliament, from 17 October to 16 January when the Bill was introduced into parliament. This corresponds with the testimony given by policy-makers that policy development surrounding the SCPO occurred over a relatively short period of time, and there was pressure to innovate driven by the demand from Number 10 for new powers. In Chapter 8, it is argued that these time constraints on innovation play an essential role in development and can compel policy-makers to engage in transfer because it is expedient to do so. The next section illustrates how policy transfer occurred throughout these stages of policy development in the creation of the SCPO, from a transfer of ideas through to the transfer of actual statutory instruments and provisions.

7.2 The preventive order model and transfer

The policy transfer framework developed in Chapter 4 proposed that in determining *What is Transferred*, 'policy' is a concept that encompasses goals, content, instruments, programmes, institutions, ideologies, ideas, attitudes, cultural values, or negative lessons (see particularly Section 4.3.1). Three of these differing conceptions of policy correspond with the three stages of policy development distinguished in Section 7.1 – *ideation* (setting the policy direction), *policy content* (bill-team development), and *policy instruments* (drafting statutory provisions). These three aspects of policy development are examined in Sections 7.2.3, 7.2.4, and 7.2.5 (respectively), to reveal any specific evidence of *direct* transfer that occurred in the development of the SCPO. Supplementing this are two initial subsections that provide responses from interviewees about the recognition and general development of the family of preventive orders (Section 7.2.1) and indirect forms of transfer in the policy-making process (Section 7.2.2).

7.2.1 Recognition of the family of preventive orders and the prominence of the ASBO

The legislative analysis in Chapter 6 has clearly demonstrated the similarity of a large body of preventive orders. However, the awareness by policy-makers of this family of preventive orders was important to examine, as it provides an essential indication of their intentions to foster a broader structure for preventive justice. Several policy-makers emphasised the differences between the SCPO and preceding orders, rather than seeing them as part of the same family. While they were aware of other orders, particularly the Control Order and the ASBO, a number of interviewees (1, 7, 10, 11, and 12) strongly expressed their dissimilarity, and resolutely emphasised the innovative nature of the SCPO. For example, one interviewee argued that the ASBO had a broader reach and involved judicial discretion:

> I think there is a difference between the sort of generality of the ASBO and the targeted nature of some of the others; that is quite a big difference. And the problem about ASBOs is that it gave the court far too much discretion. That was slightly before my time, when I became [Director] all of that stuff was just coming in. (Senior director)

Other interviewees emphasised the divergence in approach of the orders or the specific provisions of the orders. For example, a Home Office official differentiated between the SCPO and Control Order on the basis that they were not motivated by the same goal of avoiding the admissibility of intelligence evidence:

> We talked a little bit with the Control Order people, although in reality the terrorism side see their orders as really quite different, not least because we never had any intention of using information that we wouldn't share in open court in our orders.

In addition, one minister distinguished between Control Orders and other orders because they were imposed by executive rather than judicial order:

> One of the other differences between the Control Order and other orders, say like the ASBO, was that it was an executive decision to put the order on, the Control Order, whereas the courts decided based on proportionality principles for the Serious Crime Prevention Order and ASBO. So I can see that they're [control orders] a slightly more contentious order in that respect.

However, the same minister admitted an intention at the time to downplay the similarity between orders so as to distance newer orders from the perceived failures of previous ones such as the Control Order: 'I think that people can't get through the contention around Control Orders to look at the success of some of these prevention orders in other areas.'

Moreover, the minister explained how the policy intention behind the creation of different orders can be distinct:

> I would certainly hesitate because we were never great fans of Control Orders. We always saw them as something that we needed in response to Belmarsh. We always thought it was terribly unsatisfactory . . . so whereas ASBOs and SCPOs were positive developments of policy on our part, the Control Orders were simply . . . a more pragmatic response to the way the law had developed, rather than a positive response from us to try and deal with on the one level anti-social behaviour and on the other serious and organised crime.

The author's suggestion that there might be a family of preventive orders caused some of the early decision-makers to express frustration and confusion (particularly those at SOCA). They believed that their policy ideas were indisputably original and not associated with other domestic policies such as terrorism and anti-social behaviour. These ideas were argued to have evolved from within the field of organised crime control: '[W]e all felt that we lacked the ability [to respond], especially to those who facilitated organised crime' (senior policy staffer, SOCA). This confusion about the family of orders was expressed by one interviewee from senior management at SOCA:

> It wasn't intended to be a Super-ASBO; it was intended to be a preventative order. I guess you could say well ASBOs are intended to be that as well, as is a control order . . . and yes it is a control order, but it is against serious organised crime that is causing harm, rather than someone who is just a nuisance on the street and in effect it is just another way of getting an injunction against them.

While the legislative analysis in Chapter 6 has clearly demonstrated the connections between different preventive orders, it is important to consider the possibility that senior decision-makers may have drawn inspiration from elsewhere. That is, what was intended at the level of initial abstract policy ideas might become more familiar when shaped into final statutory form. This policy evolution and the point at which direct transfer occurred in developing the SCPO are examined in Sections 7.2.3 to 7.2.5.

However, one minister (different to those quoted above) did acknowledge the broader family of orders – expressing a need to scrutinise the principle behind this new model – as currently there are different levels of success and attention achieved by the various orders:

I mean it's a debate isn't it? There is a real debate to be had about these orders. Certainly, you can see it from Serious Crime Prevention Orders and Anti-Social Behaviour Orders, the use of civil orders has been something that we've used, you know, and it's been a debate about how useful they are. I mean, we are interested in them, if you want to look at an example that has been fantastically successful, nobody disputes Football Banning Orders. . . . I think now we are at the stage of trying to see how we make existing orders more effective. (Minister, Home Office)

In addition, the conception of a family of preventive orders was publicly acknowledged on a number of occasions during policy- and law-making surrounding the SCPO (particularly at the parliamentary stages). For example, it was observed in the House of Commons library research paper that the family was growing:

> Part 1 of the Bill seeks to add a new type of civil order – a serious crime prevention order (SCPO) – to the growing list of civil orders, including anti-social behaviour orders (ASBOs) and control orders, available for use in relation to the prevention of crime or anti-social behaviour. (Peck et al. 2007: 3)

Similarly, the Select Committee on the Constitution (2007: 3–5) recognised the extent of the family of preventive orders:

> The statute book now contains a growing number of examples of a different model: powers enabling individuals or public authorities to seek civil orders from a variety of courts to prohibit undesirable behaviour, backed by criminal sanctions if the subject of the order breaches the order. . . . ASBOs and other types of control order that now exist on the statute book generally deal with small-scale anti-social behaviour. . . . SCPOs will have a much wider reach. The constraints imposed by an SCPO may be wide and deep and are capable of having a considerable impact on third parties.

Furthermore, the Joint Committee on Human Rights (2007: 6) found the dominance of the ASBO in formulating the SCPO:

> The [Serious Crime] Bill creates a new type of civil order, 'serious crime prevention orders' (hereafter 'SCPOs'), modelled on anti-social behaviour orders (ASBOs), empowering courts to impose a wide range of prohibitions or requirements in order to prevent harm from serious crime.

Despite the above responses from several early key decision-makers who did not recognise the family of preventive orders, many different actors interviewed did identify the influence of preceding orders, particularly the ASBO. In particular, the vast majority of interviewees believed that the ASBO had set a solid benchmark that guided new developments. As one interviewee from the lobby group Liberty stated, the SCPO was a 'hybrid of control orders and ASBOs', and 'so we trace it back to the ASBO, and then from the ASBO all of these other orders have flowed'. Moreover, evidence of the influence of the ASBO was found in accounts by different groups of actors involved in development (politicians, officials, legal advisors, and directors). It is important to briefly delineate these overlapping accounts from diverse actors.

One minister stated that the preventive order model was 'rooted in the development of, and we would say relative success of, ASBOs. . . . I think it would be fair to say that the ultimate development of all the policy in the area grew out of the order concept around ASBOs'. Similarly, one member of the bill-team explained how the widespread knowledge about the ASBO created an impetus for the idea to spread:

> Anti-Social Behaviour Orders seem to somehow have kind of opened some kind of flood gates and now everyone is jumping on the civil order bandwagon.

Another director who was consulted directly by the Prime Minister and policy officials at Number 10 stated:

> I think fundamentally they have some core qualities that are very similar, and the ASBO was the start of it. And of course once it got beyond the initial ASBO, the people who got the first few . . . a number of agencies and forces and government got a sense this is a way we can get justice.

A departmental lawyer also maintained that '[t]he ASBO is definitely seen as a bit of the trailblazer I suppose, and then, I guess once you have got one why not have more?'. Finally, one Permanent Secretary also clearly stated that these orders were part of a family of new penalties:

> And that is the same issue of effectively putting them under curfew in terms of Control Orders on terrorism. They're all in the same family

of thinking about penalties that go beyond what we might more traditionally think of as penalties, which is anything from a fine to a prison sentence.

Accordingly, a different Permanent Secretary also took the view that the ASBO model had such prominence, even influencing the development of the Control Order when there was pressure to come up with a prompt response following the Belmarsh ruling:[8]

> Control Orders obviously emerged completely differently. They emerged from the realisation that with the way that the law had developed, particularly the Human Rights Act, you can no longer detain and expel foreigners who you didn't want. And that was overruled, you know, we were told we couldn't do that, so the question was 'so what the hell are we going to do then?' And Control Orders, yes they took elements out of the ASBO, but it was a must at that stage, it was a different set of – I mean, here we had a dozen, 20, people in Belmarsh who we didn't want to let out, and we were going to have to let them out.

While some policy-makers interviewed seemed to be aware of the broader family of preventive orders, many still perceived them as *sui generis*. Indeed, several key decision-makers found it difficult to accept the extent of the similarity between the SCPO and other orders, focusing rather on the substantive points of difference (not least the fact that different orders were developed in relation to distinct areas of crime control policy). However, all 21 interviewees acknowledged that one order, the ASBO, had influenced the development of the SCPO to a greater or lesser extent. It is the extent of influence of existing orders that forms the next four subsections.

7.2.2 Indirect transfer: Iteration, osmosis, and employee transfer

Many interviewees (1, 2, 3, 4, 9, 14, 15, 16, 18, 19, and 20) portrayed the fluid nature and interactions of actors during policy development and the overlapping organisational structure of the Home Office, as introducing more *indirect* forms of transfer. That is, policy transfer was not viewed as uncommon by policy-makers; rather it was perceived as an essential part of what many described as a process of 'iteration' (interviewees 1, 3, 4, 15, and 19). Policy development was described as occurring through a process of iteration and interaction between key decision-makers. This led one Permanent Secretary to conclude:

> I think if you go on a quest for what was the moment when this was born, I don't think you'll find that, because the way policy making works is [through] interaction. . . . So what we have here is a quite strong political focus from the top on the problem of serious organised crime, the setting up of an agency to focus on that specifically, therefore a focus on: 'I wonder if we've got, we've got the organisation now, I wonder if that organisation has all the power it needs to deal with this problem?' And out of those discussions comes a proposition for these orders.

However, while these fluid interactions make the policy-making process complex, this does not mean that instances of policy transfer cannot be discerned. The precise origin of a given policy idea can conceivably come from a wide range of sources being motivated by politics (for example, party manifestos created while in opposition), social advocacy (for example, lobbying by interest groups), and the private sector (for example, consumer organisations). In some cases, policy might even be traced back to an individual's personal experience; for example, in an interview with one Home Secretary, Jack Straw,[9] it was found that the initial genesis of the ASBO was attributable, at least in part, to personal experience:

> Well, the original idea and the driver was me. Essentially it came from me as the Home Secretary. I'd had an experience as a victim of anti-social behaviour when I was a kid living on a council estate. So that has stuck in my memory because we were faced with bad behaviour by an anti-social neighbour. The police wouldn't do anything about it. In the end my mother took out a private prosecution and I was a witness in the case. It was all pretty unpleasant. So that was the driver.

Conversely, one Permanent Secretary claimed that the task of tracing the true origin of the SCPO, and who was responsible, was potentially impossible because the dynamic of policy-making involved a great deal of iteration between various individuals.

> I think you would find – we were just talking about this as well – whenever anybody looks back at a period and says 'well who's idea was this?', probably six or eight people claim it. Because they all think, because of the process I have described that they had the idea.

And it could just as easily have come from a senior police officer, or a senior civil servant, or not so senior, or from a political person, especially an advisor or minister, it could have come from Number 10 . . . but it wouldn't have come from them, what it would have come out of was the interaction of those people.

When interviewees were asked as to who conceived of the SCPO, several decision-makers believed they had been primarily responsible for its existence. The speed at which the iterative process occurred during the development of the SCPO had a considerable impact on the resultant confusion about who was responsible for the germ of the idea. As one bill-team member described it:

You go away and you think about it and you come back and say, 'well how about this as a possibility?'; 'Oh yes, that sounds like a good idea, go away a bit more and think about that'; [or] 'No, I don't like that idea', and so it goes on . . . in this instance [for the SCPO] it took like days or weeks, because it was all very quick.

Consequently, one official in the Home Office who played a central role in the development of the SCPO expressed genuine uncertainty: 'I mean, whose idea was it first between us and SOCA? I wouldn't really be able to say.'

It is during a process of iteration like this (and perhaps especially given that time was limited) that the opportunity to engage in transfer is increased. Accordingly, one Permanent Secretary suggested that the introduction of the ASBO not only marked a significant development in the control of anti-social behaviour, but it also created a strong model that would inevitably be drawn on during this iterative search for new policy solutions:

Once [the ASBO] had been shown to be effective legally, if not universally, in practice, it was inevitable that the Home Office, and politicians, should think about using similar measures in other areas, for example, serious crime and terrorism.

Similarly, a senior official in the Home Office explained how the successes in one area of crime policy become exemplars for potential transfer:

And once you've applied it in one set of circumstances, I think it's inevitable that people will think 'oh that's an interesting example, can we actually apply it to that sort of business that we're interested in?'

However, one Home Secretary also described this inevitability of transfer as resulting from a more gradual process of osmosis, or institutionalisation of policy:

> Because what would happen is, you say, why don't you do this . . . and then gradually what happens to these concepts is they sort of go into, as it were, the fabric of an institution like the Home Office.

This supports the theories of international diffusion that were discussed in Chapter 4, Section 4.3.2, which suggest that policy can become 'systematically conditioned' (Simmons et al. 2008: 7). Accordingly, another Permanent Secretary described transfer as an osmotic occurrence whereby the ASBO simply forged a new way of thinking about crime control:

> I don't want you to misunderstand this answer – I don't think it is as simple as somebody saying, 'ooh look we've got ASBOs, let's apply them to serious criminals', but I think it did create a new way of thinking about interventions and penalties, which undoubtedly influenced these orders [SCPOs], it undoubtedly did. . . . But you couldn't read it directly across, nobody said 'ooh we've got ASBOs now, well let's see if we can apply it to serious criminals'. But it became a way of thinking, didn't it.

While these decision-makers attest to osmotic processes of transfer inevitably occurring as a result of fluid iteration, these forms of indirect transfer are more difficult to trace in the case of the SCPO.

Finally, another form of indirect transfer that conceivably occurred was through employee transfer. As discussed in Chapter 4, Section 4.3.2, when developing a policy transfer framework, employee transfer is based on the theory of mimetic modelling between organisations (DiMaggio and Powell 1983: 151). A number of interviewees (1, 2, 13, 15, and 18) suggested that there would have been an opportunity for indirect forms of transfer to occur owing to the significant overlap of key decision-makers who simultaneously worked in a number of other areas of crime policy. For example, one minister described his role as spanning across a number of policy arenas where various preventive orders were developed:

> So certainly on the development of ASBOs side, on all the paraphernalia around serious and organised crime legislation, including the

proceeds of crime and the development of SOCA, and the development of Control Orders and SCPOs, those are all under my watch.

Moreover, indirect transfer could have resulted from the particular organisational structure and employee movement in the Home Office. One Permanent Secretary argued that the Home Office has a very 'networked structure' and tends to attract long-term careers where employees frequently move around the department, which he suggested meant that there was inevitably a baseline amount of transfer occurring:

> It is quite a tight-knit group . . . [one senior civil servant] had 30 years' experience in the Home Office in criminal justice, and so you get a lot of cross transfer [through] kicking ideas around inside the Home Office, and indeed within the Home Office legal team . . . and so they would be kicking this stuff around, and that is where you would get a lot of 'well you ought to have a look at what happens in this area or that area' . . . and these were all people who know each other extremely well. . . . It is a very networked structure.

This role of departmental legal actors in transfer is particularly important for several reasons. First, as the legal department constitutes a relatively small group in the Home Office,[10] those within it might be more prone to this 'kicking ideas around', or transfer:

> Obviously the legal department is relatively small, and well if you think how big the Home Office is, you know, thousands of people, the legal department is like 60 lawyers, that's it. (Legal advisor, Home Office)

As the legal department continued to work on the particular policy from development to final drafting, this group of individuals was also perceived to have a powerful position in the law-making process. For example, the perceived authoritative position of legal actors led one interviewee from SOCA to consider the bill-team merely as 'the gateway through to the lawyers'.

In addition, the small size of the legal department means that legal actors in the Home Office will work on a greater number of criminal justice bills, when compared to other departmental officials. For example, one senior official who was central to the development of the SCPO (having written the White Paper, Green Paper, and set the policy direction) explained that Home Office officials have a compartmental-ised knowledge of crime policy:

> It is an excellent question, and I think on the policy side it is very bad, there tends to be almost total ignorance of what is going on in other areas. I mean, I am aware of these, but I am not an expert myself on how ASBOs work or how football banning orders . . . and in reality, it is the lawyers who tend to put it together because they are often crafting the same sort of instructions to counsel and they will learn a lot, and procedures that are used in one will tend to be used in the other.

In support of these propositions, the departmental lawyer on the bill-team for the SCPO explained that she had also been involved in devel-oping other criminal justice legislation and preventive orders. When asked if she worked on many other crime bills previous to this one, she replied: 'Yes, quite a few. I worked, the first one I worked on was the Criminal Justice Act 2003. . . . I was also doing Control Orders a bit.' The small size of the legal department meant that legal actors could more easily exchange knowledge and experience – the bill-team lawyer again stated with clarity:

> There is no doubt that when I was developing the [SCPO] policy, I went over to the desk of my colleague who did anti-social behaviour orders and I had a chat with her about what things they had thought about and what issues came up, and so on.

In the case of the SCPO, there was even evidence that employee transfer could have occurred by individuals moving across departments:

> The policy drive is different, because it comes from different divisions within the Home Office, but the lawyers are very similar, the lawyers are the same people. The senior lawyer at SOCA came from the Home Office, and he was involved in quite a lot of the crime legislation before he was with us. (Senior management, SOCA)

This role of legal actors as agents of transfer is clearly important, as given the relatively small pool of legal staff working inside the Home Office, their influence is inevitable across different areas of policy. The role of these legal actors in more direct transfer is discussed further, particularly in Section 7.2.5.

7.2.3 Direct transfer of ideas

As shown in the timeline in Figure 7.1, there were a number of meetings and correspondence (formal and informal) between SOCA, the Home Office, and Number 10 to generate new ideas for potential powers to be given in the Serious Crime Bill 2006–2007. It was shown that one meeting in particular brought actors from all of these bodies together, which according to many interviewees (1, 3, 4, 5, 7, 20, and 21) set the first definitive policy direction for the SCPO. However, the findings below from interviewees at the top of the hierarchy of decision-making present some mixed responses about the transfer of policy ideas. These responses do not vary in relation to whether a transfer of ideas occurred, but rather *from where* the idea for the SCPO was transferred.

Interviewees expressed a number of different views about the source of transfer at the level of ideas. There was a strong view by several decision-makers that there was a specific intention to spread the 'ASBO model', particularly emanating from the Prime Minister who saw it as 'one of the great successes':

> Different Home Secretaries would have had different views on these things. Tony [Blair] was clearly of the view that ASBOs were something that had worked, and that the model could be applied elsewhere. (Staffer, Number 10)

Two Home Secretaries who were interviewed also expressed a similar view. For example, when the author asked one Home Secretary whether he thought it was serendipitous that this model had spread, he responded:

> No, no, no, far from that, it was that it became clear that this kind of order was filling a very important gap in the criminal law . . . and that therefore, the ASBO example could be more widely used.

Another Home Secretary agreed that transfer of the ASBO was behind the spread of this model that led to the use of the SCPO against serious crime:

> Now the consequence of the civil orders for ASBOs, antisocial behaviour orders, led us to think well are there other areas that are more serious where we can get into this, where peripheral activity, where precluding people from being able to do something would protect us?

In addition, a minister from the Home Office explained how the ASBO model became indicative of seriousness and success, and was transferred to serious crime control as an expression of commitment:

> We thought the success of ASBOs as a preventative measure, that this should be at least a parallel to show how serious we were about serious and organised crime. So the SCPO is always figured as one of the central pieces of such legislation.

Other interviewees (1, 3 6, 8, 15, and 19) also mentioned the influence of other preventive orders on the development of the SCPO. One interviewee from SOCA stated:

> The SCPOs start really with the Prime Minister (a) wanting to give us and others the tools we need to do the job; and (b) keen on building on the precedent of the Control Orders and the CT [Counter-Terrorism] context . . . and it's in one of the conversations we're having down at Number 10 and in the Cabinet about this, with Charles Clarke, and we come upon the idea of defining these as preventative in nature.

Further findings about this ideology of prevention in the minds of decision-makers are presented in Section 7.3. However, it is important to note here that at the level of concept generation, each addition to the preventive order model contributed to redefining a new logic:

> The simplest example of this was stopping football hooligans going to football matches. There was a whole sort of developing thinking, which said, if you want you can put them into prison, but actually the best way of getting at football hooligans is to stop them from going to the match and really grounding them, that will really get them. (Permanent Secretary, Home Office)

There is also evidence that in developing the SCPO, the transfer of ideas came from outside the domestic policy sphere – distinct from similar orders like the ASBO. One decision-maker from SOCA, who attended the stock-take meeting at Number 10, was asked whether this meeting marked the beginning of the idea for the SCPO. He initially responded by stating that, at the level of policy ideas, it is difficult to precisely indicate a point in time, or identify one source of transfer:

> Oh, God yeah! It was certainly one of the sorts of things being floated around. . . . I mean that's, you know, the criminal lifestyle stuff that

came in, you know, it's a real development. There isn't any one time, I should think, where you can say and just suddenly – I mean ministers may have decided now you'll get a day for it, but these sorts of suggestions were floating around in the ether with people when they were talking about other things . . . you know, 'well what about it? What about orders stopping people doing it?' And how you might do it and how you might describe it. These ideas were going around for a very long time.

However, after further deliberation, this same interviewee claimed that the idea had its roots in international transfer from Japan:

Author: Can you pinpoint a time when you remember the discussion beginning about this new order?

Interviewee: [laughing]

Author: I know it is probably too difficult to remember.

Interviewee: No, it is not, it is framed in my memory because what had happened was . . . on a visit to Japan some years ago. . . . [W]e were talking with the Japanese police . . . and while we were out there we were discussing some legislation that the Japanese were putting into place through their parliament, because until that time the Japanese had no offence of conspiracy . . . and one of the things that I said was, 'Well how do you deal with organised crime? How do you deal with these issues?' And one of the things that they talked about, which I thought was really fascinating, was the Yakuza there, the Japanese organised crime [group], they set themselves up as friendly societies, like the old Ancient Order of Foresters and Buffaloes and all the rest of it. . . . So what the Japanese police did is that they started to serve notices on them, saying 'we know that you have done this, this is a civil matter but if you do this again and breach this notice, then that is a criminal matter because it was a statutory order that had been given to stop the activity'.

This interviewee went on to explain that this trip to Japan was during the period when the Japanese parliament was considering its first bill to create an offence of conspiracy.[11] According to Coulson (2006: 869), 'Japan's first bill to criminalize conspiracy was introduced in 2003 in Japan's 156th Diet session'. This suggests that the transfer of ideas (from an international origin) which led to the SCPO may have begun as early as 2003. In addition, the analysis of documentation containing the internal consultation responses also shows that one stakeholder drew policy-makers' attention to the anti-mafia laws that exist in Italy, which include similar civil restrictions on associations, movement, travel, and 'involvement in certain business activities' (barrister, response to Green Paper, internal policy document).[12] Moreover, as already discussed in earlier chapters, civil RICO powers were being considered by policy-makers at an early stage, and were mentioned in the White Paper in 2004 (see particularly Chapters 2 and 4). Therefore, international transfer may also have inspired the development of the SCPO at the level of ideation (when considering new powers). Correspondingly, the official who wrote the White Paper and attended the meeting at Number 10 in Spring 2006 (where he was charged to translate these policy ideas into policy direction for the bill-team for further development of the policy content) suggested that international transfer was most influential on ideation:

> And to be honest, although it ends up probably looking a fair bit like those other orders, I suppose on the policy side my gaze was really much more on abroad, on the States [US], on a different kind of . . . we sort of tried to start from first principles on how we would like to control people civilly, and then it gets crafted in a way that actually ends up looking like some of these other orders.

Thus at the level of ideation, it appears that policy may not have been simply transferred from one location. The inspiration for the SCPO seems to have come from a number of separate sources, both domestic and international. Nonetheless, it is clear that the mechanism of transfer, while not simply attributable to one origin, was the principal method used for developing the policy idea. This process of transfer was certainly not viewed as uncommon by those interviewed, as one interviewee from Number 10 clearly stated:

> There was a frame of mind looking for new measures, looking if you can apply measures that worked in one area, to apply in other areas in a creative way.

One Permanent Secretary also explained that it was a method commonly employed by civil servants to resist change: '[U]sually one would run to Australia or Canada – somebody must have tried this out – and then you can tell the minister that it doesn't work.' Though, another interviewee from Number 10 – reflecting on how the civil service functioned – indicated that transfer might be a more recent phenomenon (at least international transfer) that began to enhance the search for policy options, instead of always 'reinventing the wheel':

> They'd very rarely look at what's happened elsewhere and then try and draw policy from that, certainly when we came into government. Now I think there's more of a tendency for people to go and look at Sweden and the education models and say 'oh let's try and draw some ideas from that'. Even when I was in China a few years ago talking to the Communist Party School, the head of it told me he'd been sent off to Sweden to study the educational system to see if it could apply to China. . . . But now, there is a bit more – in Britain anyway, [and] I think actually probably across Europe – more actually going and looking elsewhere. Certainly when we came to government in 1997, if you asked the department to come up with policy they wouldn't really think about looking at other countries, they'd simply try and invent *ab initio* within the country.

The following section turns its focus on this civil service machinery and whether there is any evidence that transfer occurred, especially by the bill-team when developing the content of the SCPO.

7.2.4 Direct transfer by the bill-team and home office officials

Following the discussions with senior decision-makers in the Home Office, SOCA, and at Number 10, the duty to further develop the idea behind the SCPO was allocated to more junior officials in the Home Office, led primarily by the bill-team. Before this decision was made, two interviewees from the Home Office (an official and a legal advisor) worked together on setting the overall policy direction, and they in turn gave these instructions to the bill-team. The legal advisor involved in this final policy direction contended that ministers were not explicit about the use of civil preventive orders:

> I am not sure, I don't know if it is fair to say that ministers have ever said, you know, we want a civil order to tackle serious organised crime. It is a bit more iterative than that, it is more likely that ministers would have said something a bit more generic perhaps I suppose you know like: '[Y]ou need to tackle these problems, how are we going to go about it?'

Similarly, the official stated that the discussions with senior decision-makers did not produce specific direction about the kinds of powers that were desired:

> Well we knew the Prime Minister was interested in new powers and that there had been – there was a series of precedents of civil orders. But we had no particular steer in what kind of new powers he might want, that really was left, it was left for us to come up with.

Once this direction was set, the responsibility for further development was given to the bill-team. The policy official from the bill-team who worked directly on the SCPO portrayed her or his role:

> I would probably describe my role as – I was given a brief I suppose, which was, I was given the concept of a preventive civil order. I was given the kind of broad outline. My role was, I suppose, translating that into reality. So, working with SOCA, the police and other government departments as appropriate.

At this stage, this bill-team member also described the SCPO as quite underdeveloped: 'I think it's fair to say that it was probably not much more than a concept: a concept with a bit of flesh on the bones but not much.' The process of fleshing out the policy content is an intricate stage of development: '[T]here's a huge amount of detail about the appeals process, how it goes into the courts legally, and all these sorts of provisions' (senior official, Home Office). As shown in the legislative analysis in Chapter 6, there was an expansive trend seen in many provisions, and this suggests that bill-team actors played a leading role in this incremental expansion. A member of Parliamentary Counsel interviewed confirmed that these decisions (about provisions) do come from departments – being a policy decision – rather than from the drafters themselves. For example, in setting the penalty for breach, this drafter stated:

> In terms of penalty, this would be something the department would settle on . . . if we saw a penalty that looked out of line with what we knew to be what was right, you know what was common in that field, it might be something we would say, 'well are you sure it should be five years rather than two years', or the other way around. But yeah, the department would be the ones to set the provision . . . [though] ultimately parliament are the ones who will sign off on that. (Drafter, Office of the Parliamentary Counsel)

In addition, the policy lead on the bill-team explained how there was direct transfer at this stage of policy development, from the ASBO and other civil orders: '[M]y role was to translate the concept of something which is a preventive order along the same sorts of lines in terms of the theory of an ASBO.' This interviewee continued to explain how other officials who had worked on other preventive orders were also sought out for advice: '[W]e went and spoke to the policy leads on football banning orders and spoke to the policy leads on ASBOs . . . yes we talked to them, yes we learned what we could from them, but there was a lot of stuff that we had to take further.'

In addition, this bill-team official postulated that 'the person who did the most work and the person who is most responsible for this being a success was [*name redacted*, bill-team lawyer]'. The lawyer on the bill-team had a crucial role in policy development, as it is a role which merges the policy ideas into a workable statutory instrument, and mediates between various policy-makers:

> As for bill work, our main role, in terms of the policy, is the lawyer kind of sits in the middle if you like between, on the one hand the parliamentary draftsman, so it is [*name redacted*] who drafted this Bill, so [*name redacted*] is responsible for actually putting pen to paper and drafting the words that go into the bill; then, on the other side, is the policy team, so in this case that was [*name redacted*]. So you are like the go-between I suppose is the best way of describing it, effectively translating sometimes quite abstract policy ideas, sometimes more though, it depends, into something that the draftsman can actually turn into statutory language effectively. So I guess part of our role is to tease out, as much as we can, the detail of the policy if you like. (Bill-team lawyer, Home Office)[13]

This bill-team lawyer described in detail how provisions from earlier orders were directly transferred to create the final form of the SCPO:

> What happens is that – I mean, the way that the policy process tends to work, and this is definitely how it happened for Serious Crime Prevention Orders, is somebody comes to me and says, 'I want you to create a Serious Crime Prevention Order', well they don't even say that, they say 'we want a civil order', you know, we don't even have a name for it at that stage; 'we want a civil order to tackle the Mr Bigs of this world'. 'Fair enough', I say, 'okay I will go and have a think about that and come back to you'. Well immediately what I'm thinking is,

'oh, a civil order, well antisocial behaviour orders are civil orders, drinking banning orders are civil orders, football banning orders . . .', and so on. You know, I whipped out my Archibald and I start looking at them, and what the provisions are. And unsurprisingly I say, 'well we can borrow that, and we can borrow this, and we can borrow that and the other'. A lot of legislation is about the precedents that you can lay your hands on and then adapting them to your particular circumstances. So no, it is not a coincidence that they all look the same. I am sure every person that has made one of these orders will have looked at their predecessors work and adapted it.

This concept of 'policy precedents' is important to highlight, and is discussed further below. Moreover, it is again apparent that there is a predominant role of legal actors in transfer, especially when it comes to drafting the specific provisions for a new order. This direct legal transfer requires further examination.

7.2.5 Direct legal transfer

Several senior decision-makers acknowledged the central role played by legal actors in developing the preventive order model. One Permanent Secretary stated that while there was interplay between political and legal actors, it was the legal actors who gave the policy its final shape:

And now, who came up with this neat idea of switching into the civil courts? Which of course it was the lawyers at the Home Office. I mean, under political encouragement. The politicians wanted to find something new, the lawyers came up with it.

Accordingly, one senior decision-maker from SOCA explained how this interaction occurred in developing the SCPO:

There's two different things going on here. There are the people with the policy drive on it, which is the Home Office division and us [SOCA] in this case . . . with me particularly in this case, I am pushing this thing. And then there's the lawyers who want, who have this sort of, you know, let's not reinvent the wheel if we've already got a wheel that runs. So they go away and say, 'well you know we done this thing in the legislation before so let's pull those clauses along and just turn them around for this one'.

The drafter from Parliamentary Counsel argued that this relationship with policy decision-makers is fundamental as it is not the role of a drafter to develop policy, but rather to take direction:

> If ultimately they want something that is new, so long as it's deliverable and makes legal sense then we can do it. We just need to know that we're sure that that's really what they want. That's how that iterative process works.

Despite this, this drafter went on to explain that a distinction can be made here between macro and micro policy development:

> It depends what we're talking about. Sometimes I sort of think of it as macro–micro policy. The macro policy is, you know, 'we want to have serious crime prevention orders there to deal with serious crime [and that] they're preventative orders'. There's that level. And at that level, we clearly have no input into that. That's pure policy. Ministers decide that. I mean where we tend to get involved, and I don't know whether you want to characterise it as policy, or just the detail of implementation. It's the micro detail of implementing what the minister's policy is.

Therefore, depending on what is classified as policy, the eventual shape (the actual content or manifestation) of policy is determined in large part through the decisions made by legal actors. If the 'pure policy' (macro) was transferred from ideas taken from abroad (inspired by RICO from the US, or anti-organised crime laws from Italy or Japan), there was also a second (micro) level of transfer that occurred domestically in constructing the specific provisions of the act.

Again, at the micro-policy level of drafting, the process of transfer was assumed by interviewees as standard procedure. As the drafter from Parliamentary Counsel explained:

> When we are asked to produce something, like the serious crime prevention orders or whatever it is, then obviously we'll have a look at what the precedents are and take account of them.

This influence of precedents was explained by one senior decision-maker as being caused by two perceived advantages: first, there is a benefit of efficiency, 'they've already got the clauses there nicely written'; and second, there is a benefit in maintaining a certain level of consistency in the statute book 'to keep, as best you can, the legislation clean'. While drafters might believe that it is not their role to make policy, they clearly shape the ultimate substance of policy through a process of transferring statutory provisions.

Moreover, the Instructions to Parliamentary Counsel are also written by another legal actor, the departmental lawyer. In the case of the SCPO, the instructions given to drafters referred specifically to the provisions of existing preventive orders. The bill-team lawyer explained the production of these instructions as a process of 'cherry-picking' to develop the SCPO:

> I seem to remember the instructions on serious crime prevention orders said to the draftsman, 'look, there are these orders that are already out there that are very like what we want to achieve', and sort of cherry-picking, you know, it literally would say 'we don't want something like Section blah' of the Crime and Disorder Act.

An analysis of instructions to counsel (contained in an internal policy document obtained from the Home Office) to create the SCPO corroborates this process of cherry-picking.[14] In fact, these instructions consist almost entirely of a detailed comparison of the provisions (and relevant case law) of many of the preventive orders analysed in Chapter 6. Specifically, six orders were compared in the instructions: the ASBO, Football Banning Order, Travel Restriction Order, Sexual Offences Prevention Order, Financial Reporting Order, and Control Order. Interestingly, the Control Order was only mentioned once by way of comparison, to provide a reason for *not* having a definitive list of the types of conditions that the SCPO could impose. It was suggested that because the Control Order included such a list, this limited its ability to be used effectively on a number of occasions.[15] While most of these orders were mentioned only a few times, once again the ASBO was clearly dominant; referred to over 30 times in the instructions, and it was systematically assessed (provision by provision) to see which provisions could be transferred and which were not appropriate or relevant. For example, a detailed comparison was made concerning whether legal aid was provided, regarding the standard of proof, whether interim orders should be used (interim SCPO), the age of individuals on whom the order can be imposed, and so on. That is to say, it was used as the basic template for creating the SCPO, whereby the introduction to these instructions stated the following:

The precedent that is closest to the provision requested [SCPO] is probably Chapter 1 of Part 1 of the Crime and Disorder Act 1998 . . . which makes provision for anti-social behaviour orders (ASBOs).

Therefore, while definitive proof of the transfer that occurred at the level of ideas is more difficult to verify, there is indisputable evidence of direct transfer from the ASBO at the stage of drafting. It can thus be said that the results thus far have demonstrated that policy transfer, during policy development, provides a strong explanation for the spread of the preventive order model across a number of distinct areas of crime policy. However, it is less clear whether the current family of preventive orders is solely a consequence of incremental transfer by officials and legal actors in the Home Office, or if the proliferation of this model was part of a broader policy objective to reconfigure the system around preventive justice. The findings from the discussions with key decision-makers about their broader intention to create a 'preventive justice system' are considered in the next section.

7.3   Intentions of decision-makers: The preventive order model

The findings presented above about the nature of policy transfer have already provided some indication as to whether, and to what extent, the SCPO was intended to contribute to a much broader preventive structure. Based on these findings, several propositions can be made about the decision-making that occurred during policy development:

1. There was a political demand for innovative powers, though limited direction was given to civil servants about the form that these powers should take.
2. There was limited time allocated for policy-makers to produce this innovative new power.
3. Decision-makers had different views about where the initial idea for the SCPO originated (though it seems that transfer was involved, be it international or domestic).
4. Indirect transfer might also have occurred (though osmosis of ideas is less easily proved).
5. Officials and legal actors in the Home Office actively sought to draw upon the model of other preventive orders, and particularly the ASBO.

It can be inferred that the development of the SCPO therefore fundamentally resulted from 'bottom-up' decision-making, whereby, under pressure to innovate, Home Office officials and legal actors resolved to draw upon existing models. This would support the thesis that the spread of the preventive order model has occurred as a result of incremental processes of policy transfer rather than by a grander political strategy. In addition, a number of interviewees (7, 9, 12, 14, 15, 17, 18, and 19) specifically described the policy and decision-making surrounding the spread of preventive orders as having occurred through incremental developments. For example, one member of Parliamentary Counsel described this gradual change:

> It's an incremental process . . . you started off with fairly small beginning, if you like, with some of these orders. And then, gradually their value was recognised, or the potential was recognised, as a sort of, as something that fell short of criminal prosecution and something that dealt with evidence.

Furthermore, one senior director argued that the incremental spread of this model was certainly not intended to create a separate path for achieving justice:

> They would do it measure by measure, so they would say, 'Would this power be useful? Or would that power be useful? What do you think about this?' They wouldn't say, 'now let's try and develop a parallel jurisdiction here because that would be helpful for us'.

Accordingly, decision-makers made it clear that there was no real debate on justice principles that might be affected by a new body of preventive measures:

> I don't actually recall it as a wider debate of principle, about where is this going to lead if you have now got such a set of civil orders? (Permanent Secretary, Home Office)

A Home Office lawyer also agreed that during policy development, decision-makers were far less concerned about the impact of new policy measures on broader principles of justice. Rather the focus was on the detail of the policy at hand, which in the case of preventive orders was 'how best to insulate our orders against a finding of being Article 6 criminal':

> It would be a mistake to imagine that I spend my days thinking in abstract terms about whether this is going to have some fundamental

impact on the criminal law as a whole, or so on. It is a bit more, it is a bit less . . . is a bit more boring than that really [laughing]. You know, it is a bit more like, 'oh, I don't want these orders to be criminal, what can I do to make sure that this doesn't happen?' It is a bit less abstract I suppose . . . rather than thinking, what might be the consequences?

One Permanent Secretary maintained that this marked a dramatic and problematic change to the civil service structure that occurred under New Labour to make the Home Office more fertile and less critical:

> It is an institutional failing that once you have got an idea that looks like it's going to work, you tend to focus on the upside and the British system is not very good at it nowadays – it used to be very good at it; and the great criticism in the old days, when the Labour government came in 1997, their criticism was that the [civil service] system was too passive and too critical. In other words, the Home Office would think up 100 good reasons why this won't work; and, you know, over the years what has happened is they've turned that on its head, so now the great criticism, post-Iraq and so on, is that public servants don't speak out enough. And you have [David] Cameron saying that he wants to restore the position of senior civil servants to be able to speak their mind.

In addition, one policy director from Liberty suggested that this lack of a principled approach might have actually permitted the spread of preventive orders:

> If they haven't taken a principled position on the use of civil orders in this way, then it means that there is then the potential for them to spread because they are making up their mind on a case-by-case basis.

While it seems that incremental policy developments can explain the spread of preventive orders, a number of interviewees indicated some possible broader intentions in seeking to reform criminal justice. These findings are presented in the next section.

7.3.1 Reforming criminal justice

There is no doubt that there was a strong governmental intention to reform the criminal justice system. Two interviewees from Number 10 recounted the same anecdote about their initial meeting at the Home

Office, to convey a certain message that they were getting from officials – that nothing could be done about crime rates:

> When we first came into government we had a seminar with the Home Office. They'd come over to brief us on crime and told us what would happen to crime, and they had a wonderful slideshow of figures of crime going up and up. And so Tony [Blair] said to them, 'why is crime going up?'[And they replied] 'Because the economy is growing so there is more stuff to steal, so people [criminally minded] will do better then.' So I asked them, 'what happens if you've got a recession?' And they said, 'oh crime will go up – more people will be poor and need to steal stuff'. (Staffer, Number 10)

One of these interviewees from Number 10 went on to say that they were not convinced of this reasoning that crime was inevitable: 'Tony and I were never persuaded . . . our view was that crime was manageable'. This did, however, cause great frustration to be felt by decision-makers, where it became a major challenge and political priority to reconfigure the criminal justice system for 21st-century crime. This agenda to reform what the Blair government considered to be an outdated criminal justice system was well documented and publicly declared:

> For eight years I've battered the criminal justice system to get it to change. And it was only when we started to introduce special measures for anti-social behaviour, we really made a difference. And I now understand why. The system itself is the problem. We are trying to fight 21st-century crime – anti-social behaviour, drug-dealing, binge-drinking, organised crime – with 19th-century methods, as if we still lived in the time of Dickens. (Tony Blair 2005: Labour Party Conference, Brighton)

This led to a particularly close period of policy collaboration between Number 10 and the Home Office:

> [R]ebalancing the criminal justice system was actually quite an unusual bit of policy-making because it was a really intense period, I actually decamped over to the Home Office for a bit. (Staffer, Number 10)

Accordingly, one Home Secretary described the nature of deliberation about reform during this intense period:

There was discussion about what we were to do in terms of bridging the gaps, filling the holes that existed in the system which had been designed for a different era, and for different challenges which obviously over the years had changed.

While it was clear that there was a desire to manage crime by refashioning (or rebalancing) criminal justice, there was far less coherence and direction about the type of justice reform desired. That is, although decision-makers aspired to fill the gaps with new crime control measures, there was no apparent intention to redefine justice. For example, one senior director interviewed expressed that it was difficult to pinpoint the broader intention behind a discernible body of new policy developments, which included the new body of preventive orders:

> We saw a huge expansion of this type of secondary criminal justice and I can't think of a good phrase to describe it, but all those orders. . . . It wasn't visible but there was certainly a broader agenda at foot. So you couldn't find it in a manifesto but you would detect the echo in lots of discussions.

The analysis of interview data suggests three potential motivations for creating preventive orders, which also reflect key aspects of the theoretical discussion produced in Chapter 3. The three broad areas of intent expressed by interviewees were as follows: (1) to subvert the criminal justice system (by creating shortcuts to punishment), (2) to supplement the criminal justice system (by 'filling the gaps'), and (3) to create earlier forms of preventive state intervention (by extending the law to deal with non-criminal harms). The evidence for these overlapping explanations of intent are presented in the next three subsections.

7.3.1.1 Intention to subvert the criminal justice system

There was evidence from interviewees that the dissatisfaction with the criminal justice system, expressed at the time by some senior decision-makers, might have fomented a desire to undermine the criminal process completely. One senior director explained how, at the time, it was widely understood by officials that their role was to search for new ways to get around the established norms of criminal justice:

> There was a huge frustration with the criminal justice processes, and courts, the sentences and all that. You would get lots of arguments going on about that. But then it was difficult to surface well actually

seems to be a coherence here, across a number of departments
t wanting to do, wanting to circumvent, these processes. And it
:oo consistent for it to be random, so it was there.

There was notable consensus among those interviewed that this intention to subvert established procedures of justice stemmed from the most
senior levels of decision-making. As one senior staffer from Number 10
stated: 'Tony was all about fast, rapid, let's-just-get-this-sorted justice.' In
addition, one Permanent Secretary explained that the political strategy
was to be more successfully punitive:

Blair had a strategy, all of the way through, which was he knew, he
thought that the system should be more effective and punitive than it
was. And he used each occasion, each scandal, each event as a chance
to push a little bit further in the direction that he wanted to go.

Similarly, one interviewee from senior management of SOCA stated that
this was reflected in his discussions with the Prime Minister about new
powers for SOCA:

The Prime Minister wanted to extend the law to make it easier to deal
with criminals. And being less fussed than the rest of us about, you
know, the proprieties of Article 6 stuff, and saying 'well why can't we
just, you know, if we're confident that they've done X, Y & Z, why can't
we just take them to court and get an order on them so that they're all
fined or put in prison or something?' Well, we said 'because you can't,
because it's not Article 6 compliant'. 'Oh, [huff] oh dear' he said.

One senior director involved more broadly in discussions that led to
earlier preventive orders also stated that decision-makers were certainly
aware of the risks of these new measures, which fell outside the mainstream criminal justice system:

To get justice quickly and cheaply, these alternative solutions were
infringing people's liberties at the time and for me – and I did say this
to ministers and the Prime Minister – if we were to spend as much
effort on the criminal justice process to make it as efficient as possible
there probably wouldn't be a need for this.

A different director noted the political benefit as a potential reason
for this desire to reshape justice, that is, the populist element of crime

control for New Labour (and most widely accepted reasoning in the academic community):

> Yes, I think this idea, yes, that the Home Office can be a vote winning thing. You know Labour was always, in opposition, caricatured as being very soft on crime. So it was part of Tony Blair's New Labour vision that we are not going to let the Conservative party wrong-foot us on law and order. So he went for it . . . his quotes of ripping up the criminal justice system, or you know this Dickensian criminal justice system, we've got to start again, this idea that our criminal justice system was not fit for purpose.

However, this isolated expression by one decision-maker about the political rhetoric surrounding reform does not necessarily explain (by virtue of cause and effect) the spread of the preventive order model. The subversion of criminal procedures and law may not have followed a simple blueprint, as one Home Office official claimed:

> I'll be honest, I don't think there really was because, like I say, going back to the point about was this part of a concerted effort to use civil measures to get around the criminal law? . . . I think it was more incremental than driven. . . . I genuinely don't think there was a concerted desire to use – how can I put it? – I don't think there was an overarching strategy.

While the preventive order model may not have been driven by explicit directions to create a new system to subvert criminal procedure, this political rhetoric about punitiveness did at least seem to influence officials' thinking about preventive orders as shortcuts to punishment on a case-by-case basis. As one senior official in the Home Office expressed:

> There was a certain sense, and there has always been a certain sense around ASBOs that it is a quicker route into criminal justice as well, because breach of it potentially gets you [criminal punishment] – the impression that we got from Number 10 was that the Prime Minister was deeply frustrated by the slowness of the criminal justice system, and he saw this was a quicker route of actually penalising people. And we had to be careful in the way that we describe this.

Therefore, at one level, for some actors involved in policy-making, particularly those at the top ranks of decision-making, preventive orders satisfied a desire to achieve rapid forms of justice and avoid the burdens of criminal prosecution. Conversely, there was also evidence that preventive orders were intended to *supplement* the criminal justice system, discussed in the next subsection.

7.3.1.2 Intention to supplement the criminal justice system

Several decision-makers suggested that the preventive order model was intended to work with, or alongside, criminal procedure rather than intending to avoid criminal justice. There were two key categories of views expressed about the complementary role of preventive orders in supplementing the existing structures of justice. First, it was expressed by some interviewees (1, 3, 4, 6, 7, and 18) that the criminal justice system offers a limited response, simply 'prosecution or not', whereby the 'preventive orders are just looking for something in between' (senior official, Home Office). Moreover, a Permanent Secretary suggested that restrictions on liberty were being considered in preference to the default response of a deprivation of liberty: '[T]here was developing, in this period and before, this concept of trying to put constraints on people beyond simply putting them in prison.' However, in contrast, a minister made it clear that prosecution and punishment would always be more suitable where possible:

> Ultimately, even with Control Orders, we were still very much of the view that if you could catch them and have the evidence, and deal with people under the full majesty of the rule of law, all the better.

Therefore, as one member of the bill-team perhaps best described it, this filling of the gaps in the criminal justice system was intended to be complementary and used to complete the set of available state responses to crime:

> It is more about having different things in your armoury. . . . Not that you are thinking, 'oh well, prison is a complete disaster we can't be bothered with that anymore'. More just that there is some real serious harm going on here, we need to tackle it every way we can and so let's not just confine ourselves to the criminal law, let's go down as many other avenues as we can.

Second, several other interviewees (3, 4, 10, 11, 14, and 20) expressed the view that preventive orders were intended to supplement the criminal justice system by picking up the overflow of the growing prison population. One policy director from SOCA described how the SCPO was a more practical policy response to a growing prison population:

> Serious Crime Prevention Orders are just an extension of the next, or rather the precursor to the next stage, which is there aren't enough cops, courts or prisons in this country, so how do you deal with the 30 plus thousand out there who are committing serious and organised crime. You've only got the capacity to put 2,500 [per year] through the criminal justice system and the prison capacity is 82,000, and there were 81,999 there last night. That would have been the business case for these preventive measures.

Moreover, as one interviewee from Number 10 conceded, the institution of prison was not considered to be an adequate solution to criminal behaviour:

> I don't think anyone believed that you were necessarily going to stop crimes simply by tougher and tougher punishment measures. I mean maybe Michael Howard believed that it works. But I don't think many people believed it. Anyway, our prisons were getting incredibly full and the cost of building new prisons incredibly expensive. So people were looking for preventative measures.

This was particularly expressed by those decision-makers from SOCA interviewed, in relation to the SCPO and organised crime control:

> The more that we can apply preventive orders that reduce the number of people engaged, then we can focus on the ones that do have to go to prison under criminal justice procedure. (Senior management, SOCA)

This interviewee from senior management at SOCA therefore argued strongly that the SCPO is not an alternative to criminal procedure (trial, prosecution, and sentence):

> This is not an alternative, this just clears the decks so that we can get on with those that do need to go down, and go down for a long time. So we tell cops that, but they think that what we have been doing is something alternative. It's not. But the approach is not the same in other law enforcement agencies – their focus, the way they are driven and targeted, is not the right way.

Therefore, preventive orders were viewed by decision-makers as performing one of two quite antithetical tasks: either subverting established criminal procedures or augmenting and supplementing existing criminal justice procedures. Finally, it is worth examining the preventive intentions of decision-makers, as this family of orders clearly embodies a preventive disposition and a new vision of justice.

7.3.1.3   Early intervention: Preventive justice in mind?

Several interviewees (7, 14, 16, and 19) stated that preventive orders can be conceived of as expanding the reach of criminal justice. That is, preventive orders should be seen as intending to address harm by intervening earlier. In Chapter 2, it was shown how preventive orders represent state coercive action occurring temporally earlier to deal with more remote harms, rather than consummate harms (criminal offences). There was some evidence of this preventive vision and intention by senior decision-makers, as one minister stated:

> I think it stems from a belief that the use of civil powers and civil òrders to try to deal with some aspects of behaviour, that may not themselves be criminal, but can lead to criminal activity . . . why don't we intervene earlier in the process to try and prevent it from moving . . . to criminal prosecution?

However, when interviewees were asked specifically about the consideration and role of preventive ideology and preventive justice in their deliberations, it was apparent that this was generally not explicitly in mind. For example, one Permanent Secretary explained:

> What I recall is less about the prevention and more about avoiding criminalisation. That somehow you had to divert – I suppose it is prevention by another word – but I don't remember people talking about prevention as such, but whether by intervening early, before you had got to the centre of criminal offences having been conducted that themselves would have led to some kind of criminal sentence.

While early intervention and notions of prevention might be viewed as analogous, it was apparent that there were no discussions about engendering a broader alternative form of preventive justice. Rather, notions of prevention seemed to feature more in reference to the legal justification for new measures being non-punitive. As discussed in Chapter 3, it was necessary to classify the SCPO as 'preventive' in order for it to be deemed a civil order, and accepted in parliament (and indeed the courts) as a legitimate form of non-punitive control. This was also clearly expressed by various interviewees (1, 2, 3, 5, 7, and 15); for example, one senior civil servant explained:

> One of the reasons that it has to be prevention is that these are civil orders and not criminal orders . . . so it's preventive, and the orders were sold very heavily in Parliament, and I think only accepted in Parliament because they are preventive rather than a punitive measure.

Very similar expressions were made by other actors at all levels of decision-making (ministers, legal advisors, civil servants, and senior management at SOCA). For example, one interviewee from SOCA stated:

> It was because we needed to get these orders into the civil regime. They could not be punitive, so by definition they had to be something other than punitive, i.e. preventive.

Similarly, a minister stated that 'they are definitely about prevention, that is the key. If you get into punitive then they are not preventive, they are not civil orders'. These specific expressions about the role of prevention sound less like designing early intervention strategies and more like the above-mentioned intentions to subvert criminal procedure. That is, notwithstanding the preventive label, the order would be found to be criminal in substance and effect and therefore subject to Article 6 protections (evidence of the 'prevention and civil law marriage of convenience' discussed in Section 3.4.1).

The only other mention of the influence of prevention in discussions held by decision-makers was from interviewees, particularly those from law enforcement bodies, who believed that prevention became a focus in serious and organised crime control as a result of similar pre-emptive policies used for counter-terrorism:

> That thinking evolved out of some of the discussions around pre-emptive powers and controls around terrorism. And it did influence the thinking around a whole range of policies. What it did, it brought people out of a mindset of what was possible and what was not possible. And this often happens, I think policy jolts forward often as a consequence of some crisis or other, where people are broken out of the confines of their own thinking, if you will. And the Serious Crime Prevention Orders did come out of that era, I'm pretty sure they did. (Senior director)

One minister described this as 'societal acceptance' (or normalisation) of emergency powers and explained it as following fluctuating trends:

> It's almost like fashion a bit, it seems to me, it becomes more fashionable, you know the ship moves one way and then something happens and then it shifts back. You'll get a terrorist attack and peoples' sort of concept of what is acceptable moves towards greater curtailment of individual liberty. And then it drifts along a bit and people say, well I'm a bit uneasy about this.

A decision-maker from SOCA even argued that this focus on prevention, which was the primary goal of SOCA, should be a more widespread goal of all law enforcement agencies:

> And this is the debate that we're now having with our colleagues in the CT side, the counter-terrorism side, because their focus is on preventing a terrorist incident. And in serious organised crime, we're saying that that should be the same for us, that is, what the government should be asking all law enforcement agencies to do. Because actually, you don't want your house broken into, it doesn't matter how good the detection rate is, you don't want your house broken into [in the first place].

This interviewee went on to suggest that if policy-makers were to start from scratch in redesigning justice, the approach would be completely different: 'I think if we were to look at something again, it wouldn't be about law now, it would be about supercharging regulations.' Similarly, in an exchange about how the preventive order model has spread, one minister explained how targeted regulation would be effective:

> I think it is a case-by-case basis, which has come from the sort of general perception that there is an area of activity that we should be able to regulate and control, but would not necessarily do that by waiting for there to be criminal activity before you intervene. Hence, prevention. Hence, civil. In a sense it is society laying down a standard, saying you will perform to this standard, you will do this in order to behave the way that we think is appropriate. But the deal is, that if you break that, then we're saying that that's unacceptable, and that is why that is criminal, because we've laid down to you what is acceptable. What most people in this country, well most people in our society or our community abide by this, you should abide by it, and if you won't then there is a criminal penalty for it.

More specifically in the case of the SCPO, one senior civil servant also explained the broader ideological agenda as regulatory:

> We were trying to present it as something that was a new form of regulation actually. Not least, a targeted form of regulation that was only going to trouble people that were up to no good in the first place. So it was actually a more attractive approach for various sectors to blanket regulation which might be the alternative.

While there might not have been a unified single intention to create an alternative system of preventive justice, preventive orders seem to have fulfilled a number of distinct (and even opposing) aims of different decision-makers. There was unquestionably an open agenda to reform the criminal justice system, and most senior decision-makers who were interviewed (including those from Number 10) agreed that the pressure to reform was predominantly emanating from Number 10. With broad scope to apply restrictions and prohibitions on individuals involved in harmful and criminal conduct, the preventive order model was able to appease the various demands of different policy-makers – be it a shortcut to punishment, a measure to make good the shortcomings of criminal procedure, or to alleviate the criminal justice system's burden of a surplus in criminality. It is also clear that notions of prevention did not feature strongly in the deliberations of key decision-makers; far less was there any discussion of an alternative system of preventive justice. It is apparent that the existence of a family of preventive orders (and by extension, conceivably the wider body of new measures of regulation and control that restrict behaviour) is largely a product of incremental policy transfer by officials, and in particular legal advisors, on a case-by-case basis in the Home Office.

These findings have several implications for our understanding of the development of criminal justice policy. Above all, these findings demonstrate how without the broader governmental intention, and without proper consideration of the impact on principles of justice, incremental changes can dramatically reshape criminal justice. In addition, the findings have profound implications for how we conceive of innovation during policy development. These findings about the routine role of policy transfer change the way that policy-making and innovation during policy development were perceived:

> Everybody thinks that the SCPO is a new initiative and all the rest – but it's never really like that. It's more of a continuum of various ideas being developed. (Senior director)

True innovation and originality in the policy-making process is rare and policy transfer is the mechanism upon which policy-makers rely:

> It is fair to say that there is very little . . . very little room for originality and these things, there is usually something that has gone before and done something similar, and it's just easier as well from our perspective to be able to point to something and say, 'look, this is the kind of thing that we are trying to work towards'. (Legal advisor, Home Office)

Furthermore, if this process of policy transfer is recognised as a common occurrence, it could have implications for the way in which policy-making is formally structured. A deeper understanding of how policy transfer functions could have wide implications for the manner in which non-governmental actors (including academics) might influence policy, how policy-makers (civil servants, political actors, parliamentary draftsmen, and other legal actors) *engage* in policy transfer, and how transfer might be facilitated and improved without drifting into otherwise predictable pitfalls. This could even have implications for the organisational structure of the Home Office:

> But we do tend to reinvent the wheel an inordinate amount, and I think it is an error in the way that we organised the Home Office because everything is done so much by crime theme, that actually there are certain functional tasks that are really the same. And I've always thought that powers is a very good example of one, that it would make a lot of sense to have all the powers work done in one place, and effectively you say give me an order to deal with this problem, and then you design one, rather than actually having little teams that are responsible for the provisions around different powers in a dozen different parts of the department. So I think that we probably make more heavy weather of it, inventing new ones than we need to and that we don't learn enough of the lessons. (Senior official, Home Office)

These implications and others are discussed in the next and concluding chapter of this book.

8
The Power of Policy Transfer

This chapter provides an integrated discussion, combining the empirical findings in Part II of this book with the theoretical positions taken, and frameworks developed, in Part I. Final implications and conclusions are then drawn.

There are clearly many distinct policy motivations that have led to the creation of preventive orders in different areas of crime control. For example, the ASBO was a governmental reaction to widespread systemic disorder in communities across the UK, in an attempt to use the law to deal with non-criminal (yet harmful) behaviour. Quite separately, the motivation for the Control Order emerged from an urgent threat of additional acts of terrorism in the UK. Related to this, the government pursued policies which would maintain a level of control over individuals suspected of terrorism who would be released from custodial detention following the decision of the House of Lords in *A and others v Secretary of State for the Home Department* [2004] (the 'Belmarsh decision'). The motivations for the SCPO also differed from those behind orders which sought to control anti-social behaviour and terrorism. It is apparent that the SCPO was specifically designed to reach and control individuals on the fringe of organised criminality who were known to facilitate some of the most sophisticated, enduring, and destructive crimes (such as trafficking in drugs, children, and vulnerable adults). However, this book has shown that the key responses to these three quite distinct criminogenic activities have been the development of remarkably similar instruments of state control.

The increased use of preventive orders for crime control in the UK has generally been explained theoretically as being part of a governmental, ideological shift in criminal justice, giving preference to risk-based strategies and actuarial approaches to a new penology or crime control agenda (discussed in Chapter 3). Indeed, in Chapter 3 it was argued that recent preventive discourses – though they may have a long-standing historical role in criminal justice – have modified the current approach to crime control. Whether or not a pre-emptive turn in criminal justice is clearly discernible, it is apparent that the system is leaning towards a greater role for preventive jurisprudence made manifest in the broad spectrum of state action that is restricting its citizens (preventive orders) and depriving them of their liberty (preventive detention). Whereas academics and practitioners of criminal justice have tended to theorise that these actions are based on a range of disconnected rationales – including protection, pre-emption, precaution, dangerousness, regulation, risk, and security – it was argued in Chapter 3 that prevention is the single, most dominant imperative behind the state's use of new coercive methods for early intervention. Such a focus was seen to involve lesser degrees of harm to ensure justice. It was demonstrated that this state of prevention presents significant challenges to the system of criminal justice, in particular, there has been a blurring of the dividing line between the civil and criminal law, and the extent of legitimate coercive protection before such protection is seen to be punishment.

These explanations of a broader ideological shift led to the first hypothesis developed throughout this book: that the use of new preventive measures was part of a calculated government objective to expand the role of these new approaches and, in so doing, to reconfigure the justice system to deal with 21st-century crime problems. As an alternative to these claims, I developed a policy transfer framework to examine the potential for more gradual and somnambulant ('sleepwalking') processes to have been the method by which there has developed a new system governed by 'preventive justice'. That is, the examination of policy transfer presented an alternative hypothesis: that the increased role of prevention in the administration of justice occurred through incremental (even unconscious) changes.

To test these two alternative hypotheses, the approach taken in this book was to conduct a detailed case study and examination of the policy development surrounding the Serious Crime Prevention Order. While it was acknowledged that the method of process-tracing employed (focusing as it did on a single preventive order) has some limitations as to the generalisability of the findings, it was shown in Chapter 5 that the flexible case study design was well suited to the broader goal of theory testing – probing the existence of policy transfer. That is, this case study approach permitted the use of multiple sources of data collection and analysis, enabling a broader examination of the legislative developments across a number of preventive orders, and selective interviews with key elite decision-makers about the general occurrence of policy transfer during policy development.

The legislative analysis conducted in Chapter 6 left no doubt as to the influence of existing domestic crime policy on the formulation of the SCPO. There was indisputable evidence that there exists a widespread preventive order model, which, over a period of at least two decades, has propagated freely across distinct areas of crime policy. The correlations between the provisions of 19 preventive orders that preceded the SCPO showed unequivocally that this order belonged to a broad family of preventive orders, which incorporated a multitude of criminal (and non-criminal) conduct, ranging from anti-social behaviour to the most extreme cases of serious crime and terrorism. In addition, the legislative analysis demonstrated that there were a number of expansive trends within this family of preventive orders, which signified a gradual pushing of the boundaries over time. As the most recent addition to the family of preventive orders involved in this analysis, the SCPO was found to embody some of the most wide-reaching provisions when compared to earlier variants of the preventive order model. This is most obvious when the SCPO is compared with the first preventive order incorporated in the analysis, the Exclusion Order under the Licensed Premises (Exclusion of Certain Persons) Act 1980, which demonstrated a far narrower scope of application. An Exclusion Order could be imposed only on individuals post-conviction as part of criminal proceedings in order to protect the proprietor (and her/his patrons). It could have effect for no more than a two-year period (with no procedure for renewal), and breach of the order carried a maximum penalty of a one-month custodial sentence.

Through gradual expansion of the model over more than 20 years and across 20 orders, the analysis identified six trends which illustrated the path which led to the extensive scope of the SCPO. First, there was a widening of the application procedure, where the SCPO can be imposed through both criminal and civil procedure. Second, there was an extension of the *subject* of preventive orders, where the SCPO can be imposed on both individuals and companies. Third, there was an expansion of the *object* or purpose of the order, where the SCPO was intended for public protection rather than only for the protection of a specific individual(s). Fourth, there was a broadening of the type of conduct required to be committed by individuals before a preventive order could be imposed, where the SCPO is not only applicable to persons convicted of serious crime *but also* those who are deemed 'likely to facilitate' crime (whether or not such an offence was even committed). Fifth, there was an increase in the possible duration that an order could be imposed, where the SCPO can be imposed on individuals for up to 5 years *and* with unlimited potential for renewal. Sixth, there was an increase in the sanction for breaching the terms of an order, where breach of an SCPO could result in the maximum penalty of 12 months (on summary conviction) or five years (on indictment).

These findings clearly substantiate not only the occurrence of transfer operating across the provisions of domestic orders, but also the potential for gradual change to dramatically redefine the preventive order model itself. This process of change is analogous to the gradual shift in shades on a colour spectrum, which ranges from blue at one end to red at the other. The colour difference between any two adjacent incremental steps along the spectrum is imperceptible; however, the overall shift from one end to the other is dramatic (from blue to red). Similarly, the minor amendments to policy can result in a dramatic difference between the original and final product. While clearly some level of modification must necessarily be made to any given measure if it is to be employed within new circumstances, the pattern of remodelling shown across preventive orders illustrates the potential for a substantial shift to occur from the original model (and the potential to unwittingly end up 'in the red').

These findings clearly support the alternative hypothesis of incremental and unintentional policy change. Given that the spread of this model occurred over a period of at least two decades (a generation) involving numerous decision-makers, policy-makers, and law-makers, as well as governments, it is doubtful that the spread of this model can be explained as being one individual's or a small group of individuals' specific intention. It can therefore be concluded from the legislative analysis alone that structural forces, and diffuse and incremental processes of policy transfer, can have a significant impact on, and can lead to large-scale changes in, the criminal law.

In Chapter 7, the empirical analysis of the interviews conducted with elite decision-makers also supports the alternative hypothesis that emphasises the powerful structural forces at play and, accordingly, presents a strong alternative view to the oversimplified assumptions about an alleged authoritarian drive towards these new developments to undermine the principles of criminal justice. While there was certainly a declared intention to reshape criminal justice, there was little calculation and deliberation about the way in which that should or could be achieved. Two primary intentions were expressed by senior decision-makers for preventive orders: either to find ways to subvert criminal procedures (a view purportedly held largely by the Prime Minister and those at Number 10) or to supplement criminal procedures by filling the gaps and extending the law to address more remote harms. It was found that notions of preventive justice were not clearly in the minds of decision-makers. It was shown that while policy-makers in the Home Office were fully aware of a governmental desire for reform (by political decision-makers), they undertook the primary role of law-making, innovation, and the determination of new measures on a case-by-case basis, as the broader direction for reform was either (at best) ambiguous or otherwise not articulated. This corresponds with Page's (2003) thesis of the 'civil servant as legislator' (discussed further below).

It is also important to discuss the number of findings about the nature of policy transfer and policy development. There are three key characteristics of policy-making (particularly evident in early policy development) that permit policy transfer to prevail as a method of innovation:

1. A small fertile group of decision-makers
2. Time constraints
3. Policy precedents

In support of Ismaili's (2006: 261) contextual theorising about the criminal justice process, I have substantiated that policy development indeed occurs among a small group of individuals, a 'constellation of forces'. It was shown that through empirical enquiry, a policy community's subgovernment can be refined to identify the key actors that effected change. It was found that in developing the SCPO, the decision-makers of this small group engaged in what they referred to as an 'iterative process'. A similar finding was found in an empirical study by Page (2003: 665), who noted that this process of iteration was 'generally termed "toing and froing" by the officials'. The engagement of this small group of actors in a fluid process of iteration is important as it creates an environment conducive to transfer:

> A stable group may well be intellectually fertile, and it can certainly foster commitments and loyalties, but it is the instability of the small group that seems to provide the stronger immediate catalyst for the innovation and diffusion of ideas. People on the move take their histories, expertise, and experience with them, carrying knowledge from site to site. They are prone to transfer, contrast, mix, and refashion the larger common sense and practice of the organizations in which they have worked. (Rock 1995: 3)

The nature of the iterative relationship between officials and ministers is also important as there has been considerable debate about the identity of those responsible for new laws. In Chapter 4 it was shown that there was significant contention in the literature, whereby some researchers argued that a *Yes Minister!* style system was in operation, involving civil servants being seen to be the true legislators (notably Richards and Smith 2002: 61 and Page 2003), while others contended that 'we must avoid exaggerating the bureaucracy's role' (Howlett et al. 2009: 67). The findings from the research undertaken generally support the more dominant role of civil servants and legal advisers in the Home Office acting as legislators. In the case study of the SCPO, it was clear that while senior decision-makers outside the Home Office created a demand for new powers (namely, those at Number 10 and SOCA), it was the civil servants who set the policy direction and developed the policy content, and the legal advisers who developed these ideas into policy instruments. In particular, the role of legal actors in direct policy transfer was paramount. From the analysis of the Instructions to Parliamentary Counsel and the accounts from legal actors themselves, it was clear that departmental lawyers had engaged in a process of 'cherry-picking' from other preventive orders (particularly the ASBO) in an apparent 'cut-and-paste' approach to the development of the specific provisions contained in the SCPO.

Nonetheless, the role of more senior (political) decision-makers in the iterative process and policy transfer should not be diminished. It is maintained that the interaction between these actors is critical, where allocation of legislating authority cannot simply be attributed to any particular parties involved. While the initial idea and desire for new policy direction might only slightly progress a policy's development, it is a necessary part of the impetus for policy change. This is because officials themselves tend not to generate new ideas unless provoked a tendency particularly true of those in the Home Office. As one Permanent Secretary exclaimed: '[T]he basic Home Office unofficial approach was: "don't".' It is also important to note that this conservatism towards innovation by civil servants might itself explain a preference for more incremental forms of policy-making such as transfer, so as *not* to diverge too far from existing policies. Therefore, the officials' and legal advisers' role in policy transfer is clearly *reactionary*. This emphasises the relevance of the impact of the politicisation of crime on the crime control agenda, whereby it can lead to hyperbolic policy-making (hence the huge increase in legislative activity), which drove new developments through a process of policy transfer. Nonetheless, politicisation is not the only (even not the most important) factor that can explain the moves towards preventive justice, as there is no indication that this was in the minds of decision-makers themselves – though the two factors are clearly related.

The second characteristic of policy development that cultivates transfer is the *time pressures* under which decisions are made by the small group of policy-makers. In Chapter 4 it was shown that policy transfer can be conceptualised within customary rationalist policy models involving a 'search for alternatives' to select ideas or existing measures for adoption from distinct areas of policy. In these models it has been argued that, under limited conditions, policy-makers engage in a form of bounded rationality to 'satisfice' rather than optimise the search for solutions (Simon 1956: 136). The time pressures expressed by many decision-makers in this research represent an important condition which constrains innovation by policy-makers. That is, in a move to satisfy the demands of more senior decision-makers, policy-makers in the Home Office resorted to transfer as a 'short cut' to innovation (Althaus et al. 2007: 65). These imposed time pressures and those emanating from parliamentary timetabling create an environment ripe for policy transfer.

Finally, it is also important to discuss the role that policy precedents play in the process of policy transfer. While it is acknowledged that the notion of precedents in the law has a particular connotation concerning *case law* making (and it is clearly debatable as to whether *case law* even makes law or just interprets the existing law), this book has shown clearly that in terms of statute law-making, what has gone before has a powerful impact on new developments. The SCPO can be seen as resulting from two important precedents. In particular, a strong precedent was set by the creation of the ASBO, about which the vast majority of decision-makers who were interviewed expressed a similar sentiment: that this order had 'opened the flood gates' to a wider spread of the preventive order model. In addition, it could be said that a precedent was set by the Control Order, introduced as an exceptional measure, which according to many decision-makers changed the logic for serious and organised crime control. Once these two precedents were set at either end of the continuum of crime and harmful conduct, many interviewees expressed that bridging the gap was inevitable. As one departmental lawyer in the Home Office put it: '[O]nce you have got one why not have more?'

As discussed in Chapter 3, the ASBO clearly has had its critics, and there has been widespread debate about its impact on the appropriate control of anti-social behaviour. However, the broader policy implication of setting a precedent or benchmark has escaped criticism. That is, with the acceptance and popularity of any new area of innovation – in this case, the preventive order model – there is a broader potential for greater concern. Several decision-makers indicated that they had intentionally used the ASBO as a form of political gesturing (to show their commitment to serious crime). This suggests that decision-makers themselves could be accused of wearing the ASBO as a 'badge of honour'. However, clearly part of the problem was that policy-makers focused solely on developing the SCPO, and not on spreading the preventive order model. This supports Steiker's (1998) claim that if each new measure is treated as *sui generis* instead of being conceived of as part of a larger preventive framework, there might be a consequence of drifting into a new state of prevention.

Therefore, to conclude the discussion, it is apparent that the path to preventive justice is one which is not paved by careful planning and deliberation on sound foundations for each step; nor is the process cognisant of the developing cracks which inevitably emerge during construction. There was little consideration of the potential impact on the architectural environment (established criminal justice procedure), or worse still a deliberate disregard for, or subversion of, the established structures of justice. This book has argued that a preventive justice system is being constructed by expedient actions by policy-makers who seek (often with good intentions) to respond to distinct crime policy problems. In their search for solutions and innovations policy-makers take the shortest and most direct line (the critical path), 'the line of least resistance' (Rose 1991: 13). The search for inspiration will be as much at the domestic level as it will be international, though domestic ideas are more likely to be sought for transfer because of easier accessibility to reliable information. In a department such as the Home Office, a large structure with numerous competing actors and influences, the legal department forms the 'critical path' for direct transfer to occur. These legal actors work with a position of authority: they guide and advise senior decision-makers on which policies are feasible, translate final policy ideas into the desired statutory instruments, and work intra-departmentally where most other actors operate within a more compartmentalised environment. Therefore, while the SCPO can be considered an innovative measure (as shown in Chapter 2, it is indeed a novel response to organised crime control), it was the fundamental role of policy transfer which facilitated the process of innovation.

8.1 Specific responses to research questions

There were three broad research questions posed at the beginning of this book to help shape the enquiry. Firstly, how can the spread of the preventive order model be explained? Second, what can detailed policy studies contribute to the understanding of new preventive practices? Third, to what extent does policy transfer play a role in policy-making and innovation? While the discussion above has already provided some certain conclusions to these overlapping questions, it is worth briefly clarifying the response of this book to all three key questions.

Most importantly, the findings from the empirical analyses (Part II) of this book leave no doubt that domestic policy transfer occurred during the development of the SCPO. Of course, the specific findings about the origins of the SCPO alone cannot simply be generalised to explain the role of transfer in the development of other preventive orders; nor can they directly explain the rise of a new system of 'preventive justice'. However, there was compelling evidence to suggest that policy transfer occurred in the development of other preventive orders. This was found in both the legislative analysis (the apparent homogeneity of substantive provisions across orders) and in interviews with decision-makers, where policy transfer was accepted to be a common feature of everyday policy-making. To reiterate the words of the bill team lawyer:

> A lot of legislation is about the precedents that you can lay your hands on and then adapting them to your particular circumstances. So no, it is not a coincidence that they all look the same. I am sure every person that has made one of these orders will have looked at their predecessors' work and adapted it.

Such findings do emphasise the powerful structural forces of policy-making at play. These go beyond explanations based on *agency*, and present a strong objection to oversimplified assumptions about the ostensible intentions of an authoritarian state. The method of process-tracing presents a unique methodology for conducting detailed policy studies to contribute to the understanding of new preventive practices and other developments in criminal justice. In relation to the third research question, the extent of policy transfer during domestic policy-making and innovation for the SCPO depended on the stage of development. The policy transfer framework developed in Chapter 4 proposed several key questions about the dimensions of transfer – the who, what, and why of transfer. It was found that these questions overlap significantly. That is, *what* is transferred and *who* is involved in the transfer depend on the stage *when* policy is being developed. Therefore, the extent or *degree of transfer* varied. That is, at the level of ideas, inspiration was drawn from international policies as well as domestic preventive orders, while at the level of policy instruments (micro policy transfer), there was direct transfer of the provisions of existing preventive orders, particularly the ASBO. It was clear that at the early stage of idea generation, many senior decision-makers were engaging in a broad search, based on their knowledge of existing policies, both internationally (how the US, Italy, or Japan were using civil powers backed by criminal punishment to deal with organised crime groups) and domestically (namely, the ASBO, Control Order, and Football Banning Order). Therefore, the origins of transfer at the level of ideas was less conspicuous or perhaps a mixture of inspiration. However, at the level of developing policy instruments, transfer played a more palpable role. As already discussed above, at this micro level of policy development, policy-makers (officials, and particularly legal actors, in the Home Office) were found to have taken a 'cut-and-paste' approach to develop the provisions for the SCPO.

8.2   Implications and key contributions

Jones and Newburn (2002: 175) argued strongly for the need for greater empirical research to be conducted into policy formulation, postulating that there is 'much to gain from a more detailed consideration of both the idea of "policy" and more particularly, the processes through which it comes about'. This book has shown that a detailed study of the policy process can offer great benefits. There are a number of specific implications and contributions which can be drawn from the research that has been conducted into policy transfer. These findings are significant for the work of both practitioners and academics alike. These are discussed in turn.

First, my findings should persuade decision-makers of the existence of the family of preventive orders, and make them aware that the direction of gradual policy developments is leading towards a system based on preventive justice. Throughout this book, a concerted effort has been made *not* to construct any normative judgements about the desirability or value of a system of preventive justice. However, it is argued that if the system is to be reshaped, to be determined and administered by notions of prevention, it must do so along with a greater awareness of the desired system and serious thinking about the principles of justice that would be appropriate to include with it. In addition, there is great importance of the need to focus practitioners on the recognition of the actual process of transfer in which they are frequently engaged. It was evident in discussions with policy-makers that they were largely unaware of their use of policy transfer, rather it was viewed simply as part of the complex mix of an iterative process. However, it is argued that whenever possible, policy transfer should be done knowingly (to avoid the pitfalls of misappropriation).

If policy transfer was systematically recognised, there would be some important implications for the way in which the search for innovation occurs. That is, if policy-makers were more acquainted with a formally structured process of transfer, they could decide to use transfer as a policy-making *tool*, rather than haphazardly drawing upon existing models when put under pressure to innovate. That is, there is an important opportunity to systematise transfer as a mechanism of policy-making and innovation and remove the need for expediency. For example, this could have implications for creating new databases or management system tools (electronic or otherwise) that contain available policy options for decision-makers (options for transfer). This would facilitate the search for innovative solutions (both internationally and domestically) and assist in developing new ideas and instruments. In addition, as one interviewee believed (quoted at the end of Chapter 7), policy transfer could even have implications for the organisational structure of departments such as the Home Office. To restate the views of this senior official:

> But we do tend to reinvent the wheel an inordinate amount, and I think it is an error in the way that we organised the Home Office because everything is done so much by crime theme that actually there are certain functional tasks that are really the same. And I've always thought that powers is a very good example of one, that it would make a lot of sense to have all the powers work done in one place.

Recognition of policy transfer as a common part of policy-making could clearly have significant implications for how policy-making is structured and operated, so as to facilitate the search, while minimising the duplication of procedures for development. Of course, it is not claimed that policy transfer is such a foreign concept – lessons are learnt and drawn, and influence is had before any decision is made. Indeed, in writing a book, one must initially seek out what has gone before to find a suitable approach to avoid the adoption of inappropriate research methods which might produce misleading or failed conclusions. However, in the academy, there are systems in place to facilitate the complexities involved in the search for, and deliberation of, past approaches where clear reference is made to what has gone before. Despite this, policy development clearly has been shown to have more finite deadlines than writing a book – though this is arguably only more reason for developing more enhanced systems of transfer, rather than allowing development to occur through mere expedience.

In addition, there are two key implications for academic research. First, it focuses the criminal justice community on the importance of engaging in detailed policy studies. Empirical studies of the policy- and law-making processes can make an important contribution to criminological knowledge. While the academies of criminologists and legal theorists have each established a strong and important body to critique the actions and policy direction taken by governments, there is an obvious dearth of research exploring the environment under which criminal justice policy decisions are made. There is an apparent gap in the field of criminology where engagement in analyses of how statute law and policy are developed is largely missing. That is, the criminal justice community should also be looking for ways to enhance the policy-making process, with a recognition of political demands and need for efficiency. Therefore, it is contended that this book has made a substantial contribution by tackling a core mechanism of policy development. This book has also shown the benefit of using a case study research method to understand the motivations of practitioners (decision-makers) in creating new crime policy. There is much to be gained by engaging in this method of analysis to examine the under-researched 'private–public' policy process, that is, the early stages of development that occur behind closed doors.

Second, there may be a wider contribution made to researchers outside the field of criminal justice, particularly in the political sciences. This book has begun to unify the current disparate theories that explain international influence (diffusion, convergence, and learning) under one framework of policy transfer, and refocus them on an understanding of the domestic circumstances of routine policy-making. That is, while several academics have built these theories to explain the influence of policy between jurisdictions (internationally) – predominantly in the political sciences but also in studies in criminal justice (for example, Jones and Newburn 2007) – this book has demonstrated the potential for a unified framework to be developed to illuminate the more fundamental dynamics of everyday policy-making. That is, while Jann and

Wegrich (2007: 56–57) claim that 'the policy cycle framework ignores the role of knowledge, ideas and learning in the policy process', it is suggested that the notion of policy transfer can be built into rational models of policy-making, where during the search for alternatives domestic transfer is a routine process which selects ideas and existing measures for adoption from distinctly different areas of policy.

8.3 Concluding statement

> *Change is the only constant*
> *– Heraclitus of Ephesus, 6th century BC*

Policy transfer is a legitimate method of policy-making and innovation. Indeed, it could be a useful instrument to assist policy-makers in keeping pace with the highly fluid and changeable entity that is the policy-making process. However, without the proper recognition of this mechanism, and without a deeper understanding of how this method is best utilised, it will continue to operate haphazardly. The danger of expedient policy transfer is that new and specific policies and laws can be formed without proper consideration of their combined impact. Without recognition of domestic processes of transfer, the path to preventive justice will be cobbled with complexity, disparagement, and the potential breakdown of justice as it is currently perceived and known.

Appendices

Appendix 'A': Summary of the ways SCPOs have been used

This appendix includes internal documentation originally provided by the Serious Organised Crime Agency (SOCA) to the author – information that is not available publicly. While the names of individual cases where a Serious Crime Prevention Order (SCPO) has been imposed cannot be disclosed, the summary below provides an interesting account of some of the terms and conditions imposed under these orders which are not published elsewhere. Existing SCPOs can be categorised into two groups: (1) restrictions on those in custody; and (2) restrictions on those *not* in custody. These are summarised in the table below.

Examples of the types of restrictions and conditions used under an SCPO	Description of restrictions
Individuals in custody	
Restrictions on prison bank accounts	Unless previously authorised by the SOCA, the subject of this order must not have a sum of money in excess of £250 in any prison bank account (to include any spending account, earnings account, or private cash account that has been set up by the prison).
Notification of prison visitors and correspondence	The subject of this order must notify the SOCA of the details of all third parties (other than legal representatives) that they wish to have visit the prison, or have correspondence with (including name, date of birth, home address, relationship to subject, and reason for visit). Correspondence includes the acts of both sending and receiving mail.
Restrictions on using the prison telephone system	The subject of this order must notify the SOCA of details of their Personal Identification Number System (PINS). These details include the registered telephone numbers, name of person or persons being contacted on that telephone number, home address of person or persons being contacted on that telephone number, and reason for contacting and relationship with the person(s). In addition, the subject must only use his or her own PINS number, may not make a call that diverts to another telephone number, may not conduct conference calls, and may only speak to the person(s) who habitually reside(s) at the address to which the telephone number (landline) relates and who is already an approved contact in accordance with his PINS list.

(continued)

211

Examples of the types of restrictions and conditions used under an SCPO	Description of restrictions
Prohibition of communication devices	The subject of this order must not be in possession of any communication device. In conjunction with Rule 34 and 51 of the Prison Rules 1999, an offender must not own, possess, control, or use any mobile communication device. This includes mobile communication devices such as mobile telephone handset and/or SIM card; mobile Voice Over Internet Protocol (VOIP); Portable Digital Assistance (PDA); any other mobile communication device or component thereof, equipped to send and/or receive data; or any device manufactured, adapted, or improvised for the use of charging a mobile communication device. If the subject is found in possession, use, or control of such a device this will constitute a breach of the SCPO and this order shall take precedence over any Prison Rules 1999.
Restrictions on training	The subject of this order must not participate in, or undertake, any training or educational courses while in prison that permit access to the Internet.
Restriction on personal and business bank accounts	The subject of this order must not be a signatory to one or more business or personal bank accounts. The restriction and notification procedures are the same as those summarised below for subjects *not* in custody (see description below for 'Restriction on bank accounts').
Prohibition of third-party financial accounts	The subject of this order must not access, or have control of, any bank accounts held by third parties.
Individuals *not* in custody	
Restriction on bank accounts	The subject of this order must not be a signatory of more than one current bank account (including savings accounts). This account must be with a financial institution in the UK. This includes business accounts, personal accounts, and joint accounts (shared with a third party). The subject must notify the SOCA when accounts are closed or opened. If a new account is opened a number of details must be sent to the SOCA in writing (e.g. account name and number, sort code, bank name, branch location, and opening balance).
Restrictions on third-party bank accounts	The subject of this order must not have access to third-party accounts. If access is desired, the SOCA must first be notified of the details of the third party (e.g. name of account holder and their residential address, bank account name and number, sort code, bank name, and branch location).

(continued)

Examples of the types of restrictions and conditions used under an SCPO	Description of restrictions
Restriction on loans	The subject of this order must not apply for a loan, borrow, or in any other way receive a sum of money in excess of £3000 without notifying the SOCA. This loan includes an overdraft facility, borrowing against a mortgage, and borrowing through the use of a credit card. The notification to the SOCA should set out a number of details, for example, from where the money will be borrowed (details of person or institution), the exact sum of money that will be received, the purpose of the loan, and a plan to pay back the loan. The subject must also give written notice to the lender regarding the conviction or fraud-related activities in which the subject has been involved in the past (i.e. the reasons why the SCPO was imposed).
Restrictions on mortgages	The subject of this order must apply for a mortgage without giving prior notice to the SOCA. This notification should include the purpose for seeking the mortgage, full and accurate copies of the completed mortgage application form, and any supporting documentation used in the mortgage application. The subject must also give written notice to the mortgage lender regarding the conviction or fraud-related activities in which the subject has been involved in the past (i.e. the reasons why the SCPO was imposed).
Restriction on travel outside the UK	The subject of this order must not travel outside the UK unless written notification is given to the SOCA at least 28 days in advance of travel. This notification must include the location, purpose, and duration of the travel, and complete details of the accommodation during the time abroad.
Restrictions on possession of money	The subject of this order must not be in possession of a sum of money (in any currency) in excess of £1000, unless written notification is given to the SOCA. The notification must include details about the full sum of money, the source of the money, and the purpose for obtaining this large sum of money.
Restrictions on removal of money from the UK	The subject of the order must not be involved in the transfer of money outside the UK, unless written notification is given to the SOCA. The notification must include details about both the source and destination of the sum of money, the full amount that will be transferred, and the reason for transfer.
Restriction on association	The subject of this order must not associate by any means, directly or indirectly, with [name of third party removed].
Notification of premises	The subject of this order must notify the SOCA of the details of any rented or owned property. This definition is taken broadly to include *any* 'proprietorial interest' including premises rented, owned, occupied, leased, or used for any purpose of storage.

Appendix 'B': Parliamentary process

The parliamentary process is illustrated in Figure A.1. A bill can enter either the House of Commons or the House of Lords, and then must pass through several prescribed stages in both houses (the same five stages in each house). A précis of the purpose and procedure at each stage is as follows (see also Lord Rippon 1992: 8–10; Zander 2004: 53–57; and UK Parliament Website: www.parliament. uk [December 2014]). The first reading serves as a pronouncement of the bill and its title, and a formal notice of presentation. The second reading provides the occasion for a general debate on the principles contained in the bill. The debate of specific clauses then occurs in committee and report, where amendments can be made. The third reading is the final debate of the bill – including any amendments – then the House may pass the bill. If passed, the bill moves to the other House in order to proceed through each of these stages once more (first reading, second reading, committee, report, and third reading). Once passed through the second House, any contentious amendments are discussed via an exchange of notes between the Houses to reach an agreement (a stage known as 'ping-pong'), before a bill can proceed to the final stage of Royal Assent, where it is formalised as an Act of Parliament.

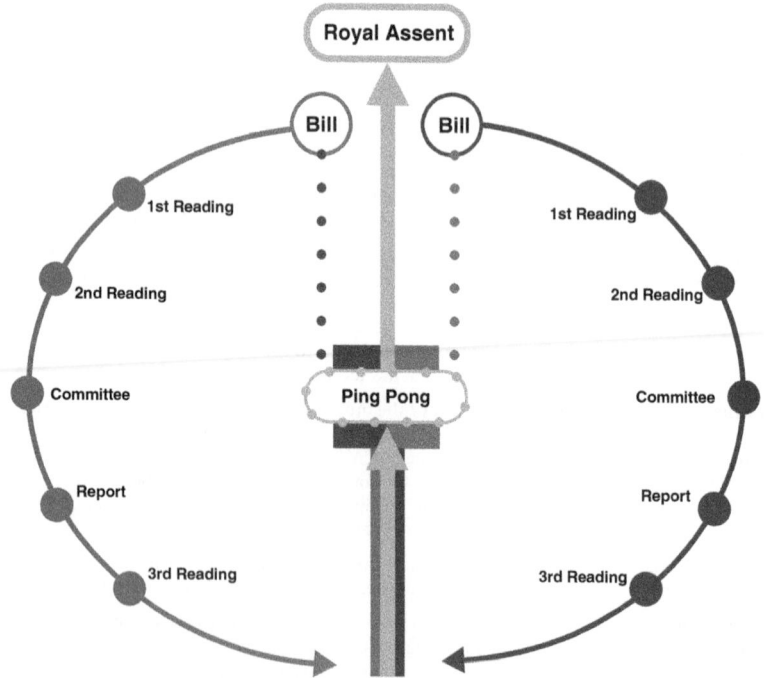

Figure A.1 Formal stages of the parliamentary process

Appendix 'C': Example of interview transcript with indicative questions

Introductory statement

The focus of this interview is on some developments in crime policy (in the academic literature) that seem to have occurred in the last decade. A number of policies introduced during this period seem to suggest a greater inclination towards preventive or future-orientated measures that expand on the more customary retrospective procedures of the criminal justice system such as investigation, criminal trial, and punishment.

My focus is on the civil preventive order model – the most famous example is the Anti-Social Behaviour Order (ASBO) – but as you probably know there are other variants. During your term as Home Secretary, several {insert number} civil preventive orders were developed (or partially developed – that is, carried over from the previous Home Secretary) {insert names of orders}.

I hope to understand the policy processes which have led to the use of civil preventive orders across a range of diverse areas of crime control policy in the UK. *In particular, by way of a case study, I will focus on the policy- and law-making process which led to the formulation and development of the Serious Crime Prevention Order, one of the more recent civil preventive orders.*

Might also need to mention:

- My central interest is in describing and explaining the policy development during this early gestation period. During the interview discussion about the process that occurred, specific people, Units of the Home Office, or other organisations involved in the process might be mentioned. It would be very useful for me to hear as much of this detail as you can recall, as I seek to understand the inner workings of the policy practices and procedures which have taken place.
- I should also reiterate here my confidentiality and anonymity assurances. In the writing up and analysis of these interviews complete anonymity is assured. No details which might identify you directly (including, for example, your name and position) will be used in portraying the accounts of the process given by you or any other person that I interview. The same applies to other people (third parties) that might be mentioned. In the event that I might find it especially valuable to attribute direct quotations to your name or position, I would only do so after first contacting you and seeking your approval to write up such segments.
- I also acknowledge that often my questions focus on small detail, which you might not clearly recollect. I am aware that the Serious Crime Prevention Order (SCPO) is but one of many policies measures that you have been involved in developing.
- So, are you okay to proceed?

☐ **Opening questions**
   ☐ You have worked in the Home Office {or insert other organisation} for {insert number of years} – is this correct?

▢ During this period, how would you describe your role/roles in the organisation, *in terms of policy-making*?

▢ Is there a pattern/group of individuals who worked closely with you in this capacity? [advisers, assistants, consultants, other directors from other units] [note these people down to ask again for their details later in the interview to speak to]

▢ **Events and circumstances leading to the SCPO**

The following questions are trying to create a timeline of important events in policy gestation period (early stages of formulation). [*Note*: Timeline would include plotting the White Paper in 2004, Green Paper in 2006, when Bill begins, when consultation occurs, when bill ends . . . also interviewee's period of employment in Home Office or other relevant organisation]

▢ When do you recall the first discussions being held about the SCPO?

▢ In your view, what brought the SCPO onto the agenda?

▢ Who were the central proponents of this measure?

▢ Was a 'policy bill team' or 'handling bill team' allocated for development of the SCPO (or more precisely, for the Serious Crime Act 2007)?

• Typically, how is a bill team assembled or selected?

• How was it selected for the Serious Crime Act 2007?

• If it was a handling bill team, who was the 'policy lead' [typically a senior civil servant]?

• How many legal advisers were involved?

• Who else was allocated on the 'bill team' for the SCPO? How many people? Names if possible?

▢ What other responses were initially considered?

▢ What support did they have?

▢ Why were they not adopted?

▢ Why was the SCPO selected as a response over other potential responses? *[e.g. why did you ask the PM for this particular type of measure over others?]*

▢ **Focused questions on policy transfer**

One of the things I am interested in is how, and at what level, information, knowledge, and ideas are shared across differing areas of crime control policy.

▢ Is it common/possible for an individual to work simultaneously on different bill teams, or is a position on a bill team considered 'full-time' (for the period until passage)?

▢ Were you involved in any capacity in the development of other civil preventive orders, for example, Control Order, Football Banning Order, ASBO, and so on?

• Did you have direct dealings with those who were?

• Was the introduction of civil preventive orders just a matter of common knowledge, or were there explicit discussions about its applicability to different areas of crime control?

▢ How much overlap is there generally between the set of people working on antisocial behaviour *{insert other field if necessary}* and those working on serious crime *{insert other field if necessary}*?

❑ Modes of communication questions: Describe how decisions are made? Where are they made? Informal and formal locations?

  • Could you provide me with a picture of the varied forms of communication used with respect to the development of new policies in your department/organisation/unit (meetings, emails, memos, etc)?

❑ **Preventive justice and ideology in policy-making**

  ❑ What role, if any, would you say that broader government policy goals have played in formulating or initiating the SCPO?
    • What were these goals?
    • At what level of government or policy decision-making do such articulations take place?

  ❑ Language questions: Regarding policy-makers' use of concepts such as prevention, security, risk, harm, public protection, and so on. What broader policy objectives lie behind civil preventive orders? Which of these terms, if any, tend to dominate the policy agenda when thinking about new measures?

  ❑ By my estimations, there are now 12 civil preventive orders *[need to list these orders and explain criteria for inclusion]* – do you believe that this was the initial intention or just serendipity?

  ❑ Would you say that there was an articulated effort to use civil preventive orders as a model for responding to various areas of crime control? If so, could you explain?
    • Who or what would you consider to be the 'drivers' of this broader civil preventive order model?
    • Is there an opportunity for particular individuals (or groups) to champion a policy idea, such as the civil preventive order, as a model for various areas of crime control?

❑ **Normative worth of the civil preventive order model**

  ❑ What qualities/advantages did these orders add that weren't available previously?

  ❑ How has the advent of civil preventive orders impacted negatively on crime control policy?

  ❑ Why is the UK leading when compared to other (common law) jurisdictions in adopting these preventive orders/measures?
    • Are you at all aware whether this model has been adopted in other countries?

  ❑ What impact, if any, on established criminal law protections do you see as flowing from these preventive measures?
    • Were these considered in the policy-making process? (Prompt: Strasbourg case law on 'anti-subversion'?)

  ❑ When responding to crime through developing crime control policy, do you believe there is a clear distinction to be made between preventive measures and punitive measures?
    • *Note:* preventive measures (target *harmful acts* and managed through the civil courts); punitive measures (target *criminal acts* and managed through the criminal courts).

- ☐ Are there dangers in the blurring of distinctions between preventive measures and punitive measures?
  - And does this matter?

☐ **Future of civil preventive order model**

- ☐ Could the civil preventive order model become a more dominant force in policy development?
- ☐ What, in your view, is the future of civil preventive orders in the UK in the next 10 years?
- ☐ Is there more room in other areas of crime policy to use the civil preventive order model? (examples/elaborate)
- ☐ Are there particular individuals/stakeholders championing the spread of this statutory instrument?

☐ **Mention in closing statement**

- ☐ *I really value your time; this has been enormously helpful. Would I be able to call/contact you in the future, if necessary, to clarify or sharpen some things?*
- ☐ *Who else should I interview? What about {insert name of person}? Would it be okay for me to use your name as a reference when contacting others in the Home Office [other office/organisation]?*

Notes

1 Introduction

1 This was also the last piece of criminal justice legislation of the Blair administration.
2 For example, Ashworth and Redmayne (2005: 147–153), particularly in sections 6.2 and 6.3, note the substantial increase in 'Out-of Court Penalties' over the last few decades.
3 Other similar dichotomies have been put forward to identify this perceived trade-off, for example, the 'Human Rights Act vs public protection', and rights to 'liberty vs security'.
4 This 2006 Home Office paper encompassed a number of proposals including expanding the support to victims and witnesses, tougher sentences for violent offenders, increase in prison spaces, and a more efficient system of licence conditions (broader application of restrictions, enhancing enforcement on breach, and tougher penalties when breach occurs).
5 Linked to the New Right movement, the Conservative Party became known as the 'party for law and order'. For years the Labour Party was criticised for not taking the issue of crime control seriously, until New Labour made the issue a priority. See the work of Stephen Savage, particularly Savage and Nash (1994), Savage, Atkinson, and Robbins (1994), Savage (1998), and Savage and Nash (2001).
6 At the time of embarking on the research for this book, this civil preventive order was enacted as one of the newer additions to the preventive order family. Other preventive orders have since been enacted which are emphasised in Chapter 6.
7 The terrorism 'Control Order', enacted under the Prevention of Terrorism Act 2005, played a marked role in the development of the preventive order model, being one of the furthest-reaching and most intrusive measures in this family. It was replaced by the Terrorism Prevention and Investigation Measure (TPIM) under the Terrorism Prevention and Investigation Measures Act 2011, which limited some of the state's powers under the Control Order (branded 'Control Orders-lite'). Given the empirical focus of this book is on the development of the Serious Crime Prevention Order (SCPO), the preceding Control Order is an important part of the detailed examination, particularly in Chapters 6 and 7 (legislative and interview analyses). For a detailed comparison of the similarities and differences between the Control Order and TPIM, see Ashworth and Zedner (2014: 181–192).

2 'Serious' Shifts in Organised Crime Control

1 Since conducting the research for this book, the SOCA was abolished and replaced by the National Crime Agency by enactment of the Crime and Courts Act 2013 (Royal Assent on 25 April 2013). The National Crime Agency

219

merged SOCA and the Child Exploitation and Online Protection Centre, and absorbed *some* responsibilities from the UK Borders Agency and the (abolished) National Police Improvement Agency. The SOCA is still often used and referred to throughout this book, particularly as the measure under examination (SCPO) was developed as a central power for SOCA, and many of those who were interviewed while completing research for this book were operating under this agency.

2   At the time of publication, the Serious Crime Bill 2014–15 was introduced into the House of Lords which will make amendments to the SCA 2007, among other existing pieces of legislation (for example, the Proceeds of Crime Act 2002 and Computer Misuse Act 1990). The provisions in the Bill are likely to extend elements of the SCA 2007 to Scotland, and to broaden the potential application of an SCPO to include new offences such as firearm possession, 'computer misuse', and 'cultivation of cannabis plants'.

3   This phrase pre hoc is used to describe state intervention that comes 'before the fact' (preventive), to distinguish from those which are post hoc ('after the fact'). The 'fact' here refers to any criminal activity.

4   The retrospective element also meant this provision applied to offences that may have occurred before the establishment of the 1986 Act.

5   The Law Commission produced two detailed reports which form the basis of Part 2 of the SCA 2007: Law Com No. 300, Inchoate Liability for Assisting and Encouraging Crime (2006); and Law Com No. 305, Participating in Crime (2007).

6   The Crown or High Court may issue an SCPO on application by the Director of Public Prosecution, the Director of Revenue and Customs, the Director of the Serious Fraud Office, or the Director of Public Prosecution in Northern Ireland (s.10(4)), or as a result of a conviction in the Magistrates' Court issued for sentencing (s.19).

7   In the Explanatory Notes (November 2007: 20) for the SCA 2007, the following is stated: 'R (McCann) v. Crown Court at Manchester [2003] 1 AC 787, the leading case on anti-social behaviour orders, the House of Lords held that although the civil standard of proof would apply in relation to an application for an anti-social behaviour order the standard is a flexible one ranging from proof on the balance of probabilities, at the lowest level, to beyond reasonable doubt, at the highest. The House of Lords stated that they would expect a high standard of proof to be applied in relation to anti-social behaviour order applications, particularly in relation to whether a person has acted in an anti-social manner, and the same principle is likely to apply in relation to applications for serious crime prevention orders.' The blurring of the civil and criminal standards of proof are discussed in greater detail in Chapter 3 of this book (specifically Section 3.4.1).

8   There is an additional section of the Act (s.2(2)(b)) which allows the court to use its discretion in considering what might also be deemed 'sufficiently serious'. This exception is discussed later in the chapter.

9   One of the most prominent examples of serious fraud in the UK is the case of the Bank of Credit and Commerce International (BCCI), founded in London and eventually closed by the Bank of England in 1991: 'BCCI . . . [provided] banking services to money launderers, drug traffickers, arms dealers, coffee smugglers, tax evaders, political offenders, dictators, and intelligence agencies around the globe' (Passas 1996: 58). See also Anderson (1993: 298).

10 Essentially, SOCA responded to Level 3 crime, while Level 1 crime remained the remit of local and metropolitan policing. There has been some concern raised about a potential 'Level 2 Gap' – that is, the regional constabularies' capacity to respond to this level of crime ('cross-border issues . . . at force and inter-force level') (John and Maguire 2004: 3).

11 An enterprise, according to s.1961(4), 'includes any individual, partnership, corporation, association, or other legal entity, and any union or group of individuals associated in fact although not a legal entity'.

12 These areas of cooperation and assistance have been fostered by bodies such as the UN Interregional Crime and Justice Research Institute and the UN Office on Drugs and Crime. See Boyle and Schmid (2010: 19).

13 This provides additional evidence for the discussion above regarding the current shift away from the language of 'organised crime', as the SCPO itself was originally drafted as an 'organised crime' prevention order.

14 While the centrepiece of the SOCPA 2005 was the establishment of SOCA, there are various additional police powers that accompanied this Act, which were arguably largely overlooked or submerged in parliamentary debate by SOCA's pre-eminence (for further discussion on this point, see Owen et al. 2005: Ch. 1).

15 Section 5(3) states: 'Despite the references to serious organised crime in section 2(1), SOCA may carry on the activities in relation to other crime if they are carried on for the purposes of any of the functions conferred on SOCA by section 2 or 3.'

16 Section 48(3) states that 'the offence *or offences* by reference to which those matters are proved must be of the offences specified in the indictment' (emphasis added). This sole reference to an indictment is the only possible indication of Part 2 applying only to indictable offences (that is, more serious offences). While the legislatures' intentions are unclear, this may in the future be used as grounds to acquit any inchoate (encouraging or assisting) offences, which are heard summarily under this Act.

17 In Chapter 3, the SCPO and other hybrid orders are analysed as manifestations of the 'preventive state'. In Chapter 6, a legislative analysis is conducted to demonstrate expansive trends across the statutory provisions of a number of preventive orders across a diverse range of areas of crime control.

18 The actual motivation might not be to disrupt, but rather that pre hoc provisions for liability are simply easier to prove. This alternative motivation is discussed in Chapter 3.

19 This echoes the infamous story of Al Capone, a Chicago gangster, who was finally convicted of income tax evasion, after years of managing to avoid prosecution for a range of alleged criminal activities. See Yaniv (1999: 28); see also Calder (1992).

20 The idea that the SCPO and other preventative orders might be punitive is examined in Section 3.4.2.

3 A State of Prevention

1 A more detailed account of similar orders is given in Chapter 6, where a legislative analysis of the specific statutory provisions of these orders is conducted.

2 'Other entity' relates specifically to the SCPO, which can also be applied to companies and organisations (s.30, Serious Crime Act 2007).

3 See also Ashworth and Zedner (2010) on the criteria for preventive measures more generally, and Ramsay (2009a: 109) on the criteria for 'civil' preventive orders in particular.

4 For a fuller description of these established limits, see Steiker (1998: 772–773).

5 Also refer to Figure 3.5, which depicts the degrees of harm and state intervention.

6 Ericson (2007) conceived two forms of counter-law, *Counter-law I* and *Counter-law II*, to embody both *new laws* and *surveillance infrastructures* (respectively). Both are argued to 'erode or eliminate traditional standards, principles, and procedures of criminal law that get in the way of preempting imagined sources of harm' (Ericson 2007: 24).

7 Specifically referring to the practice of preventive detention.

8 This phrase dates back to early theorists such as Blackstone. See Section 3.3 on historical conceptions of prevention.

9 This 'principled framework' is specifically discussed in relation to the state's justification for its pursuit of security.

10 These decisions relate to three separate House of Lords cases of appeal: see respectively, *Secretary of State for the Home Department v. JJ and others* [2007: para. 105]; *Secretary of State for the Home Department v E and another* [2007: para. 11]; and *Secretary of State for the Home Department v MB and others* [2007: para. 10].

11 The schedule of offences qualifying for an IPP was also reduced by the Criminal Justice and Immigration Act 2008.

12 Though the rate of increase is slowing considerably after the amendments in the 2008 Act (see Jacobson and Hough 2010: 11).

13 That is, the detention will end after the criminal procedure is complete.

14 This is also true of the IPP prior to the amendment in the Criminal Justice and Immigration Act 2008, which removed the mandatory sentencing requirement.

15 See also Tadros (2007), who argues that the preventive function was dominant in early models of policing, and that this should not be overlooked in making new claims about the preventive state.

16 For example, this is evident in the Hansard debates in parliament on the Serious Crime Bill 2006–2007, analysed in Chapter 7.

17 See also the joint project 'Design Out Crime' from the Home Office's Design and Technology Alliance Against Crime and the Design Council. Available online: www.designcouncil.org.uk (June 2014).

18 This distinction between 'general' and 'specific' crime prevention can be thought of as analogous to 'general' and 'specific' deterrence theories of punishment. This concept also reflects Slobogin's (2005: 123) belief that 'individual prevention' should be the focus of the criminal law.

19 Essentially subcontracting out crime control, investigation, and detention of individuals to other countries.

20 This phrase was originally coined in this legal context by Justice Holmes in a majority decision, *Schenck v United States*; see Lowe (2005: 185–186).

21 Ackerman (2004: 1060) concludes that an actual attack must occur before coercive preventive action can be taken by the state.

22 However, in the case of *Secretary of State for the Home Department v AF and another* [2009], the courts have held that secret evidence could not be used in Control Order cases. This now raises profound questions about the use of intelligence information in the UK.

23 For a discussion of this normalisation process in respect of other law enforcement powers, see also Hillyard (1994) and Stuntz (2002).

24 Though, as discussed below, the Strasbourg 'anti-subversion' doctrine affirmed the need to go behind these simplistic labels to find intent – established in *Engel and others v Netherlands* [1976].

25 Specific deterrence refers to the deterring of convicted individuals from reoffending, while general deterrence refers to deterring the general public by example.

26 Anleu (1998: 22) states that 'there appears to be less faith in rehabilitation as a goal of criminal sanctions, and the policies and programmes are oriented to crime prevention'.

27 This is evidenced by, for example, the institutional purpose to 'correct' bad character. This is even reflected in the naming of institutions as 'correctional facilities'.

28 See Monahan (1982) on a 'Modified Desert Model'.

29 See Duff (2001) on 'Punishment, Communication, and Community'.

30 Zedner points this out in relation to Control Orders, though this is arguably true across a number of other preventive orders.

31 This point about the balance between liberty and security was made in *AS (Pakistan) v Secretary of State for the Home Department* [2008: para. 24].

32 As discussed in Section 3.4.2.2, it follows that preventive orders at sentencing, which aim to secure, should be based on more solid principles of justice such as necessity and proportionality.

33 This term is taken from Beck (1992).

34 As discussed in Chapter 2, there were also changes made under the SCA 2007 to include inchoate offences of 'encouraging and assisting' crime.

35 This question is answered in Part II following the empirical analyses (see particularly Chapter 7, Section 7.3).

36 See Appendix 'A' for a description of types of conditions that were imposed by SOCA under SCPOs, and a summary of the restrictions and conditions used.

37 Though these preventive justice principles would not necessarily have to be derived from the criminal law, it would seem to be an appropriate point of reference.

38 For a more detailed discussion of 'regulatory justice', see Kagan (1978), Macrory (2006), and Crawford (2009: 2). For the 'regulatory state', see Goldstein (1992: 1895), Steiker (1998: 799), and Ashworth and Zedner (2008: 38).

39 Though some exceptions have been discussed, for example, dangerous driving. For a more detailed discussion of those remote harms addressed by the criminal law, see Simester and von Hirsch (2009: 90) and von Hirsch (1996).

40 The exception here of course is the development in criminal law of inchoate offences (attempts, conspiracy, facilitation, etc.), which, as shown in Figure 3.5, are to some degree lower than actual consummate harms (though still blameworthy).

41 The budgetary cuts to the probation service and National Offender Management Service (NOMS) are estimated to be between 20 and 40 per cent under New Labour, and a total of 50 million expected in 2009/2010 and 2010/2011 (Ledger 2010: 419). See also Bawden (2009).

4 Policy Transfer and Everyday Policy-Making

1 See also Solomon (1981), who similarly points out this dearth.
2 In particular, for the actors in the subgovernment who developed the SCPO, see Figure 5.1 in Chapter 5.
3 See, in particular, Lasswell (1936), Simon (1956, 1976), and Easton (1979).
4 This assertion was made in reference to the importance of acknowledging the method of incrementalism. However, the sentiment equally applies to the acknowledgement of policy transfer.
5 This procedure is explained further (and represented diagrammatically) in Appendix 'B'.
6 *Yes Minister!* is a satirical British TV sitcom depicting a senior minister's struggles to effect (legislative and departmental) change, impeded by his civil servants. See also Page (2003) for a similar picture depicted to that of Richards and Smith (2002).
7 Lord Rippon (1992: 14) states that the parliamentary process is not an effective system of checks and balances: 'Parliamentary processes are not well designed to secure the passage of better legislation . . . debates in Commons and in committees emphasise political confrontation rather than scrutiny of practicalities and detail.'
8 A bill-team can often have several policy leads if there are a number of distinct areas of policy covered in one bill.
9 Though, as discussed in Section 3.3.3, many reviewers in the criminal justice community have criticised this controversial claim by Garland (2001). See, for example, Edwards and Hughes (2005: 346) and Jones and Newburn (2002: 177).
10 Nonetheless, UK officials were still visiting US Boot Camps in the 1990s when these programmes were already much criticised in the US. This suggests that unsuccessful policies in one jurisdiction might still be considered for transfer to another jurisdiction.

5 Process-Tracing: Case Study and Method

1 Since beginning the analysis of the SCPO, further preventive orders have been enacted including the Violent Offender Order under the Criminal Justice and Immigration Act 2008, the Gang-Related Violence Injunction under the Policing and Crime Act 2009, and the Terrorism Prevention and Investigation Measure under the Terrorism Prevention and Investigation Measures Act 2011.
2 See also Woliver (2002: 678).
3 'Other entity' relates to the provision for the SCPO to apply to companies and organisations s.30, Serious Crime Act 2007.

4 Each of these criteria is explained further in Chapter 6.

5 Halsbury's Laws is the authoritative encyclopaedia of statute law.

6 The asterisks for search terms indicates truncation for search terms, to include, for example, 'prevent', 'prevention', 'preventive', 'prevents', and so on.

7 For example, Non-Molestation Orders (under the Family Law Act 1996) and Disqualification Orders for company directors (under the Company Directors Disqualification Act 1986).

8 Indeed this snowballing technique was employed for selecting the sample of interviewees in this book, as discussed in Section 5.3.2.2.

9 Available online: www.parliament.uk/business/publications/ (June 2014).

10 For example, access was denied to any policy documents used to brief ministers. The precise number of these documents remains unknown.

11 Yin (2003: 114) argues that case descriptions focus on general characteristics, which means that this strategy is not as analytically rigorous and localised as the other two strategies.

12 The first coder was the primary researcher and author of this book. The second coder was a colleague studying a Master's in International Relations. This second coder was selected as she was familiar with the field of social (political) science, but working outside the specific subject area under analysis. This coder selection improves 'the criterion of intersubjectivity' (Crittenden and Hill 1971: 1073–1074).

13 For a further discussion of positional and alternative types of criteria, see French (1969).

14 In addition to the documentary materials used for the analysis, discussed above, media releases and articles were also employed to identify key actors to include in the population.

15 One of these three initially responded, but after requesting more information, they did not respond despite several follow-up attempts by the author.

16 During the fieldwork period, respondents were particularly busy because of the 2010 election build-up and subsequent change of government. See also Rivera et al. (2002: 684), who experienced similar problems, arguing that this was 'a problem endemic to all elite interviewing – the extraordinarily busy lives of the respondents'.

17 The online resource of KnowUK was used to search government profiles and biographies, [available online]: www.knowuk.com (June 2014).

18 It was found that many politicians and senior civil servants were part of the author's university alumni network. It must be acknowledged that these networks undoubtedly facilitated the process of gaining access.

19 For the latter two examples, see also Goldstein (2002: 671).

20 On a more sociologically reflexive note, the personal circumstances of the author were also potentially important here in achieving this goal. For example, being Australian, and therefore foreign to the domestic British processes under discussion, undoubtedly assisted in creating the appearance of some degree of naivety.

21 The research ethics approval number is CUREC1 09-101.

22 This transparency is particularly important for researchers wishing to replicate this method to trace the process involved in other areas of policy development.

6 The Proliferation of the Preventive Order Model

1 Originally in the Public Order Act 1986, and amended by the 1994 Act.

2 For example, the Exclusion Order for offences committed on licensed premises (Licensed Premises [Exclusion of Certain Persons] Act 1980) is argued to be the earliest preventive order to fit these criteria (see Figure 6.1).

3 One order listed in Figure 6.1 does not fit into these five categories of conduct, the Driving Disqualification Order, under the Road Traffic Act 1988. Consequently, this order is discussed separately at the end of Section 6.3.5.

4 The Violent Offender Order, Criminal Justice and Immigration Act 2008, can only be applied to individuals previously convicted of a relevant violent offence (as specified in section 98(3)) and who have served an imprisonment term of at least 12 months for that offence (s.99(4)). An application can be made either by a chief officer of police to the Magistrates' Court (s.100(1)) or by order of the Secretary of State (s.100(4)) if it is deemed that the previously convicted individual has 'acted in such a way as to make it necessary to make a violent offender order for the purpose of protecting the public from the risk of serious violent harm' (s.101(3)). The duration of an order must be no less than 2 years and no more than 5 years (s.98(1)(b)), where the maximum imprisonment term is 12 months on summary conviction and 5 years on indictment and/or a fine (s.113).

5 Terrorism Prevention and Investigation Measures Act 2011.

6 The Gang-Related Violence Injunction, Policing and Crime Act 2009, can be applied to an individual where a court is satisfied that the individual has 'engaged in, or has encouraged or assisted, gang-related violence' (s.34(2)). The prohibition contained in an order can include those pertaining to geographical exclusion zones (s.35(2)(a)), associations with other individuals (s.35(2)(b)), possession of a dangerous animal (s.35(2)(c)), wearing gang clothing (s.35(2)(d)), and Internet use (s.35(2)(e)).

7 Each of the orders listed in Figure 6.1 contains provisions for England and Wales, Scotland, and Northern Ireland. On occasion, there are slight variations between these jurisdictions (particularly with regard to the sanction for breach). While some notes are made in respect of these variations, the account below focuses primarily on the substantive elements of the orders as they apply in England and Wales.

8 As amended by the Football (Offences and Disorder) Act 1999 and later amalgamated with the *International Football Banning Order*, as simply a 'Banning Order' under the Football (Disorder) Act 2000 (see summary of the *Banning Order* below).

9 Though section 30(3)(b) states that an order can be applied 'in addition to a probation order or an order discharging him absolutely or conditionally'.

10 As amended by the Football (Offences and Disorder) Act 1999 and later amalgamated with the *Domestic Football Banning Order*, as simply a 'Banning Order' under the Football (Disorder) Act 2000 (see summary of the *Banning Order* below).

11 Though section 15(3)(b) states that an order can be applied 'in addition to a probation order'.

12 Though the commencement order was issued in 2009.

13   To be sure the attention has been for other important reasons, not least their explicit focus on young people, as well as the broad range of nuisance, non-criminal behaviour to which they have been applied.

14   Powers in respect of the CRASBO were further amended and broadened under the Anti-Social Behaviour Act 2003 and the Serious Organised Crime and Police Act 2005. These amendments also made provision for *Interim Orders* to be made (in cases requiring adjournment).

15   Though section 47 outlined procedures for 'arrest for breach of order', which could be made by either a constable without warrant if there was 'reasonable cause' that there was a breach (ss.6), or 'substantiated on oath' that there was a breach on application by the 'respondent' (ss.9).

16   The duration of an order is for an indefinite period; however, applications can be made to discharge an order under sections 31 and 32. Breach constitutes an offence subject to a maximum imprisonment term of six months on summary conviction and five years on indictment and/or a fine (s.35(6)).

17   The duration of an order must not exceed six months (s.117(1)) and if breached the offender is guilty of an offence and is subject to a maximum imprisonment term of six months on summary conviction and five years on indictment and/or a fine (s.122(2)).

18   Section 123(3) includes the following subsections: '(a) engaging in sexual activity involving a child or in the presence of a child; (b) causing or inciting a child to watch a person engaging in sexual activity or to look at a moving or still image that is sexual; (c) giving a child anything that relates to sexual activity or contains a reference to such activity; (d) communicating with a child, where any part of the communication is sexual'.

19   The duration of an order must not exceed two years or until further order (s.123(5)(b)) and breach constitutes an offence punishable for a maximum imprisonment term of six months on summary conviction and five years on indictment and/or a fine (s.128).

20   Perhaps an exception here, discussed above, is the Football Banning Order, as it contains a requirement on individuals to surrender their passport on the occasion of designated international matches. The Football Banning Order can also make other negative (prohibitory) requirements and restrictions.

21   While Control Orders could have been either *non-derogating* or *derogating*, the description herein refers only to those non-derogating orders (unless specifically stated otherwise). The distinction here is whether or not an order contained obligations which derogated from the European Convention on Human Rights, Article 5 (right to liberty) (s.10(a)). No derogating Control Orders were ever issued.

22   This is an interesting departure from previous preventive orders, even though the distinction is superficial given that prior conviction for involvement in terrorism activity would provide the necessary grounds for suspicion (analysed further below).

23   This increase on summary conviction to a maximum of 12 months rather than 6 months as formally stipulated in a number of the preventive orders outlined above is the result of a general increase in summary conviction powers of the Magistrates' Court by virtue of the Criminal Justice Act 2003 (s.154(1)) rather than a reflection of an actual increase due to the

circumstances of Control Orders per se. Note that this increase initially occurred only in England and Wales, so in some cases might differ in respect of Northern Ireland and Scotland.

24 For example, driving while over the legal limit of alcohol or drugs (s.5 and s.6); reckless driving offences (s.1 and s.2); accumulation of points (more than 12) in relation to other traffic offences (such as speeding); or failure to provide a specimen for testing alcohol levels in the blood (s.7).

25 Cf. Police Reform Act 2002 (n.26).

26 Since these orders are strictly civil, they are somewhat analogous to the earlier Disqualification Orders for company directors under the Company Directors Disqualification Act 1986.

27 Prevention of Terrorism Act 2005 (s.1(9)).

28 This indeterminate period, particularly through the statutory phrasing of 'until further order', was adopted in a number of orders; see, for example, the Non-Molestation Order, 1996 Act s.42(7); Restraining Order, 1997 Act s.5(3); Anti-Social Behaviour Order, 1998 Act s.1(7); Disqualification Order, 2000 Act s.31 and s.32; and Sexual Offences Prevention Order, 2003 Act s.107(1)(b).

29 Accordingly, earlier preventive orders such as the Non-Molestation Order and Football-Related Orders were also subsequently amended or replaced with new provisions which increased the punishment for breach (respectively, under section 1 of the Domestic Violence, Crime and Victims Act 2004 and the Football (Disorder) Act 2000). Breach for some preventive orders also constitutes an offence triable summarily only.

30 Clause 2(1)(c) relates to the determination of 'involvement in serious crime': 'has conducted himself in a way that was likely to facilitate the commission by himself or another person of a serious offence in England and Wales (whether or not such an offence was committed)'. See Hansard HL vol.691 col.668 (25 April 2007) (Lord Lloyd of Berwick).

7 Policy Analysis: Elite Interviews and Early Policy Documents

1 A summary of the latter findings about the usage of the SCPO by SOCA is presented separately in Appendix 'A'.

2 In the interviews conducted, some dates were estimated based on interviewees' memory while others referred directly to their diaries, for example, about scheduled meetings and notes indicating when documents were received.

3 'Policy customer' was a phrase used by several interviewees to refer to the person or organisation who would have most to gain by the policy; in this case, SOCA was considered to be the primary policy customer (though other law enforcement agencies could apply to impose an SCPO, as described in Chapter 2).

4 A detailed description of these four powers is outside the necessary scope of this book. The important point to note here is that powers were announced but there was no mention of the SCPO at this stage.

5 The bill-team lawyer explained that several legal actors interact: 'There tends to be more than one, so what tends to happen is that you tend to have one

lawyer who, sort of, takes the lead amongst the lawyers if you see what I mean. So in relation to the Serious Crime Act, I was sort of taking the lead in relation to the Bill. But there were other lawyers, not working for me, because we are all at the same level, but perhaps just less involved . . . so maybe three or four lawyers working on it maximum, of which I was the lead. I mean, initially I was just working on Serious Crime Prevention Orders, and then the chap who was working on the asset recovery agency stuff, at the end of the Bill, retired and so I took that on as well.'

6 One interviewee explained how the junior handler is normally a graduate fast-streamer: '[W]hen it comes to bills you tend to have a fast-streamer on the team . . . [to do] for example, things like putting together all the brief packs for ministers and that sort of thing. It's a crap job but you need someone who's not going to muck it up' (bill-team official).

7 This claimed 'rapidity' at this part of the process is important to highlight, as it suggests pressure on the bill-team to rely on precedents (that is, engage in policy transfer). The correlation between 'time pressures' and 'policy precedents' – two key characteristics of the policy environment that foster transfer – is discussed further in Chapter 8, Section 8.1.

8 In December 2004, the House of Lords ruled in favour (an eight to one majority) of nine appellants detained in Belmarsh Prison without trial under counter-terrorism laws. This meant that these individuals (who government intelligence agencies believed to be involved in terrorist activities) were facing release back into the community. (*A and others v Secretary of State for the Home Department [2004]*)

9 As an exception to the 'non-attributable' anonymity principle followed in writing this book, permission was obtained from the Right Honourable Jack Straw MP to directly attribute this quotation. The passage concerns a personal childhood experience and was difficult to conceal the interviewees identity because of unique references made (such as living on council estate) which would narrow the pool of Home Secretaries interviewed.

10 The total number of staff employed in the Home Office is approximately 31,455 (Home Office Annual Report 2011: 112).

11 The name of this bill and its translation are as follows: 'Hanzai no koku-saika oyobi soshikika ni taisho suru tame no keihou nado no ichibu wo kaisei suru horitsuan [Bill to Revise Part of the Criminal Law to Deal with Internationalisation and Increased Group Criminal Activity], Diet Session 156, Bill No. 85 of 2003' (see Coulson 2006: 869).

12 Though, as argued above, the consultation responses might not have had time to be adequately considered, and thus probably played a lesser role in influencing the initial idea for the SCPO.

13 Departmental lawyers do not just work on bill-teams, they have three other roles in the Home Office: 'We basically have four things that we do. Broadly speaking, bills, which is what we are talking about now. . . . The other three things, just so you know, are we draft secondary legislation, so I was involved in implementing the Bill as well as that involved drafting quite a bit of secondary legislation. We also work only – because the Home Office is an advisory department, it basically means that all our litigation is done outside the department by the Treasury Solicitors Department, we effectively employ them as our solicitor to do our litigation, but we do high-profile cases that

might have an impact on government policy. And then finally we do give just ad hoc legal advice on policy matters, so you know someone will come to you and say "the minister wants to do X, Y and Z, are there any legal issues?", or please could you clear this press line or whatever for legal matters and so on. So those are the other three things.' (Departmental lawyer, Home Office)

14   This internal policy document was obtained on the condition that the body of the document (policy material) was not cited directly. Nonetheless, a précis of this policy content is provided to corroborate policy transfer and the 'cut-and-paste' approach that was undertaken by policy-makers.

15   The instructions did not provide a more specific reason for making this claim, merely that a list of conditions was not desired as experience with the Control Order caused concern that the discretion of the Secretary of State had been restricted. It is likely that there were stronger grounds for excluding this list, but on this occasion the author's limited access to internal policy documents meant that this detail could not be verified.

References

Aberbach, J. D. & Rockman, B. A. 2002. Conducting and Coding Elite Interviews. *PS: Political Science & Politics* 35, 673–676.

Ackerman, B. 2004. The Emergency Constitution. *Yale Law Journal* 113, 1029–1091.

Allum, F. 2008. Special Edition on Organized Crime. *Policing* 2, 2–6.

Althaus, C., Bridgman, P. & Davis, G. 2007. *The Australian Policy Handbook*. Allen & Unwin.

Anderson, M. 1993. The United Kingdom and Organised Crime – The International Dimension. *European Journal of Crime, Criminal Law and Criminal Justice* 1, 292–308.

Anleu, S. L. R. 1998. The Role of Civil Sanctions in Social Control: A Socio-Legal Examination. *Crime Prevention Studies* 9, 21–43.

Ashworth, A. 2000. Is the Criminal Law a Lost Cause? *Law Quarterly Review* 116, 225–256.

Ashworth, A. 2004. Social Control and "Anti-Social Behaviour": The Subversion of Human Rights? *Law Quarterly Review* 120, 263–291.

Ashworth, A. 2005. *Sentencing and Criminal Justice*. Cambridge University Press.

Ashworth, A. & Von Hirsch, A. 2005. *Proportionate Sentencing: Exploring the Principles*. Oxford University Press.

Ashworth, A. & Redmayne, M. 2005. *The Criminal Process*. Oxford University Press.

Ashworth, A. & Zedner, L. 2008. Defending the Criminal Law: Reflections on the Changing Character of Crime, Procedure, and Sanctions. *Criminal Law and Philosophy* 2, 21–51.

Ashworth, A. & Zedner, L. 2010. Preventive Orders: A Problem of Undercriminalization? *In:* Duff, R., Farmer, L. L., Marshall, S., Renzo, M. M. & Tadros, V. (eds.) *The Boundaries of the Criminal Law*. Oxford University Press: USA.

Ashworth, A. & Zedner, L. 2011. Just Prevention: Preventive Rationales and the Limits of the Criminal Law. *In:* Duff, R. D. & Green, S. (eds.) *Philosophical Foundations of Criminal Law*. Oxford University Press.

Ashworth, A. & Zedner, L. 2014. *Preventive Justice*. Oxford University Press.

Atkinson, R. & Savage, S. 1994. The Conservatives and Public Policy. *In:* Savage, S., Atkinson, R. & Robins, L. (eds.) *Public Policy in Britain*. Macmillan: London.

Auerhahn, K. 2003. *Selective Incapacitation and Public Policy: Evaluating California's Imprisonment Crisis*. State University of New York Press.

Ayres, I. & Braithwaite, J. 1992. *Responsive Regulation*. Oxford University Press.

Ball, W. 1992. Critical Social Research, Adult Education and Anti-Racist Feminist Praxis. *Studies in the Education of Adults* 24, 1–25.

Bawden, A. 2009. No Quick Fix for Probation's Problems. *Guardian*. London.

Beck, U. 1992. *Risk Society: Towards a New Modernity*. Sage Publications Ltd.

Bennett, A. & Elman, C. 2006. Qualitative Research: Recent Developments in Case Study Methods. *Annual Review Political Science* 9, 455–476.

Bennett, C. J. 1991a. How States Utilize Foreign Evidence. *Journal of Public Policy* 11, 31–54.

what is being prevented?
How? offending? victimisation?

Bennett, C. J. 1991b. What Is Policy Convergence and What Causes It? *British Journal of Political Science* 21, 215–233.

Bentham, J. 1843. Principles of the Civil Code. *Jeremy Bentham, The Works of Jeremy Bentham (John Bowring ed.)* 1, 415.

Bergelson, V. 2009. *Victims' Rights and Victims' Wrongs: Comparative Liability in Criminal Law.* Stanford Law Books.

Berry, F. S. & Berry, W. D. 2007. Innovation and Diffusion Models in Policy Research. *In:* Sabatier, P. A. (ed.) *Theories of the Policy Process.* Westview Press: USA.

Berry, J. M. 2002. Validity and Reliability Issues in Elite Interviewing. *PS: Political Science & Politics* 35, 679–682.

Blackstone, S. W. 1922. Commentaries on the Laws of England: In Four Books. *In:* Lewis, W. D. (ed.) *Yale Law School.* Rees Welsh and Company: Philadelphia.

Blair, T. 2005. Labour Party Conference, Brighton. [available online] http://news. bbc.co.uk/1/hi/uk_politics/4287370.stm [June 2014].

Boyle, M. & Schmid, A. 2010. A Global Compact for Counter-Terrorism: Towards a Robust Multilateral Counter-Terrorism Regime. University of St. Andrews. [available online] http://www.ibrarian.net/navon/paper/A_Global_Compact_for_Counter_Terrorism.pdf?paperid=16289328 [April 2015].

Braithwaite, J. 2002. Rewards and Regulation. *Journal of Law and Society* 29, 12–26.

Braybrooke, D. & Lindblom, C. E. 1963. *A Strategy of Decision: Policy Evaluation as a Social Process.* Free Press of Glencoe.

Bridgman, P. & Davis, G. 2004. *The Australian Policy Handbook.* Allen & Unwin.

Brimelow, K. 2007. Serious Crime – Who is Taking Liberties? *Parliamentary Brief* (13 June). [available online] http://www.parliamentarybrief.com/2007/06/serious-crime-who-is-taking-liberties#all [June 2014].

Burke, L. 2011. Revolution or Evolution? *Probation Journal* 58, 3–8.

Cairney, P. 2009. The Role of Ideas in Policy Transfer: The Case of UK Smoking Bans Since Devolution. *Journal of European Public Policy* 16, 471–488.

Calder, J. D. 1992. Al Capone and the Internal Revenue Service: State-Sanctioned Criminology of Organized Crime. *Crime, Law and Social Change* 17, 1–23.

Castellano, T. & Gould, J. 2007. Neglect of Justice in Criminal Justice Theory: Causes, Consequences, and Alternatives. *In:* Duffee, D. E. & Maguire, E. R. (eds.) *Criminal Justice Theory: Explaining the Nature and Behavior of Criminal Justice.* Routledge: New York.

Chamberlin, H. B. 1932. Some Observations Concerning Organized Crime. *Journal of Criminal Law and Criminology* 22, 652–670.

Coffee, J. C., Jr. 1992. Paradigms Lost: The Blurring of the Criminal and Civil Law Models. And What Can Be Done About It. *The Yale Law Journal* 101, 1875–1893.

Cole, D. 2004. The Priority of Morality: The Emergency Constitution's Blind Spot. *Yale Law Journal* 113(8). 1753–1800.

Cole, D. & Lobel, J. 2007. *Less Safe, Less Free.* New Press.

Corrado, M. L. 1996. Punishment and the Wild Beast of Prey: The Problem of Preventive Detention. *The Journal of Criminal Law and Criminology (1973–)* 86, 778–814.

Coulson, C. 2006. Criminal Conspiracy Law in Japan. *Michigan Journal of International Law* 28, 863.

Crawford, A. 2006. Networked Governance and the Post-Regulatory State?: Steering, Rowing and Anchoring the Provision of Policing and Security. *Theoretical Criminology* 10, 449–479.

Crawford, A. 2007. Perceptions of Crime and Insecurity: Urban Policies in an Era of Hyperactivity and Ambiguity. *In:* Groenemeyer, A. & Rousseaux, X. (eds.) *Assessing Deviance Crime and Prevention in Europe, Report of the First General Conference of CRIMPREV.* Guyancourt: GERN, 66–80.

Crawford, A. 2009. Governing Through Anti-Social Behaviour. *British Journal of Criminology* 49, 810–831.

Crittenden, K. S. & Hill, R. J. 1971. Coding Reliability and Validity of Interview Data. *American Sociological Review* 36, 1073–1080.

Davies, P. H. J. 2001. Spies as Informants: Triangulation and the Interpretation of Elite Interview Data in the Study of the Intelligence and Security Services. *Politics* 21, 73–80.

Del, H. 1940. "Preventive Justice". Bonds to Keep the Peace and for Good Behavior. *University of Pennsylvania Law Review and American Law Register* 88, 331–347.

Dershowitz, A. 1970. The Law of Dangerousness: Some Fictions about Predictions. *Journal of Legal Education* 23(1), 24–47.

Dershowitz, A. 1973. Preventive Confinement: A Suggested Framework for Constitutional Analysis. *Texas Law Review* 51(7), 1277–1324.

Dershowitz, A. 2006. *Preemption: A knife that Cuts both Ways.* Norton & Company: New York.

Dexter, L. A. 2006. *Elite and Specialized Interviewing.* ECPR Press.

Di Maggio, P. J. & Powell, W. W. 1983. The Iron Cage Revisited: Institutional Isomorphism and Collective Rationality. *American Sociological Review* 48, 147–160.

Dolowitz, D. & Marsh, D. 1996. Who Learns What from Whom: A Review of the Policy Transfer Literature. *Political Studies* 44, 343–357.

Dolowitz, D. P. 2000. Introduction. *Governance* 13, 1–4.

Dolowitz, D. P. & Marsh, D. 2000. Learning from Abroad: The Role of Policy Transfer in Contemporary Policy-Making. *Governance* 13, 5–23.

Dorussen, H., Lenz, H. & Blavoukos, S. 2005. Assessing the Reliability and Validity of Expert Interviews. *European Union Politics* 6, 315–337.

Duff, A. 2001. *Punishment, Communication, and Community.* Oxford University Press: USA.

Duke, K. 2002. Getting Beyond the 'Official Line': Reflections on Dilemmas of Access, Knowledge and Power in Researching Policy Networks. *Journal of Social Policy* 31, 39–59.

Easton, D. 1979. *A Framework for Political Analysis.* University of Chicago Press.

Edwards, A. & Hughes, G. 2005. Comparing the Governance of Safety in Europe. *Theoretical Criminology* 9, 345–363.

Ericson, R. V. 2007. *Crime in an Insecure World.* Polity Press: Cambridge.

Explanatory Note Serious Crime Act. 2007. Great Britain: Stationery Office: London.

Feeley, M. M. & Simon, J. 1992. The New Penology: Notes on the Emerging Strategy of Corrections and its Implications. *Criminology* 30, 449–474.

Finkelstein, C. 2003. Is Risk a Harm. *University of Pennsylvania Law Review* 151, 963–1001.

Fitzpatrick, D. 2006. Crime Fighting in the Twenty-First Century? A Practitioner's Assessment of the Serious Organised Crime and Police Act 2005. *Journal of Money Laundering Control* 9, 129–140.

234   *References*

Floud, J. & Young, W. 1981. *Dangerousness and Criminal Justice*. Heinemann: London.
Flyvbjerg, B. 2006. Five Misunderstandings about Case-Study Research. *Qualitative Inquiry* 12, 219.
Foote, C. & Frankel, L. H. 1970. Comments on Preventive Detention. *Journal of Legal Education* 23, 48–55.
Fortson, R. 2008. *Blackstone's Guide to the Serious Crime Act 2007*. Oxford University Press: Oxford.
Foucault, M. 1980. Power and Strategies. In: Gordon, C. (ed.). *Power/Knowledge: Selected Interviews and Other Writings, 1972–1977*. Pantheon Books: New York.
French, R. M. 1969. Effectiveness of the Various Techniques Employed in the Study of Community Power. *The Journal of Politics* 31, 818–820.
Garland, D. 2001. *The Culture of Control: Crime and Social Order in Contemporary Society*. University of Chicago Press.
Garrett, E. 1998. Legal Scholarship in the Age of Legislation. *Tulsa Law Journal* 34, 679.
Garrison, A. H. 2009. The Influence of Research on Criminal Justice Policy Making. *Professional Issues in Criminal Justice* 4, 9–21.
George, A. L. & Bennett, A. 2005. *Case Studies and Theory Development in the Social Sciences*. The MIT Press.
Gilmour, S. 2008. Understanding Organized Crime: A Local Perspective. *Policing* 2, 18–27.
Goldstein, A. S. 1992. White-Collar Crime and Civil Sanctions. *The Yale Law Journal* 101, 1895–1899.
Goldstein, K. 2002. Getting in the Door: Sampling and Completing Elite Interviews. *PS: Political Science & Politics* 35, 669–672.
Gross, O. 2003. Chaos and Rules: Should Responses to Violent Crises Always Be Constitutional? *Yale Law Journal* 112, 1011–1134.
Hall, R. 2004. *Applied Social Research: A Guide to the Design and Conduct of Research in the 'Real World'*. University of New South Wales.
Harfield, C. 2006. SOCA: A Paradigm Shift in British Policing. *British Journal of Criminology* 46, 743–761.
Harfield, C. 2008. Paradigms, Pathologies, and Practicalities-Policing Organized Crime in England and Wales. *Policing* 2, 63–73.
Harmsen, R. & Wilson, T. M. 2000. Introduction: Approaches to Europeanization. *Yearbook of European Studies* 14, 13–26.
Hebenton, B. & Seddon, T. 2009. From Dangerousness to Precaution. *British Journal of Criminology* 49, 343–362.
Hill, M. 2014. *The Policy Process: A Reader*. 2nd Edition. Routledge: New York.
Hillyard, P. 1994. The Normalisation of Special Powers: From Northern Ireland to Britain. In: Lacey, N. (ed.). *A Reader on Criminal Justice*. Oxford University Press: Oxford.
Hobbs, D. 1988. *Doing the Business: Entrepreneurship, the Working Class, and Detectives in the East End of London*. Oxford University Press: USA.
Home Office. 2004. One Step Ahead, A 21st Century Strategy to Defeat Organised Crime. *White Paper*. Stationary Office: London.
Home Office. 2006a. New Powers Against Organised and Financial Crime. *Green Paper*. Stationary Office: London.
Home Office. 2006b. *Rebalancing the Criminal Justice System in Favour of the Law-Abiding Majority Cutting Crime, Reducing Reoffending and Protecting the Public*. Stationary Office: London.

Home Office. 2010. *Design Out Crime*. Home Office Design and Technology Alliance Against Crime and the Design Council. [available online] http://www.designcouncil.org.uk/our-work/challenges/security/design-out-crime/ [June 2014].

Home Office. 2011a. *Annual Report and Accounts 2010–11*. [available online] http://www.homeoffice.gov.uk/publications/about-us/corporate-publications/annual-report-201011?view=Binary [September 2011].

Home Office. 2011b. *Prevent* Strategy. *Home Office*. Stationary Office: London.

Homeshaw, J. 1995. Policy Community, Policy Networks and Science Policy in Australia. *Australian Journal of Public Administration* 54, 520–532.

Hood, C., Scott, C., James, O., Jones, G. & Travers, T. 1999. *Regulation Inside Government: Waste-Watchers, Quality Police, and Sleaze-Busters*. Oxford University Press: USA.

Howlett, M. & Ramesh, M. 2003. *Studying Public Policy: Policy Cycles and Policy Subsystems*. Oxford University Press.

Howlett, M., Ramesh, M. & Perl, A. 2009. *Studying Public Policy: Policy Cycles and Policy Subsystems*. Oxford University Press.

Ismaili, K. 2006. Contextualizing the Criminal Justice Policy-Making Process. *Criminal Justice Policy Review* 17, 255–269.

Jacobson, J. & Hough, M. 2010. *Unjust Deserts: Imprisonment for Public Protection*. Prison Reform Trust: London.

James, M. & Pearson, G. 2006. Football Banning Orders: Analysing Their Use in Court. *Journal of Criminal Law* 70, 509–530.

James, O. & Lodge, M. 2003. The Limitations of 'Policy Transfer' and 'Lesson Drawing' for Public Policy Research. *Political Studies Review* 1, 179–193.

Jann, W. & Wegrich, K. 2007. Theories of the Policy Cycle. *In:* Fischer, F., Miller, G. & Sidney, M. S. (eds.) *Handbook of Public Policy Analysis*. CRC Press.

Janus, E. 2004. The Preventive State, Terrorists and Sexual Predators: Countering the Threat of a New Outsider Jurisprudence. *Criminal Law Bulletin* 40, 576–582.

John, T. & Maguire, M. 2004. The National Intelligence Model Key Lessons from Early Research. Home Office Online Report.

Joint Committee On Human Rights (Eighth Report). *Serious Organised Crime and Police Bill*. [available online] http://www.publications.parliament.uk/pa/jt200405/jtselect/jtrights/60/6005.htm [April 2015].

Joint Committee On Human Rights (Twelfth Report). *Serious Crime Bill*. [available online] http://www.publications.parliament.uk/pa/jt200607/jtselect/jtrights/91/9103.htm [April 2015].

Jones, T. & Newburn, T. 2002. Policy Convergence and Crime Control in the USA and the UK. *Criminology and Criminal Justice* 2, 173–203.

Jones, T. & Newburn, T. 2007. *Policy Transfer and Criminal Justice: Exploring US Influence over British Crime Control Policy*. Open University Press: England.

Jordan, G. 1977. Grey Papers. *The Political Quarterly* 48, 30–43.

Kagan, R. A. 1978. *Regulatory Justice: Implementing a Wage-Price Freeze*. Russell Sage Foundation: New York.

Keyzer, P., Pereira, C. & Southwood, S. 2004. Pre-Emptive Imprisonment for Dangerousness in Queensland Under the Dangerous Prisoners (Sexual Offenders) Act 2003: The Constitutional Issues. *Psychiatry, Psychology and Law* 11, 244–253.

Kezar, A. 2003. Transformational Elite Interviews: Principles and Problems. *Qualitative Inquiry* 9, 395–415.

Knowuk. 2011. [Available online] http://www.knowuk.com [July 2014].

Lacey, N. 2007. *The Prisoners' Dilemma: Political Economy and Punishment in Contemporary Democracies*. Cambridge University Press.

Lacey, N. 2009. Historicising Criminalisation: Conceptual and Empirical Issues. *Modern Law Review* 72(6), 936–960.

Lasswell, H. 1936. *Politics: Who Gets What, When, How*. McGraw Hill: New York.

Law Commission. 2006. *Inchoate Liability for Assisting and Encouraging Crime*. The Stationery Office: London.

Law Commission. 2007. *Participating in Crime*. The Stationery Office: London.

Lawson-Cruttenden, T. & Addison, N. 1997. *Blackstone's Guide to the Protection from Harassment Act 1997*. Blackstone: London.

Ledger, J. 2010. Rehabilitation Revolution: Will Probation Pay the Price? *Probation Journal* 57, 415–422.

Leech, B. L. 2002. Asking Questions: Techniques for Semistructured Interviews. *Political Science & Politics* 35, 665–668.

Leng, R., Taylor, R. D. & Wasik, M. 1998. *Blackstone's Guide to the Crime and Disorder Act 1998*. Blackstone: London.

Levi, M. 1998. Perspectives on 'Organised Crime': An Overview. *Howard Journal of Criminal Justice* 37, 335–345.

Levi, M. 2006. The Preventive Control of Organised Crime in Europe: The Emerging Global Paradigm? *In:* Aromaa, K. & Viljanen, T. (eds.) *International Key Issues In Crime Prevention and Criminal Justice: Papers in Celebration of 25 Years of Heuni*. Criminal Justice Press: Helsinki.

Levi, M. & Maguire, M. 2004. Reducing and Preventing Organised Crime: An Evidence-Based Critique. *Crime, Law and Social Change* 41, 397–469.

Levi, M. & Smith, A. 2002. A Comparative Analysis of Organised Crime Conspiracy Legislation and Practice and Their Relevance to England and Wales. *Online Report*. Home Office.

Li, D. & Walejko, G. 2008. Splogs and Abandoned Blogs: The Perils of Sampling Bloggers and Their Blogs. *Information, Communication & Society* 11, 279–296.

Lilleker, D. G. 2003. Interviewing the Political Elite: Navigating a Potential Minefield. *Politics* 23, 207–214.

Lindblom, C. E. 1959. The Science of "Muddling Through". *Public Administration Review* 19, 79–88.

Lindblom, C. E. 1979. Still Muddling, Not Yet through. *Public Administration Review* 39, 517–526.

Loader, I. 1997. Thinking Normatively About Private Security. *Journal of Law and Society* 24, 377–394.

Loader, I. & Sparks, R. 2011. *Public criminology?* Routledge.

Loader, I. & Walker, N. 2004. State of Denial? *Punishment & Society* 6, 221–228.

Loader, I. & Walker, N. 2007. *Civilizing Security*. Cambridge University Press.

Lowe, V. 2005. Clear and Present Danger: Responses to Terrorism. *International and Comparative Law Quarterly* 54, 185–196.

Macrory, R. 2006. *Regulatory Justice: Making Sanctions Effective: Final Report*. Cabinet Office: London.

Marsden, G. & Stead, D. 2011. Policy Transfer and Learning in the Field of Transport: A Review of Concepts and Evidence. *Transport Policy* 18, 492–500.

Matthews, R. & Young, J. 2003. *The New Politics of Crime and Punishment*. Willan Publishing: Oregon.

Maxfield, M. G. & Babbie, E. R. 2005. *Research Methods for Criminal Justice and Criminology*. Wadsworth: USA.

Mcburney, D. H. & White, T. L. 2009. *Research Methods*. Wadsworth: USA.

McSherry, B. 2009. Expanding the boundaries of inchoate crimes: The growing reliance on preparatory offences. *In:* McSherry, B., Norrie, A. & Bronitt, S. (eds.) *Regulating Deviance: The Redirection of Criminalisation and the Futures of Criminal Law*. Hart Publishing: Portland.

Menard Jr, A. R. 1953. Legislative Bill Drafting. *Rocky Mountain Law Review* 26, 368–385.

Monahan, J. 1982. The Case for Prediction the Modified Desert Model of Criminal Sentencing. *International Journal of Law and Psychiatry* 5, 103–113.

Morris, N. 2006. Blair's 'Frenzied Law Making': A New Offence for Every Day Spent in Office. *The Independent*. [August].

New, C. 1995. Punishing Times: Reply to Smilansky. *Analysis* 55, 60–62.

Nicol, A. 1988. Confiscation of the Profits of Crime. *Journal of Criminal Law* 52, 75–83.

O'leary, V. 1987. Probation: A System in Change. *Federal Probation* 51, 8–11.

O'malley P. 1992. Risk, Power and Crime Prevention. *Economy and Society* 21, 252–275.

O'malley, P. 1996. Risk and Responsibility. *In:* Barry, A., Osborne, T. & Rose, N. (eds.) *Foucault and Political Reason: Liberalism, Neo-Liberalism and Rationalities of Government*. UCL Press: London.

O'malley, P. 2004. *Risk, Uncertainty and Government*. The Glasshouse Press: London.

O'malley, P. & Hutchinson, S. 2009. A Genealogy of Fire Prevention. *Legal Studies Research Paper: Sydney Law School Research Paper No. 09/89*, 205–229.

Owen, T., Bailin, A., Knowles, J. B., MacDonald, A., Ryder, M., Sayers, D. & Tomlinson, H. 2005. *Blackstone's Guide to the Serious Organised Crime and Police Act 2005*. Oxford University Press.

Page, E. C. 2003. The Civil Servant as Legislator: Law Making in British Administration. *Public Administration* 81, 651–679.

Parsons, W. 1995. *Public Policy: An Introduction to the Theory and Practice of Policy Analysis*. Edward Elgar: Cheltenham, UK.

Passas, N. 1996. The Genesis of the BCCI Scandal. *Journal of Law and Society* 23, 57–72.

Peabody, R. L., Hammond, S. W., Torcom, J., Brown, L. P., Thompson, C. & Kolodny, R. 1990. Interviewing Political Elites. *PS: Political Science and Politics* 23, 451–455.

Peck, M., Horne, A. & Danby, G. 2007. *The Serious Crime Bill*. House of Commons Library Research Paper. House of Commons Library: London.

Plowden, P. & Kerrigan, K. 2002. *Advocacy and Human Rights: Using the Convention in Courts and Tribunals*. Cavendish Pub. Ltd.

Powell, R. 2012. The Concept of Security. *Socio-Legal Review*, University of Oxford. [available online] http://www.csls.ox.ac.uk/oslr/Papers/Entries/2012/6/21_Rhonda_Powell_files/Powell%20%282012%29%20The%20Concept%20of%20Security.pdf [March 2015]

Pross, A. P. 1986. *Group Politics and Public Policy*. Oxford University Press.

Radaelli, C. M. 2000. Policy Transfer in the European Union: Institutional Isomorphism as a Source of Legitimacy. *Governance* 13, 25–43.

Ramraj, V. V. 2008. *No Doctrine More Pernicious? Emergencies and the Limits of Legality.* Cambridge University Press: Cambridge.

Ramsay, P. 2009a. The Theory of Vulnerable Autonomy and the Legitimacy of the Civil Preventative Order. *In:* McSherry, B., Norrie, A. W. & Bronitt, S. (eds.) *Regulating Deviance: The Redirection of Criminalisation and the Futures of Criminal Law.* Hart Publishing: Oxford.

Ramsay, P. 2009b. Why Is It Wrong to Breach an ASBO? *Society and Economy Working Paper Series* 20, 1–20.

Ramsay, P. 2012. Imprisonment Under the Precautionary Principle (IPP). *In:* Dennis, I. & Sullivan, R. (eds.) *Seeking Security: Pre-empting the Commission of Criminal Harms.* Hart Publishing.

Reiner, R. 1992. Policing a Postmodern Society. *The Modern Law Review* 55, 761–781.

Renzo, M. 2010. A Criticism of the International Harm Principle. *Criminal Law and Philosophy* 4, 1–16.

Rhodes, D. 2004. Is Britain Sleepwalking Into a Surveillance Society? *Solicitors Journal* 148, 1020.

Richards, D. 1996. Elite Interviewing: Approaches and Pitfalls. *Politics* 16, 199–204.

Richards, D. & Smith, M. J. 2002. *Governance and Public Policy in the United Kingdom.* Oxford University Press.

Richards, E. P. 1989. The Jurisprudence of Prevention: The Right of Societal Self-defense Against Dangerous Individuals. *Hastings Constitutional Law Quarterly* 16, 329–392.

Rippon, Lord. 1992. *Making the Law: The Report of the Hansard Society Commission on the Legislative Process.* Hansard: London. [available online] http://www.hansardsociety.org.uk/wp-content/uploads/2012/10/Making-the-Law-1992.pdf [January 2015].

Rivera, S. W., Kozyreva, P. M. & Sarovskii, E. G. 2002. Interviewing Political Elites: Lessons from Russia. *Political Science & Politics* 35, 683–688.

Robinson, P. H. 2001. Punishing Dangerousness: Cloaking Preventive Detention as Criminal Justice. *Harvard Law Review* 114, 1429–1455.

Rock, P. 1995. The Opening Stages of Criminal Justice Policy Making. *British Journal of Criminology* 35, 1–16.

Rock, P. 1998. *After Homicide: Practical and Political Responses to Bereavement.* Oxford University Press.

Rock, P. 2004. *Constructing Victims' Rights: The Home Office, New Labour, and Victims.* Oxford University Press: New York.

Rose, R. 1991. What Is Lesson-Drawing. *Journal of Public Policy* 11, 3–30.

Rose, R. 1993. *Lesson-Drawing in Public Policy: A Guide to Learning Across Time and Space.* CQ Press: New Jersey.

Ruback, T. J. 2010. 'Let Me Tell the Story Straight On': *Middlemarch*, Process Tracing Methods and the Politics of Narrative. *The British Journal of Politics & International Relations* 12, 477–497.

Rush, M. 1993. Making Better Law: A Review of the Hansard Society Commission on the Legislative Process. *Statute Law Review* 14, 75–83.

Savage, S. & Nash, M. 2001. Law and Order Under Blair: New Labour or Old Conservatism? *In:* Stephen, S. & Atkinson, R. (eds.) *Public Policy Under Blair.* Palgrave: New York.

Savage, S. P. 1998. Politics and Policy in Criminal Justice. *In:* Mckenzie, I. (ed.) *Law, Power, and Justice in England and Wales.* Praeger Publishers: New York.

Savage, S. P. & Nash, M. 1994. Yet Another Agenda for Law and Order: British Criminal Justice Policy and the Conservatives. *International Criminal Justice Review* 4, 37–51.

Seldon, A. 1996. Elite Interviews. *In:* Brivati, B., Buxton, J. & Seldon, A. (eds.) *The Contemporary History Handbook.* Manchester University Press: Manchester.

Select Committee on the Constitution (Second Report). *Serious Crime Bill.* [available online] http://www.publications.parliament.uk/pa/ld200607/ldselect/ldconst/41/4103.htm [April 2015].

Semaan, S., Lauby, J. & Liebman, J. 2002. Street and Network Sampling in Evaluation Studies of HIV Risk-Reduction Interventions. *Aids Review* 4, 213–223.

Serious Crime Bill. 2006–07. [Available online] http://www.publications. parliament.uk/pa/pabills/200607/serious_crime.htm [June 2014].

Serious Organised Crime Agency. 2007. *Annual Report 2006/2007.* [available online] http://www.soca.gov.uk/about-soca/library?start=10 [July 2012].

Simester, A. & Von Hirsch, A. 2009. Remote Harms and Non-constitutive Crimes. *Criminal Justice Ethics* 28, 89–107.

Simester, A. P. & Von Hirsch, A. 2006. Regulating Offensive Conduct through Two-Step Prohibitions. *In:* Simester, A. P. & Hirsch, A. V. (eds.) *Incivilities: Regulating offensive behaviour.* Hart Publishing: Oxford.

Simmons, B. A., Dobbin, F. & Garrett, G. 2008. *The Global Diffusion of Markets and Democracy.* Cambridge University Press.

Simon, H. A. 1956. Rational Choice and the Structure of the Environment. *Psychological Review* 63, 129–138.

Simon, H. A. 1976. *Administrative Behavior: A Study of Decision-Making Processes in Administrative Organization.* The Macmillan Company: New York.

Simon, J. 2007. *Governing Through Crime: How the War on Crime Transformed American Democracy and Created a Culture of Fear.* Oxford University Press: New York.

Slobogin, C. 2005. The Civilization of the Criminal Law. *Vanderbilt Law Review* 58, 121–168.

Smilansky, S. 1994. The Time to Punish. *Analysis* 54, 50–53.

Smith, K. E. 2006. Problematising Power Relations in Elite Interviews. *Geoforum* 37, 643–653.

Smith, G. & May, D. 2014. The Artificial Debate Between Rationalist and Incrementalist Models of Decision Making. *In:* Hill, M. (ed.) *The Policy Process: A Reader.* 2nd Edition. Routledge: New York.

Solomon Jr, P. H. 1981. The Policy Process in Canadian Criminal Justice: A Perspective and Research Agenda. *Canadian Journal of Criminology* 23, 5–26.

Statman, D. 1997. The Time to Punish and the Problem of Moral Luck. *Journal of Applied Philosophy* 14, 129–136.

Steiker, C. S. 1998. Foreword: The Limits of the Preventive State. *The Journal of Criminal Law and Criminology* 88, 771–808.

Stelfox, P. 1998. Policing Lower Levels of Organised Crime in England and Wales. *Howard Journal of Criminal Justice* 37, 393–406.

Stern, J. & Wiener, J. B. 2006. Precaution Against Terrorism. *Journal of Risk Research* 9, 393–447.

Stone, D. 2004. Transfer Agents and Global Networks in the 'Transnationalization' of Policy. *Journal of European Public Policy* 11, 545–566.

Strang, D. & Meyer, J. W. 1993. Institutional Conditions for Diffusion. *Theory and Society* 22, 487–511.

Stuntz, W. J. 2002. Local Policing After the Terror. *The Yale Law Journal* 111, 2137–2194.

Tadros, V. 2007. Justice and Terrorism. *New Criminal Law Review* 10, 658–689.

Tansey, O. 2007. Process Tracing and Elite Interviewing: A Case for Non-probability Sampling. *PS: Political Science and Politics* 40, 765–772.

Thumala, A., Goold, B. & Loader, I. 2011. A Tainted Trade? Moral Ambivalence and Legitimation Work in the Private Security Industry. *The British Journal of Sociology* 62, 283–303.

Varese, F. (ed.). 2010. *Organized Crime (Series: Critical Concepts in Criminology)*, 4 vols. Routledge: London.

Von Hirsch, A. 1971. Prediction of Criminal Conduct and Preventive Confinement of Convicted Persons. *Buffalo Law Review* 21, 717–758.

Von Hirsch, A. 1996. Extending the Harm Principle: 'Remote' Harms and Fair Imputation. *In:* Simester, A. P. & Smith, A. (eds.) *Harm and Culpability*. Oxford University Press.

Walker, J. L. 1969. The Diffusion of Innovations Among the American States. *American Political Science Review* 63, 880–899.

Watson, A. 1974. *Legal Transplants: An Approach to Comparative Law.* University of Georgia Press: Georgia.

Williams, J. C. 2009. *The Path of the Law and the Common Law.* Kaplan Publishing: New York.

Williams, P. 1980. Interviewing Politicians: The Life of Hugh Gaitskell. *Political Quarterly* 51, 303–316.

Woliver, L. R. 2002. Ethical Dilemmas in Personal Interviewing. *PS: Political Science & Politics* 35, 677–678.

Woodiwiss, M. 1999. Organized Crime: The Dumbing of Discourse. *In:* British Criminology Conference; Selected Proceedings, Liverpool, July 1999. [available online] http://eprints.uwe.ac.uk/18726/ [January 2015].

Yaniv, G. 1999. Tax Evasion, Risky Laundering, and Optimal Deterrence Policy. *International Tax and Public Finance* 6, 27–38.

Yin, R. K. 2003. *Case Study Research: Design and Methods (Applied Social Research Methods)*, Vol. 5. Sage Publications: USA.

Zander, M. 2004. *The Law-Making Process.* Cambridge University Press.

Zedner, L. 2003. The Concept of Security: An Agenda for Comparative Analysis. *Legal Studies* 23, 153–175.

Zedner, L. 2006. Opportunity Makes the Thief-Taker: The Influence of Economic Analysis on Crime Control. *The Politics of Crime Control: Essays in Honour of David Downes* 147–172.

Zedner, L. 2007a. Preventive Justice or Pre-Punishment? The Case of Control Orders. *Current Legal Problems* 60, 174–203.

Zedner, L. 2007b. Pre-Crime and Post-Criminology? *Theoretical Criminology* 11, 261–281.

Zedner, L. 2009. Fixing the Future? The Pre-emptive Turn in Criminal Justice. *In:* McSherry, B., Norrie, A. W. & Bronitt, S. (eds.) *Regulating Deviance: The Redirection of Criminalisation and the Futures of Criminal Law*. Hart Publishing: Oxford.

Index

Printed and bound by CPI Group (UK) Ltd, Croydon, CR0 4YY